Betty Groff's
Country Goodness Cookbook

To Joan, -- Enjoy and
Happy Cooking!
Betty Groff
4-9-94

Betty Groff's Country Goodness Cookbook

by

BETTY GROFF

Designed by Flat Tulip Studio
Illustrated by Thomas M. and Cheryl B. Wise

Full color art seen on chapter pages is available for purchase as signed prints and counted cross stitch kits. For a colored brochure containing prices and more information write Pond Press.

Coordinator — Barbara Adams

GFE
POND PRESS

650 Pinkerton Road
Mount Joy, Pennsylvania, 17552

Books by Betty Groff

GOOD EARTH AND COUNTRY COOKING
BETTY GROFF'S COUNTRY GOODNESS COOKBOOK
BETTY GROFF'S UP-HOME DOWN-HOME COOKBOOK

Designed by FLAT TULIP STUDIO

SECOND EDITION / NEWLY REVISED

Library of Congress Cataloging in Publication Data

Groff, Betty
Betty Groff's Country Goodness Cookbook

Includes index
1. Cookery, American.   2. Cookery, Pennsylvania Dutch
3. Menus.   I. Title.   II. Title.   III. Title:
Betty Groff's Country Goodness Cookbook

ISBN: 0-943395-00-3
Library of Congress Catalog Card Number 87-081549
Copyright © 1987
Printed in the UNITED STATES OF AMERICA

To my mother, who taught me to love food and its preparation and who never stopped teaching or caring.

To my son John for being my son John.

They both left this life too early, but in doing so influenced our lives all the more.

To my father, my constant inspiration and example of living life to the fullest. Your sharp sense of humor and business acumen is only surpassed by your desire to serve your fellowman. Enjoy Dad!

To Hazel, many thanks for being a special part of our family.

Contents

These recipes follow the cooking methods of my family. We've changed many of our eating habits, especially using less salt. Please feel free to reduce or eliminate the use of salt in all recipes except the pickles and relishes.

THE PRESENT

Betty Groff has never forgotten a childhood story she read about a man who traveled the world in search of riches, only to find a pouch of diamonds in his garden at home. For she, too, has found the equivalent of diamonds in her own backyard.

Pennsylvania's best-known country cook, with the help of culinary greats James Beard and Craig Claiborne, long ago realized her true wealth was her heritage, a heritage that has enabled her to make a career of what she loves most—meeting and entertaining people.

When she and her husband Abe first decided to serve a few dinners in their farmhouse to Lancaster County visitors who wanted to meet a farm family and taste the area's famous Pennsylvania Dutch cuisine, they had no idea they were about to change their lives forever.

But with the start of what would become the internationally known Groff's Farm Restaurant 27 years ago, they happily abandoned any chances they might have had to go the way of the somber farm couple who posed for the classic painting "American Gothic."

Using the farm restaurant as the keystone of their activities, Abe and Betty Groff and their family have continued to grow, pursuing new interests while never losing sight of the importance of the past and how it relates to the present.

Their historic Cameron Estate Inn, originally to be a bed and breakfast for visitors to the farm restaurant, has developed its own identity. The stately and historic federal-style inn transports guests to a more tranquil time and enables them to rediscover themselves and their relationships without such modern interruptions as televisions, telephones and computers.

And the couple's rich Lancaster County heritage, spanning ten generations, has inspired a Groff's Farm Collection of home furnishings that encompasses everything from wallpaper and fabric prints to carpeting and linens.

Noted Betty, "Our ancestors knew a good thing when they saw Lancaster County. They settled here and never left." That the county should have inspired so many present projects with ties to the past should come as no surprise to those who are familiar with this south-central section of Pennsylvania. There are few places in the United States where as much of the past remains visible in the present.

Thanks largely to the Groffs' Amish neighbors who do not accept modern ways, the vignettes awaiting visitors can never be forgotten. Picture a bearded Amishman reining four muscular work horses to pull a heavily laden farm wagon on a cold winter morning when the horses' breath forms billowy clouds that obscure their muzzles; Amish boys and girls in somber colored, old-fashioned clothing spending their lunchtime skating on the farm pond next to their one-room school; the husband and wife who hand-plant their crops from a horse-drawn plough or the ubiquitous horse-drawn black buggies that traverse the curving country roads through some of the nation's richest farmlands. One begins to think there will be another Currier & Ives print come-to-life around every corner.

In such a setting, dinner at the Groffs' Farm Restaurant becomes another slice of Americana that's to be savored by all those who visit. The late James Beard, who visited the farm several times, said, "I think of Groffs' farm as a wonderful example of how great American food can be."

All the rooms save one in the 1756 fieldstone farmhouse have been converted to dining rooms. Betty points to that one bedroom, and says with the same reverence a colonial innkeeper has for George Washington, "James Beard slept here."

As Beard and the countless thousands of visitors who have managed to find their way to the sleepy little hamlet of Mount Joy discovered, the farm on Pinkerton Road is the perfect setting for a hearty regional meal that includes such classics as "sweets and sours" (assorted pickled fruits and vegetables), home-baked breads and cakes, fresh vegetables with browned butter, creamy dried corn, Chicken Stoltzfus, home-cured and smoked ham and fork-tender prime rib.

Betty said, "We've always cooked for guests the way we cook for our family, using only the finest ingredients. When they tell us the food brings back memories of the way foods used to taste or say that eating at Groffs' Farm is like eating at their grandmother's house, these are the greatest compliments they can give us."

Most first-time visitors to the farm will order the full-scale, old-fashioned meals that are hearty enough to keep a farmhand going from dawn till dusk. But these days, there is also a new, leaner and lighter a la carte menu for those who don't want to eat enough in one night to last for the week.

Although Betty doesn't spend nearly as much time in the kitchen anymore, the restaurant's best-known dishes remain true to their heritage. How did she manage that? By making sure there's a capable second-generation of Groffs to carry the three-star restaurant into its second quarter of a century.

These days, the Groffs' son Charles and his wife Cindy oversee the day-to-day operation of the farm restaurant. "I don't have to taste the foods every day to make sure they're right because Charlie remembers and knows how they should taste," Betty commented. And Cindy, who has worked in the restaurant since her high

school days, pitches in where needed to insure a smooth front-of-the-restaurant operation.

Charlie, and the Groffs' younger son John (who died in a tragic accident on his 18th birthday) and their adopted son Bob Rote literally grew up in the farm restaurant's kitchen. Betty said, "When I was doing the bulk of the cooking for the restaurant and the family, I couldn't run back and forth to a family room to check on the boys. They played in the kitchen with lids to pots and pans, mixing bowls and toy rolling pins."

"I'm delighted with the trend toward the kitchen as the great room of the house. Children who watch their parents and are encouraged to help will develop life-long interests in the preparation of food. It might take a little longer to finish whatever you're working on, but it'll be time well spent," Betty said.

She remembers an evening when Johnny, then 11, proudly came into the house carrying a large trout he'd just caught in the farm pond. He asked his mother how a trout is stuffed and then vanished into the kitchen. "My curiosity got the better of me after an hour and a half," Betty said. "When I opened the kitchen door, there was a beautifully cleaned and stuffed trout, even garnished with the lemon twists and parsley sprigs."

Bob, who had worked in the orphanage's kitchen before joining the Groffs, loved pastry and learned to bake a delicious carrot cake with some coaching from Betty.

Charlie knew his way around the kitchen at an early age, too. His mother said, "When he was 5, he was discussing the proper ways to slice grapes with our kitchen staff. When he was 9, he hurried through the farm chores so he could get back into the kitchen. Crop rotation and cattle breeding didn't interest him, but trying new recipes and making special desserts did."

Although his parents never encouraged or discouraged the idea of Charlie becoming a chef, they admit they always hoped he would follow them into the restaurant business.

Betty said, "One afternoon Abe and I were relaxing before guests began arriving for dinner and Abe asked me if Charlie had said anything about his plans following graduation. He hadn't, but we got our answer that afternoon."

Charlie arrived at the living room door and announced, "Mom, Dad, I have something to tell you." He held an official-looking brown envelope in his hand and said, "I've come to tell you that I've signed up for the CIA."

Abe and Betty gasped and said at the same time, "You what!" They had taken the bait. Charlie smiled and said, "The CIA—the Culinary Institute of America."

Today, as Charlie cooks, his sons Matthew, 6, and Travis, 2, play in the kitchen and dining room. Could it be that a third quarter century for Groff's Farm Restaurant is already insured?

Matthew, in particular, has his grandmother's gift for gab and loves talking to farm restaurant visitors who have included such notables as senators and congressmen, actors and actresses, sports stars and Supreme Court Justices.

When Sandra Day O'Connor arrived for dinner one evening, Matthew thoroughly interrogated the nation's first woman Supreme Court Justice. "Are you here for a reservation or did you come for information or are you just looking around?" he asked. When she answered, "We have a reservation," he commented, "Oh, well, then you'd better go in the front door now before Grandma sees me holding you up." After dinner, the Justice posed with Matthew for a picture and sent it to him.

He has charmed his share of international visitors, too, and has received invitations to visit them in Germany and Italy. Trouble is, his hosts will have to figure out how to get him back and forth to Mount Joy in time for bed every evening.

With Matthew and his parents in command at the farm restaurant, Abe and Betty have directed more of their time to the family's other two projects—the Cameron Estate Inn and the Groffs' Farm Collection of home furnishings—though they're still in the dining room most nights to greet farm restaurant visitors.

The Inn, just four miles from the farm restaurant, is a dream come true for the Groffs. "When it first went up for sale in 1961, we just couldn't afford it. But when it went back on the market in 1981, I was desperate to buy it," Betty said.

She was entranced by the stately mansion, the 15 acres of mature trees and the two streams that converged in front of the dining room windows. Abe, the practical half of this twosome who relaxes with a paint brush in one hand and a hammer in the other and loves remodeling challenges, was impressed by the quality of construction that went into the 181 year-old-building and the ease with which it could be heated.

The Inn was theirs in March of 1981. In a matter of days, Abe organized a team of 24 local painters, electricians and plumbers who swarmed over the building's three floors and had it ready to open in just a little more than three months.

Betty noted, "Abe began working at the inn at 7 a.m. each day. He'd keep at it until it was time to clean up and dress to meet guests in the farm restaurant at 7:30 p.m. When he arrived in the dining room, so tired he was nearly dragging, people would look at him and say, "It must be wonderful to have a son in the business so you don't have to work anymore."

The inn has had its share of ghostly happenings. Some guests have heard the voice of a little boy who supposedly died in the house. During renovations, violin music was heard in the hallways but the source was never found. And finally, the first Christmas the inn was open, a lone white sheep spent several weeks on the inn property. Suggested one friend, "Perhaps the white sheep is a sign from old Simon Cameron (Lincoln's infamous Secretary of War and one-time owner of the building) that he approves of what you've done." Abe and Betty just shrug it off. After all, Simon was such a rascal that the sheep at least should have been black!

Abe, an unlikely looking repairman who does his best work in a suit and tie and arrives in a vehicle with a bulging tool kit in the trunk, still does much of the maintenance work around the inn. Whether it means tinkering with the furnace or fixing a leaking skylight, he is always where the action is. Betty noted that newsman Roger Mudd was amazed to look out and see Mr. Groff cleaning spoutings and helping to dig up an electrical line.

Although other people use the inn as an "escape," Abe says he can never rest there because he sees too much that needs to be done. And even if they stop in for a few hours, the Groffs can't resist talking to the guests who want to know more about their experiences and life in Pennsylvania Dutch country. Betty laughs and says, "We've learned that half the world would like to own a restaurant and the other half dreams about opening an inn."

Shortly after renovations on the inn were completed, an article about Betty and several other successful Lancaster County women inspired a designer to give the Groffs a call. Roche Fitzgerald said, "I know you have the farm restaurant and the inn, the cookbooks and a line of relishes. I envision a little Groff's Farm Country Store in department stores around the country." He wanted to do a series of wallpaper designs, based on the Groffs' heritage.

Betty said, "We listened to his proposal and I laughed and said, 'far out.' But then I looked at Abe and could see he was interested. Perhaps it was the thought of the fun he'd have putting all those wallpapers to use that appealed to his remodeling spirit. At any rate, we were on our way."

The inspiration for the first of the wallpapers came from Betty's great-grandmother (who was also Abe's great great aunt). "I had Susan Groff's needlework framed and hanging on a wall at the farm when Roche saw it. It contained chrysanthemums, strawberries, forget-me-nots, roses and tulips."

Ideas for more designs were easy to come by, thanks to a Lancaster County custom that could be likened to filling hope chests. Betty said, "Every Christmas, from the day I was born, my grandmother gave the children (both boys and girls) heirloom needlework for their chests. There were hooked and braided rugs, hand-crocheted pillow tops, pieces of embroidery and specially laid out and designed patchwork quilts."

Today, the collection has grown to include area rugs, tea towels and mitts, place mats, bedspreads, coverlets, ovenware, china and pottery. The Kroehler Furniture Company of Canada is using the upscale country patterns from the Groff family's past for an entire line of home furnishings.

That the farm, and eventually the inn, should showcase the design as well as the regional foods made famous in Pennsylvania Dutch County is a natural evolution according to Betty who notes, "They give you an insight into past lifestyles of the land, so fitting when warmth of home and hearth are in again."

WINTER IN LANCASTER COUNTY, Watercolor

*Winter in Lancaster County brings with it a clean
precise light. It conveys the mood of January
with its frozen soil and remains
of the last fallen snow.*

1

APPETIZERS

APPETIZERS

Artichokes with Melted Butter
Brandied Apricots
Broiled Cheese and Olive Rye Squares
Broiled Grapefruit and Oranges with Brown Sugar
Matty's Easter Pie
Melon Balls in Champagne
Glazed Bacon
Jim Bobb's Steak Tartare
Quiche
Ruth Adams' Shrimp Puffs
Shrimp Cocktail with Hot Sauce
Fresh Vegetables in Sour Cream and Vegetable Dip
Tomato Juice
Thelma Hess' Cheese Olives

SANDWICHES

Chipped Ham and Cheese Sandwiches
Watercress and Cheese Sandwiches

BEVERAGES

Iced Vanilla Coffee
Mulled Cider
Old Fashioned Lemonade
Spiced Tea

ARTICHOKES WITH MELTED BUTTER

Choose medium-size artichokes for serving, 1 per person. Wash carefully. With a sharp knife, cut about 1″ off the top of each artichoke. Trim off dark leaves around the outside, and cut bottom so it is flat. Place the artichokes in a covered pan and add enough water to make it 1″ deep. Add 1 tablespoon salt per 6 artichokes. Cover and bring to a boil. Reduce heat to medium and cook approximately 20 minutes until the hearts are tender when pricked with a fork, or when the leaves pull away easily. Serve piping hot with individual cups of melted butter. The plates should be large enough to accommodate all the leaves after the tender bits at the base have been consumed.

When eating artichokes, begin at the outside, dipping each leaf base into the butter and scraping out the pulp with your teeth. When you come to the center, remove the hairy section with a spoon and discard. Eat the delicious bottom, the heart, cutting it into bite-size pieces after dipping it into the butter.

1 per person

BRANDIED APRICOTS

When preserving a few jars of any fruit, such as apricots or peaches, the open-kettle method is best. It saves space, energy, and jars, yet does not require a lot of time. "Open kettle" means cooking the fruit in boiling sugar water until it becomes clear. As soon as fruit "gives" a bit when pressed to the side of the pan with a spoon, it is ready to be placed in the sterilized jars.

In a 6-quart saucepan, or dutch oven, heat sugar and water to boiling point. Add apricots. Bring to a boil, and continue to cook over medium heat for 7 minutes. Spoon fruit gently into sterilized jars. Add brandy, then the syrup, filling to the neck of each jar. Seal by placing lid tightly on jar. (When preserving, *always* use new lids; otherwise jars will not seal properly. You may use jar rings over, but always buy new inserts.) Leave jars to cool for at least 12 hours before moving to storage area, to prevent seals from breaking.

Fills 3 quart or 6 pint jars

2 cups sugar

3 cups water

4½ pounds apricots, washed but not pitted

2-4 tablespoons brandy per jar, depending on preference

BROILED CHEESE AND OLIVE RYE SQUARES

Dottie and Jack Askew made these for us while we were their guests in Myrtle Beach, S.C. Dottie is an excellent cook and avid antique collector.

Butter the rye squares and place under the broiler for 2 minutes, or until toasted on both sides. In a bowl gently blend the cheese, olives, onions, and mayonnaise until well mixed. Spoon the mixture onto the toasted rye bread and place under the broiler for 3 minutes, or until the cheese bubbles. Serve hot.

MICROWAVE: Prepare and place on serving plates, microwave for approximately 25 seconds.

Makes 12 squares

Butter for spreading on bread
Rye bread, cut in 2½-inch squares
¾ cup shredded Cheddar cheese
½ cup sliced ripe olives
¼ cup chopped onions
¼ cup mayonnaise

BROILED GRAPEFRUIT AND ORANGES WITH BROWN SUGAR

Arrange fruit sections in individual plates, in a design, for instance every other one an orange. Sprinkle with brown sugar and garnish with cherries. Place under the broiler for approximately 3 minutes, or until sugar bubbles. Serve hot.

MICROWAVE: Place the grapefruit and oranges on a serving plate. Microwave 2½ minutes until it is heated through.

Serves 4

2 cups grapefruit sections
2 cups orange sections
½ cup light brown sugar
Marachino cherries for garnish (optional)

MATTY'S EASTER PIE

Easter Pie is similar to a fancy quiche. This particular recipe may be served in very small slices as an appetizer, or in larger squares as part of a main course. It is an old Italian recipe, given to us by the McNiffs. Originally the ingredients were not measured, but, like most old recipes, passed on with a motion of the hand—"about this much of each meat and cheese." We experimented until we found the proper proportions for a successful pie. Some Italian families use pizza dough instead of pastry crust.

Beautiful when cut, the individual pieces look like ribbons of red and yellow.

Mix all the ingredients with a fork in a medium-size bowl until well blended and until the dough forms a ball. Roll out on floured surface or between waxed paper until ¼″ thick and large enough to line a 9″ x 13″ baking pan. This dough is very rich. If it breaks while being rolled out, put all the pieces in the pan and pat until the pan is completely lined.

To save time, line the meats up on a working surface with the cheeses in the center. Place the beaten eggs next to the pastry-lined baking pan, each slice to be dipped in the eggs. Start with half of the sliced ham, placing a layer on the bottom, following with a layer of cheese, then a layer of half of the hard salami, then a layer of cheese, then a layer of half of the cooked salami, then a layer of cheese, half the pepperoni, layer of cheese, alternating provolone and mozzarella, etc., until everything has been used. Any leftover egg should be poured over the top. Bake in a preheated slow oven 325° F. for 2 hours. Cool and refrigerate. Serve small portions, about ½″ thick, as this is very rich. Pie will keep for at least a week in the refrigerator. Perfect when served with a light wine either as an appetizer or as a light lunch.

Serves 24-60   Fills 9″ x 13″ baking pan

PASTRY

1⅔ cups all-purpose flour
2 teaspoons baking powder
1 teaspoon salt
⅓ cup salad oil
¼ cup milk

FILLING

12 eggs, well beaten
¾ pound ham (prosciutto or home-cured, sliced thinly)
¾ pound hard salami, sliced thin
¾ pound cooked salami, sliced thin
¾ pound pepperoni, sliced thin
1½ pounds provolone cheese, sliced
1 pound mozzarella cheese, grated

MELON BALLS IN CHAMPAGNE

Clean and remove the seeds from the cantaloupe and melon. Use small melon baller to make balls. Refrigerate, covered. When ready to serve, fill sherbets with fruit. Pour the champagne over the fruit, nearly filling each glass. Serve chilled.

1 cantaloupe
1 honeydew melon
Champagne to fill sherbets

Serves 6

GLAZED BACON

While I served on the Board of Directors of Nationwide Life Insurance Co., I discovered this unbelievable glazed bacon. This is my version, and be sure to make plenty. Normally I prepare 5 pounds of bacon for a party of 30. It should not be refrigerated or tightly covered. If it does get a bit limp, refresh it by placing in broiler until it bubbles again.

Put the bacon in a large cake pan and bake in a preheated 350° F. oven for 10 minutes. Drain off the fat. At this point, before you add the glaze, the bacon should be almost crisp—be sure not to underbake it. In a small bowl, mix the sugar, mustard, and wine until smooth. Pour half of this glaze over the bacon and return to the oven. Bake at 350° for 10 minutes. Turn the bacon; cover with the remaining glaze and continue to bake until golden brown. Remove and place on waxed paper. Serve warm or cooled.

½ pound bacon, sliced
½ cup light brown sugar, packed
1 tablespoon Dijon mustard
2 tablespoons red or white wine

Makes 6 servings

JIM BOBB'S STEAK TARTARE

Mix all the ingredients, except the meat and garnish, in large bowl until well blended. A food processor does this nicely. Add the meat and mix well. Mold into a mound. Cover with plastic wrap or waxed paper. Refrigerate for 8-10 hours. When ready to serve, garnish with whole anchovies and fresh parsley. Serve with party rye bread, pumpernickel, or toasted bread squares.

Serves 30

- ½   cup finely chopped onions
- ¼   cup finely chopped shallots
- 2   tablespoons capers
- 2   tablespoons chopped fresh parsley, or 1 tablespoon dried
- 1   teaspoon chopped fresh thyme, or ½ teaspoon dried
- 6   anchovies, mashed
- 1   tablespoon oil from anchovy can
- 2   teaspoons Worcestershire sauce
- 2   teaspoons soy sauce
- 2   tablespoons melted butter, or olive oil
- 2   egg yolks, whipped
- 1   teaspoon lemon juice
- 2   teaspoons salt
- ½   teaspoon pepper
- 2   pounds fresh, lean sirloin, ground 3 times
- 4   whole anchovies for garnish

Fresh parsley sprigs for garnish

QUICHE

Prebake the pastry crust for 5 minutes in a preheated 350° F. oven; this prevents it from becoming soggy. Sprinkle the shredded cheese evenly over the pastry shell. Grill the bacon or fry it in a heavy skillet until crisp; remove and drain on paper towels. Crumble the bacon and add to cheese. Use the bacon fat to sauté the onions, mushrooms, and parsley until golden brown. Add the flour and salt and stir until well blended. Add to the cheese and bacon. Beat the eggs lightly in a bowl. Add the cream. Pour over the cheese mixture. Bake in a 375° F. oven for 45 minutes, or until firm and golden brown. Serve warm.

Serves 6

- 1   (9") pastry crust
- 1½ cups shredded Cheddar or Swiss cheese*
- 8   slices crisp bacon, crumbled
- 2   tablespoons chopped parsley
- ¼   cup chopped onions (optional)
- 1   cup sliced mushrooms
- 1   tablespoon flour
- ½   teaspoon salt
- 4   eggs
- 1½ cups light cream

* Chilled cheese is easier to shred or grate.

RUTH ADAMS' SHRIMP PUFFS

Mix butter and cream cheese and blend well. Add flour. Form into a ball and chill for at least 1 hour. Roll very thin and cut with a round cookie cutter. Spread rounds with Shrimp Filling. Fold in half and pinch edges together. Bake on ungreased cookie sheets in a preheated 400° F. oven for 10 minutes. Serve hot.

Mix all ingredients together. Add a little mayonnaise if too thick. Put ½ teaspoon of the mixture in each puff.

VARIATION

Baked ham, crab meat, or anchovies may be substituted for the shrimp.

Makes 40 puffs

½ cup butter or margarine
3 ounces cream cheese
1 cup flour

SHRIMP FILLING

1 cup shrimp, cooked, cleaned, rinsed, and diced
¼ cup finely diced celery
½ teaspoon lemon juice
1 tablespoon chopped parsley
¼ teaspoon salt
⅛ teaspoon pepper
⅛ teaspoon cayenne pepper
◆ Dash Worcestershire sauce
2 tablespoons tartar sauce
Mayonnaise (optional)

SHRIMP COCKTAIL WITH HOT SAUCE

Put the raw shrimp in a large saucepan and cover with beer. Add salt and seafood seasoning. Bring to a boil. Reduce heat to medium and simmer for 4-5 minutes, or until shrimp turn white. Drain and cool. Peel and devein. Refrigerate, covered, until ready to serve.

Blend all ingredients thoroughly. Refrigerate in a covered container. This sauce will keep for weeks, refrigerated.

Serves 12

3 pounds raw shrimp
1 (12-ounce) bottle beer
½ teaspoon salt
1 teaspoon seafood seasoning

HOT SAUCE

1 cup catsup
¼ cup ground horseradish
1 tablespoon lemon juice
1 teaspoon Worcestershire sauce
¼ teaspoon salt
◆ Dash tabasco

FRESH VEGETABLES IN SOUR CREAM AND VEGETABLE DIP

This is a great example of entertaining with ease. Reba Hammond is so organized and an excellent cook and entertainer. She and Ron both work hard at their hardware business, but they always have time to entertain friends. She plans her food ahead and always looks so relaxed when guests arrive— a rare talent.

½ cup mixed dried vegetables
2 cups sour cream
½ teaspoon seasoned salt
Fresh vegetables, such as asparagus, celery, carrots, zucchini, or tender young green beans

Mix the dried vegetables, sour cream, and salt together and let stand, covered, in the refrigerator for 1 hour. Serve as a dip with any fresh vegetables that are tasty raw.

If you do not dry your own vegetables, you will find them packaged in the grocery stores, usually near the salad mixes, etc.

Serves 6

TOMATO JUICE

5 pounds ripe tomatoes
2 cups water
5 stalks celery, chopped
2 medium onions, sliced or chopped
2 teaspoons salt
½ teaspoon pepper

Wash the tomatoes, remove the cores, and cut in quarters. Put the tomatoes in a large kettle with 1 cup of the water. Simmer on low heat until soft. Put through a sieve, strainer, or food mill, then put the juice in a pan with the remaining water, celery, onions, salt, and pepper. Bring to a boil; reduce heat and simmer 15 minutes or until the onions and celery are soft. Strain the liquid through a very fine sieve or cheesecloth. Either bottle and refrigerate or reheat and pour into hot sterilized jars before sealing.

Makes 3 pints

CHIPPED HAM AND CHEESE SANDWICHES

Butter the dinner rolls. Fill with the thinly sliced ham and cheese, or spread the herb cheese on the rolls and add the ham.

Baked ham, very thinly sliced
Swiss cheese, thinly sliced, or herb cheese (see Index)
Butter
Small dinner rolls

WATERCRESS AND CHEESE SANDWICHES

Be sure the cream cheese is at room temperature. Put in a bowl and add 1-2 tablespoons mayonnaise or sour cream to soften the cheese enough to spread easily. Blend well. Spread on 1 side of the slices of bread. Place a generous amount of cleaned watercress on top of the cheese. Sprinkle with seasoned salt and cover with a second slice of cheese-spread bread. Cut in desired shapes and serve chilled.

When using these sandwiches for a party, remove the crusts from the bread, cutting the sandwiches smaller.

Cream cheese
Mayonnaise or sour cream
Watercress, washed, trimmed, drained, and coarsely chopped
Seasoned salt
White or whole wheat bread

ICED VANILLA COFFEE

This is one of my favorite summer coolers. You don't need cream or sugar, just enjoy!

Fill glasses with crushed ice. Add 1 tablespoon vanilla extract and fill with coffee. Some folks will prefer to add a bit of sugar.

THELMA HESS' CHEESE OLIVES

In a mixing bowl, blend the cheese and butter together until light and fluffy. Add the worcestershire sauce and mix well. Stir in the flour, mixing to form a ball. Using about 1 teaspoon of this dough for each olive, shape around the olive, and seal by rolling in the palm of the hands. Place on ungreased baking sheets and bake in a preheated 400° F. oven for 12–15 minutes, or until golden brown.

Serves at least 12

1 (5-ounce) jar bacon-cheese spread
4 tablespoons butter
◆ Dash Worcestershire sauce
¾ cup flour
30 medium-size stuffed green olives

MULLED CIDER

Combine sugar and 2 cups of the cider in a large kettle and stir until the sugar is dissolved. Add the orange and lemon slices and bring to a boil. Simmer approximately 6 minutes until the rinds are clear. Add the remaining 4 cups of cider and the wine and heat but do not boil. Pour into a serving bowl. If using crystal punch bowl, do not pour all in at one time, but pour gradually over a metal spoon or ladle to absorb the heat. This will prevent cracking the bowl.

Serve with cinnamon sticks for stirrers.

Serves 12

1 cup granulated sugar
6 cups apple cider
1 orange, seeded and sliced thin
1 lemon, seeded and sliced thin
2 cups white or rosé wine
Cinnamon sticks (optional)

OLD FASHIONED LEMONADE

The old fashioned flavor comes from squeezing the sugar into the lemon rind. The oil from the rind gives it extra zest. The dash of nutmeg was a tradition at our house. Try it, you'll love it!

Squeeze 4 of the lemons and reserve the juice. Slice the remaining lemons ¼″ thick. Using a wooden mallet or old-fashioned potato masher, press the sliced lemons into ⅓ cup of the sugar, in the container in which the lemonade is to be served. Allow the slices to stand in the sugar for 15 minutes. Add the water, the lemon juice, and the remaining sugar. Stir until the sugar is dissolved. Add the ice cubes and grate nutmeg over the top. Garnish with sprigs of fresh mint.

Makes 1¼ gallons

6 lemons
1⅓ cups sugar
1 gallon water
Grated nutmeg
Sprigs of fresh mint

SPICED TEA

Alma Bobb has given friends decorated jars of this recipe for years. An excellent housewarming gift or holiday treat.

Mix all ingredients together. Store in an airtight container. Add cold or boiling water and serve with cinnamon-bark stirrers.

1 cup instant tea
½ cup granulated sugar
2 cups Tang
1 (3-ounce) package instant lemonade mix
1 teaspoon ground cinnamon
½ teaspoon ground cloves
Cinnamon sticks

Robert Frederick Long ~ Arline Carrie Moll
Were united in marriage in America, state of
Pennsylvania, town of Frackville on the 30th
day of April, 1924. The ceremony was held at
Trinity United Evangelical church of
Frackville by the Rev. William H.
Schlappich.
Arline Carrie Moll Long was
the daughter of Richard Moll
and Lydia E. Edwards Moll.

DECORATIVE CERTIFICATE, MARRIAGE FRAKTUR

*Frakturs are decorative certificates which note many
special occasions. The Marriage Fraktur records an
occasion when two families gather to celebrate
the union of their son and daughter.*

2

SOUPS & GOODIES

SOUPS

Basic Beef Stock
Basic Chicken Stock
Beef Vegetable Soup
Betty's Chicken Rice Soup
Broccoli Soup with Chicken Broth
Chicken Corn Soup
Corn and Clam Chowder
Corn "Rivvel" Soup
Crab Soup
Cream of Cauliflower Soup
Cream of Celery Soup
Cream of Mushroom Soup
Cream of Tomato Soup
Gazpacho (Spanish Cold Vegetable Soup)
Cream of Watercress Soup
Green Bean Soup with Beef
Green Bean and Ham Soup
Ham and Bean Soup
Martha Garber's Mushroom Chowder
Mary's Onion Soup
New England-Style Clam Chowder
Pear and Noodle Soup
Potato Soup
Snapper Soup
Sour Cream and Potato Soup
Split Pea and Tomato Soup
Vichyssoise (Cold Potato Soup)
"Goodies" to Serve with Soup

BASIC BEEF STOCK

Place beef in a pan and roast in a preheated 400° F. oven for approximately 30 minutes until brown. Remove. Put the meat and bones in a stockpot with the other ingredients. Bring to a boil. Reduce the heat to medium and simmer for 1-2 hours. Cool. Skim the fat from the top and strain. Refrigerate, or freeze, for future use.

VARIATION

To clarify the stock, whip 2 egg whites with dash of vinegar until frothy. Whip into the broth and slowly bring to a boil. When it reaches the boiling point, remove from heat and strain through double cheesecloth.

Makes about 1 quart

2-3 pounds beef bones with meat (rib bones, leftover beef roasts, or rib roasts)

6 cups water

1 tablespoon salt (less if the meat was seasoned)

½ teaspoon black pepper (less if the meat was seasoned)

1 bay leaf

1 tablespoon chopped parsley

¼ cup chopped celery with leaves

1 teaspoon thyme

1 small onion, diced

BASIC CHICKEN STOCK

Put all ingredients in a stockpot and bring to a boil. Reduce heat to low and simmer for 1 hour. Strain through a cheesecloth. Cool. Refrigerate, or freeze for future use.

Makes about 1 quart

3 pounds chicken pieces, backs, wings, necks, etc., including hearts and gizzards but not livers

4 cups water

◆ pinch saffron

1½ teaspoons salt

½ teaspoon pepper

½ teaspoon thyme

◆ pinch of tarragon

1 teaspoon chopped parsley

¼ cup chopped celery with leaves

1 tablespoon diced celery root (optional)

¼ cup chopped onions (optional)

BEEF VEGETABLE SOUP

There are three secrets to making excellent soup. First, the quality of the meat, which should not be boiled, but browned or roasted. Use meat with the bones to guarantee a rich broth. Second, the blending of fresh (or dried) herbs to enhance the flavor. The amount of herbs used is important—too much will overpower the meat and vegetables. The correct amount of herbs will give the soup a subtle and pleasant taste. Third, the freshness of the vegetables is of the utmost importance. My mother always said, "Nothing comes out better than when it was put in."

This soup may be varied to suit your mood, and the ingredients you have on hand.

Put the beef stock in a 6-quart pot and bring to a boil. Add the remaining ingredients and simmer for 45 minutes.

NOTE: Unless you have ripe flavorful tomatoes, use canned Italian plum tomatoes.

MICROWAVE: Combine green beans, celery, potatoes, and onion with ½ cup of beef stock in a 4-quart glass casserole. Cover. Microwave for 8 minutes on high stirring twice. Add the rest of the ingredients and cook for 12 minutes longer. Let stand for 5 minutes before serving.

Makes 6–8 servings

2 quarts very strong beef stock
3 cups roast or boiled beef, cut into small pieces
1 cup peeled, seeded, and diced tomatoes or drained canned tomatoes
1 cup green or yellow beans, cut up
½ cup chopped celery
½ cup diced potatoes
½ cup thinly sliced carrots
¼ cup pearl barley
2 tablespoons fresh chopped herbs of your choice*
1 tablespoon chopped onion (optional)

* I use as many as 8 or 10 different fresh herbs, including 3 kinds of thyme, sweet basil, marjoram, dill, chives, and, when available, a leaf of lovage. Lovage is a potherb, used in cooking for centuries. It is a hardy perennial which looks like overgrown celery. It can be grown in the garden and one leaf is enough to flavor a soup or stew.

BETTY'S CHICKEN RICE SOUP

"The richer the chicken, the better the soup!" my Mother used to say. It is true! This recipe is simple, but so often the simplest things in life are the best. The roaster chicken and saffron are the answer. As I like to say, "Why waste time and energy cooking a tough old stewing hen when you can get more flavor with a tender roasting chicken in half the cooking time?"

To make the stock double strength, boil it down after it has been made until it is reduced by half. Bring this double-strength stock to a boil in a 3-quart saucepan. Add the celery, onion, and rice. Reduce heat and simmer about 20 minutes until the rice is soft. Add the chicken and heat through. Serve in heated soup bowls, garnished with chopped parsley.

MICROWAVE: Microwave the double-strength stock in a 3-quart covered casserole for approximately 8 minutes until it comes to a boil. Add celery, onions, and rice. Microwave them for 5 minutes until rice is soft. Add chicken and heat 2 minutes. Let stand 5 minutes before serving.

Makes 6 servings

- 4 cups double-strength chicken stock
- ¼ cup celery, chopped
- ½ small onion, chopped
- 1 cup uncooked long-grain rice
- 2 cups diced cooked chicken
- 1 tablespoon finely chopped fresh parsley for garnish

BROCCOLI SOUP WITH CHICKEN BROTH

If using fresh broccoli, wash, trim, and set aside. Melt the butter in a heavy 2-quart saucepan. Blend in the flour, salt, celery seed, and pepper, stirring until well mixed. Remove from the heat and add the chicken broth, stirring with a wire whisk. Add the broccoli and simmer on low heat for 10-12 minutes, depending on how well vegetable is to be cooked. Serve piping hot and garnish with grated cheese and croutons.

Serves 6

- 2 cups fresh broccoli buds or flowerets, or 1½ cups pureed cooked broccoli
- 3 tablespoons butter
- 2 tablespoons flour
- 1 teaspoon salt
- ½ teaspoon celery seed
- ¼ teaspoon pepper
- 3 cups rich chicken broth
- 1 tablespoon finely chopped onion

Grated cheese and croutons for garnish (optional)

CHICKEN CORN SOUP

Put the chicken in a large kettle. Cover with enough water to make at least 4 cups stock. Add saffron, salt, and pepper. Bring to a boil and simmer until tender. Let chicken cool enough to handle. Remove the skin from the chicken and debone. Cut the meat into bite-size pieces. Measure 2 cups of the chicken, saving the remainder for chicken salad, etc. Bring 4 cups broth to a boil. Add the corn, celery, and parsley. Boil for 5 minutes. Add the chicken. Check seasoning. Add more salt and pepper if needed.

Serves 6

1 (2½-pound) chicken
Water
◆ **Pinch saffron**
2 teaspoons salt
¼ teaspoon pepper
2 cups corn kernels
1 cup chopped celery
1 tablespoon chopped parsley
◆ **Dash freshly ground pepper**

CORN AND CLAM CHOWDER

When our children were young, we used to take them to the Chesapeake Bay to dig for clams. The large clams we found were used for chowder. The smaller clams we steamed or enjoyed raw. Large Chesapeake clams make lots of broth, which is excellent for chowder. If you do not have enough broth with your clams, add bottled clam broth. Fresh and frozen clams are equally good in this recipe.

Melt the butter in a heavy 4-quart pot, add the onion, and sauté until soft. When using fresh clams, chop them, and reserve the clam juice separately. There should be 2 cups of liquid. When using canned clams, drain them and add enough bottled clam broth to make up the 2 cups. Add the clam liquid, the chopped clams, corn kernels, salt, pepper, and parsley to the onion and bring to a boil. Stir in the milk and evaporated milk. Reduce the heat and simmer for approximately 30 minutes, stirring often to prevent the milk from sticking. The longer the soup simmers, the thicker it becomes and the better it tastes.

1	tablespoon butter
1	small onion, sliced thin
12	large fresh clams or 2 cups chopped clams, plus 2 cups clam broth
8	cups fresh or frozen white or yellow corn kernels
1	teaspoon salt
¼	teaspoon freshly ground black pepper
1	tablespoon chopped fresh parsley
4	cups milk
⅓	cup evaporated milk

VARIATION

For a really thick chowder, add 2 potatoes, peeled and thinly sliced.

MICROWAVE: Melt butter in a covered 4-quart glass pot and add the onion. Follow the above recipe and bring to boil—about 8 minutes. Stir in milk and cook about 7 minutes. Stir in clams and let stand for 3 minutes before serving.

Makes 6 servings

CORN "RIVVEL" SOUP

This was always served as the main dish for summer meals. We served this hearty soup with homemade bread, cold cuts and fresh fruit.

Bring the water to a boil in a 4-quart pot. Add the corn, salt, pepper, basil, and 1 tablespoon parsley. Simmer for 3 minutes, then add the milk, cream, and half of a 13-ounce can of evaporated milk.

Beat the flour, eggs, remaining evaporated milk, and salt in a bowl until smooth. When the soup is boiling, pour the batter through a sieve, or a dipper with holes, directly into the boiling soup. Move the bottom of the sieve around over the pot, so the rivvels do not all fall in one spot. Push them about with a wooden spoon so they do not stick together. Reduce heat, cover the pan, and simmer on low heat for 5 minutes. Just before serving, add the butter. Serve in heated soup bowls, garnished with parsley.

- 4 cups water
- 6 cups fresh, frozen, or canned corn kernels
- 1½ teaspoons salt
- ◆ Few grains black pepper
- 1 teaspoon chopped fresh basil or pinch dried basil
- 1 tablespoon chopped fresh parsley
- 2 cups milk
- 1 cup light cream
- 6½ ounces evaporated milk
- 1 tablespoon butter

RIVVEL BATTER

- ½ cup flour
- 2 eggs
- 6½ ounces evaporated milk
- ½ teaspoon salt
- 2 tablespoons chopped parsley for garnish

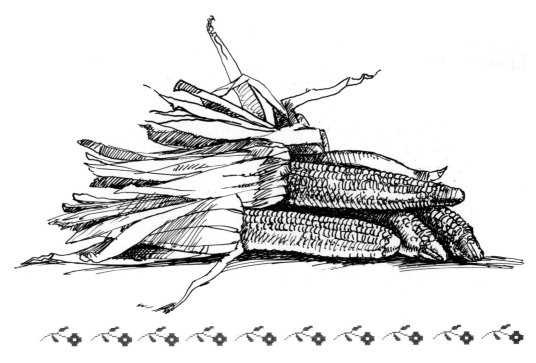

CRAB SOUP

A strange thing about this soup, which is one of my all-time favorites: no matter how much I make —even to tripling the recipe—there is never a drop left next day! Our son John would reheat any left over in the microwave oven. Whenever crab meat is on sale, I take advantage of the saving and buy some for the freezer. Cut off enough to make soup and save the rest for later. Alaska king crab is generally the least expensive crab meat available. It makes an excellent and colorful soup.

Sauté the onion in the butter in a large, heavy soup kettle. Add the water, potatoes, celery, parsley, salt, pepper, and seafood seasoning. Cook, uncovered, for 12 minutes until tender. Most of the liquid will have evaporated. Sprinkle the flour over the potatoes and stir. Add the crab meat, evaporated milk, and milk and simmer on very low heat for 30 minutes more until the potatoes fall apart and thicken the soup.

NOTE: Be sure to check crab meat carefully for shell pieces before adding it to the soup.

MICROWAVE: Microwave the onions in the butter in a large covered casserole for about 1 minute. Add balance of your ingredients as above. Cook, covered, in a microwave oven on high for about 5 minutes until tender. Continue to follow the recipe and cook on high for about 5 minutes after adding crab meat and milk, etc. At this point the potatoes should fall apart and the soup thicken.

Makes 6 servings

½ cup chopped onion
3 tablespoons butter
2 cups water
2 medium potatoes, cut in julienne strips
1 cup finely chopped celery
1 tablespoon chopped parsley
2 teaspoons salt
Freshly ground pepper to taste
¼ teaspoon seafood seasoning, preferably Old Bay brand
2 tablespoons flour
2 cups diced crab meat
½ cup evaporated milk
4 cups milk

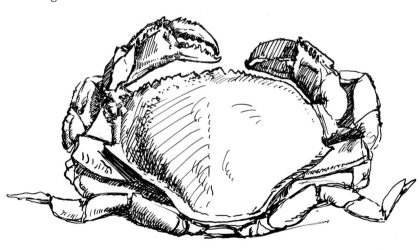

CREAM OF CAULIFLOWER SOUP

Puree the cooked cauliflower and add the onion salt in food processor, blender, or food press. Set aside. In a heavy 2-quart saucepan, melt the butter. Blend in the flour, salt, and pepper, stirring until well mixed. Remove from heat, and add chicken broth and milk, stirring with a wire whisk. Gradually add the cauliflower to the milk mixture. Simmer on low heat, stirring constantly to prevent sticking, until soup is the consistency desired—approximately 10 minutes. Serve piping hot, garnished with freshly grated cheese or a dash of paprika.

Serves 6

1½ cups cooked cauliflower
3 tablespoons butter
2 tablespoons all-purpose flour
1 teaspoon salt
¼ teaspoon pepper
2 cups rich chicken broth
2 cups milk
½ teaspoon onion salt
Freshly grated cheese (optional)
Paprika (optional)

CREAM OF CELERY SOUP

Puree the cooked celery with the onion salt in a food processor, blender, or food press. Set aside. Melt the butter in a 2-quart heavy saucepan. Blend in the flour, salt, celery seed, and pepper, stirring until well mixed. Remove pan from heat. Add the chicken broth and milk, stirring with a wire whisk. Gradually blend in the pureed celery. Return to stove and simmer on low heat until soup is consistency desired—approximately 10 minutes—stirring constantly to prevent sticking. Serve piping hot with a dash of celery seed on each portion.

MICROWAVE: Microwave instructions applicable for both soups. In a 2½-quart covered glass casserole melt butter on high for 30 seconds. Stir in flour, then milk, broth, cauliflower, and seasonings. Microwave on high, covered, for 6 minutes, stirring twice.

Serves 6

1½ cups pureed celery
½ teaspoon onion salt
3 tablespoons butter
2 tablespoons all-purpose flour
1 teaspoon salt
½ teaspoon celery seed
¼ teaspoon pepper
1 cup rich chicken broth
2½ cups milk
Celery seed for garnish (optional)

CREAM OF MUSHROOM SOUP

Melt the butter in a heavy 2-quart saucepan. Blend in the flour, salt, and pepper, stirring until well mixed. Remove from the heat and add the chicken broth and the milk. In a separate pan melt the butter and sauté the chopped mushrooms. Season with the onion salt. Add to the milk mixture. Simmer approximately 10 minutes on low heat until all flavors are blended, stirring constantly. Serve piping hot with a slice of fresh mushroom or minced parsley.

MICROWAVE: In a 3-quart casserole, melt butter for 30 seconds; stir in flour, then broth, and then milk and seasonings. Microwave on high, covered, for 6 minutes, stirring 3 times. Add mushrooms; microwave 1 minute, let sit for 3 minutes, covered.

Serves 6

3 tablespoons butter
2 tablespoons all-purpose flour
1 teaspoon salt
¼ teaspoon pepper
2 cups rich chicken broth
2 cups milk (1 cup each milk and cream may be substituted for extra rich soup)
1½ cups finely chopped mushrooms
2 tablespoons butter
½ teaspoon onion salt
Minced parsley (optional)
Sliced fresh mushrooms (optional)

CREAM OF TOMATO SOUP

Melt the butter in heavy 2-quart saucepan. Slowly add the flour, stirring until well blended. Add tomatoes and onion and simmer on low heat for 5 minutes. Then add the baking soda, salt, and pepper and bring to a boil. Pour in the milk and simmer on low heat until it comes to a boil, stirring constantly. Do not overcook. Serve piping hot with croutons.

Serves 6

3 tablespoons butter
2 tablespoons flour
2 cups strained cooked tomatoes
2 tablespoons grated onion
¼ teaspoon baking soda
1 teaspoon salt
⅛ teaspoon pepper
4 cups milk
Croutons

GAZPACHO (SPANISH COLD VEGETABLE SOUP)

In a deep bowl, combine cucumbers, tomatoes, onion, green peppers, garlic, and crumbled bread; mix together thoroughly. Stir in water, vinegar, and salt. Ladle the mixture, 2 cups at a time, into blender or food processor and blend at high speed for 1 minute, or until reduced to a smooth puree. Pour into a bowl and with a whisk, beat in the olive oil and tomato paste.

Cover the bowl tightly with foil or plastic wrap, and refrigerate for 2 or more hours, until thoroughly chilled. Before serving, stir the soup lightly to recombine it. Ladle into a large chilled tureen or into individual soup plates.

Serve the gazpacho with the bread cubes and the vegetable garnishes, presented in separate serving bowls to be added to the soup at the discretion of each diner.

VARIATION

If you prefer very crisp croutons for the garnish, fry the bread cubes. In a 6"–8" skillet, heat ¼ cup olive oil over moderate heat until a light haze forms. Drop in the bread cubes and, turning them frequently, cook until they are crisp and golden brown on all sides. Seasoned salt may be added for extra flavor. Drain on paper towels and cool.

Serves 6–8

2 medium cucumbers, peeled and coarsely chopped

5 medium tomatoes, peeled and coarsely chopped

1 large onion, coarsely chopped

1 medium green pepper, cleaned and coarsely chopped

2 teaspoons finely chopped garlic

4 cups coarsely crumbled French or Italian bread, trimmed of crust

4 cups cold water or 2 cups water and 2 cups chicken broth

¼ cup red wine vinegar

2 teaspoons salt

4 tablespoons olive oil

1 tablespoon tomato paste

Garnish

GARNISH

1 cup ¼" bread cubes, trimmed of crusts and toasted in oven till crisp

½ cup finely chopped onions

½ cup peeled and finely chopped cucumbers

½ cup finely chopped green peppers

CREAM OF WATERCRESS SOUP

Melt the butter in a heavy 2-quart saucepan. Blend in the flour, salt, and pepper, stirring until well mixed. Remove from the heat and add the chicken broth and the rich milk. Stir in the watercress. Simmer mixture over low heat, stirring constantly to prevent sticking, until the soup is of the consistency desired—approximately 10 minutes. Serve piping hot with a sprig of fresh watercress and croutons, if desired.

Serves 6

3 tablespoons butter
2 tablespoons flour
1 teaspoon salt
⅛ teaspoon pepper
2 cups rich chicken broth
2 cups half-and-half (milk and cream)
1½ cups finely chopped watercress
6 sprigs watercress (optional)
Croutons (optional)

GREEN BEAN SOUP WITH BEEF

During the summer, next to zucchini, green beans are probably the most available vegetable for the longest time. Green beans are inexpensive, nutritious, but seldom used in unusual ways. I like to use the foods which are most available in as many different ways as possible. We particularly enjoy the use of herbs with the green beans in this delicious soup.

Bring the beef stock to a boil in a 2½-quart saucepan, add the chopped beef, potatoes, carrots, celery, beans, onion, thyme, and rosemary. Taste before adding salt and pepper. If the beef stock is salty, less seasoning will be needed. Simmer for 30 minutes. Add the cream or evaporated milk and heat through. Taste before serving. If necessary, adjust seasoning.

NOTE: You may use canned green beans. In this case, add the beans when the soup has cooked for about 20 minutes.

Makes 6 servings

4 cups very strong beef stock (see Index)
1 cup chopped cooked beef
2 medium potatoes, diced
2 carrots, sliced thin
1 stalk celery, sliced thin
1½ cups green beans, cut into 1″ pieces
1 small onion, chopped
1 teaspoon chopped fresh or ¼ teaspoon dried thyme
1 sprig chopped fresh or ¼ teaspoon crumbled dried rosemary
1 teaspoon salt
¼ teaspoon freshly ground black pepper
1 cup heavy cream or evaporated milk

GREEN BEAN AND HAM SOUP

The combination of fresh green beans and spices with the ham adds a refreshing variety to the soup family. It is a hearty soup, too, perfect on a cold day.

Cover the ham hock with water in a 4-quart pot. Bring slowly to a boil and skim off. Reduce heat and simmer about 1½ hours until the meat is tender. Remove the meat and chill the ham broth. When cooled, remove fat from the top. Cut the meat from the cooled ham bone and chop in 1″ pieces. Put the fat-free ham broth back in the pot and bring to a boil. Add the ham, vegetables, and spices wrapped in a cheesecloth or placed in a tea infuser. Reduce the heat and simmer for 30 minutes. Add the evaporated milk and again bring to a boil, stirring constantly. Serve in heated soup bowls.

Makes 6 servings

1 (2-pound) ham hock
3 potatoes, peeled and sliced
3 carrots, peeled and sliced
1 small onion, chopped
4 cups green beans, cut into 1″ pieces
10 black peppercorns
1 teaspoon whole cloves
½″ cinnamon stick
◆ Sprig fresh or ¼ teaspoon dried summer savory
½ cup evaporated milk

HAM AND BEAN SOUP

Heat the milk in a heavy 4-quart saucepan. Stir in the beans, including the liquid from the can, the ham, celery, pepper, and parsley. Simmer at least 30 minutes. Serve with homemade or French bread and butter.

NOTE: Canned beans make a better soup because they stay firm. Dried beans may break apart after soaking. Be sure to include the liquid from the canned beans when preparing this dish. It will help to thicken the soup as it cooks.

Serves 6

2 cups milk
2 cups canned Great Northern beans with liquid
1 cup chopped baked country cured ham
¼ cup chopped celery
½ teaspoon coarsely ground black pepper
1 tablespoon chopped parsley

MARTHA GARBER'S MUSHROOM CHOWDER

Melt the butter in a large heavy saucepan. Sauté the mushrooms, onion, potatoes, celery, and carrots for approximately 7 minutes. Cover and reduce heat to medium. Simmer for 10 minutes. Add salt, pepper, parsley, and chicken stock and bring to a boil. Add flour moistened in water. When slightly thickened, add diced chicken.

Approximately 10 minutes before serving, add the milk and bring to boiling point, but *do not boil*. Sprinkle each serving with cheese. Croutons may be added, too.

This soup may be made ahead, but be sure not to add the milk until serving time.

Serves 6

½ cup butter
1 pound fresh or canned mushrooms
½ cup chopped onion
1 cup diced potatoes
1 cup coarsely chopped celery
1 cup coarsely chopped carrots
2½ teaspoons salt
½ teaspoon pepper
1 teaspoon chopped fresh or dried parsley
3 cups chicken stock
1 tablespoon flour
2 tablespoons water
3 cups diced cooked chicken
1 cup milk
¼ cup Parmesan cheese
Croutons (optional)

MARY'S ONION SOUP

Sauté the onions in butter in a heavy skillet for approximately 15 minutes on medium heat until light brown. Reduce the heat to low and add the beef stock. Simmer for 15-20 minutes. Check for seasoning, and add more salt and pepper if needed. When serving, place toast on top of the soup in the individual bowls. Top with the cheese. If using commercial grated cheese, place under the broiler for a few seconds to melt and brown the cheese.

MICROWAVE: Microwave butter and onions, covered, in a 3-quart casserole about 12 minutes until onions are colored. Add broth and seasonings; cover; cook an additional 10 minutes.

Serves 6

4 tablespoons butter or margarine
2 cups peeled and thinly sliced onion
2 tablespoons flour
4 cups seasoned beef stock, clarified
Thin slices buttered toast
Grated Parmesan cheese
Sherry (optional)*

* I prefer a generous dash of sherry in the soup before adding the toast and cheese.

NEW ENGLAND-STYLE CLAM CHOWDER

Melt the butter in a 3-quart soup kettle. Sauté the onion and celery about 5 minutes until clear. Add salt, pepper, and seafood seasoning. Add the diced potatoes. Cover with water and cook, uncovered, on medium heat approximately 15 minutes until potatoes are soft, stirring occasionally to keep from sticking. After most of the water has evaporated, add parsley, milk, and evaporated milk. Simmer on low heat until almost boiling. Add clams and juice, and continue to cook over very low heat. Do not overcook. Serve piping hot.

MICROWAVE: Microwave butter, onion, celery, and potatoes in 4-quart glass casserole, covered. Cook on high for 6-7 minutes. Stir halfway through cooking time. Add clam juice and water to casserole. Cover. Microwave on high for 10 minutes. Add milk and seasonings. Cover, cook 5 minutes on high. Stir in clams, let stand 2 minutes, covered, before serving.

Serves 6

3 tablespoons butter
1 medium white onion, coarsely chopped
2 stalks celery, chopped
1 teaspoon salt
¼ teaspoon pepper
½ teaspoon seafood seasoning
4 medium raw white potatoes, peeled and diced
2 cups water
1 tablespoon chopped parsley
2 cups milk
1½ cups evaporated milk
2 cups chopped clams with juice

PEAR AND NOODLE SOUP

When our Mennonite friends from Kansas come for their annual visit, we invariably talk about food. Many of this group have a German-Dutch background and like noodles as much as I do. They shared this soup recipe with me, and I was really eager to try it, as it sounded quite unusual. It is important to use firm pears. The combination of the pears and noodles is delightful and surprisingly tasty. To me, the soup is equally good served cold, but the Kansas Mennonites traditionally serve it hot with cold sliced meats. My dad and Abe like this soup with chopped celery and parsley, which I add for color and texture.

In a heavy pan over low heat, cook the noodles in the milk with salt and nutmeg, stirring occasionally. Meanwhile, put the pears in a pan with water to cover. Cook until just done, but not soft, adding the sugar toward the end of the cooking time. Drain the pears. Add to the cooked noodles and milk. Stir gently to mix evenly.

VARIATION

Add 3 tablespoons finely chopped celery and 1 tablespoon chopped parsley for crunchiness.

Makes 8-10 servings

1½-2 **cups uncooked noodles**
5 **cups milk**
½ **teaspoon salt**
¼ **teaspoon freshly grated nutmeg**
3 **large firm, ripe Bartlett pears, peeled, cored, and quartered**
4 **tablespoons sugar**
Watercress for garnish (optional)
3 **tablespoons finely chopped celery (optional)**
1 **tablespoon chopped fresh parsley (optional)**

SOUR CREAM AND POTATO SOUP

Melt the shortening in a soup kettle. Add the onion and the celery. Sauté until lightly browned. Add the potatoes, cloves, salt, and 5 cups water. Cover and cook approximately 15 minutes until potatoes are tender. Moisten the flour with ¼ cup water to make a smooth paste. Add to slightly thicken the soup. In a separate bowl, remove 1 cup of the soup and gently combine with the sour cream. Return to the soup kettle and heat. Do not bring to a boil, or the sour cream will separate. Add pepper and serve in heated soup bowls.

Serves 4-6

2 **tablespoons butter, margarine, or bacon fat**
¼ **cup chopped onion**
¾ **cup chopped celery**
4 **medium white potatoes, peeled and cut into strips, as for julienne**
2 **whole cloves or ¼ teaspoon grated nutmeg**
1½ **teaspoons salt**
5 **cups water**
2 **tablespoons all-purpose flour**
¼ **cup water**
½ **cup sour cream**

SNAPPER SOUP

Put the veal knuckle, carrots, onions, celery, and fat in a large baking pan or roaster pan. Add the thyme, bay leaves, cloves, and saffron. Bake in a preheated 375° F. oven for approximately 45 minutes. When brown, sprinkle flour over the top and return to the oven for approximately 15 minutes until well browned. Transfer to a large soup kettle. Add broth and tomatoes. Simmer on low heat for 3½ hours. Remove the veal knuckle and debone. Chop the meat fine and add to the soup. Dice the turtle meat. Put in a heavy 2-quart saucepan with half the sherry, lemon slices, salt, pepper, Tabasco, and Worcestershire sauce. Simmer 5 minutes over medium heat. Remove the lemon slices and the bay leaves from the stock and add to the soup kettle. Simmer 15 minutes. Add the chopped eggs and the remaining sherry. Serve hot with extra sherry on the side.

Serves 8-12

- 2 **pounds veal knuckle**
- 2 **medium carrots, finely diced**
- 2 **medium onions, finely chopped**
- 3 **stalks celery, finely chopped**
- ½ **cup chicken fat or vegetable shortening**
- ½ **teaspoon thyme**
- 2 **bay leaves**
- ½ **teaspoon ground cloves**
- ◆ **Pinch saffron**
- 1 **cup flour**
- 1 **gallon beef, veal, or chicken broth**
- 6 **tomatoes, peeled and diced**
- 2 **pounds snapper turtle meat**
- 2 **cups sherry**
- 3 **slices lemon**
- 2 **teaspoons salt**
- ½ **teaspoon pepper**
- ◆ **Dash Tabasco**
- ½ **teaspoon Worcestershire sauce**
- 2 **hard-boiled eggs, peeled and chopped**

POTATO SOUP

It is amazing how few recipes are available for good, old-fashioned potato soup. Many of our guests have requested my recipe. It is marvelous on days when you may need a lift. This is "heart and soul" food which requires little preparation.

Bring the water to a boil in a 3-quart saucepan. Add the potatoes, celery, onion, chives, salt, and pepper. Reduce heat and simmer slowly for 25 minutes. Stir in the evaporated milk and bring to a boil. Just before serving, add the butter. This recipe reheats nicely.

Makes 6 servings

- 6 **cups water**
- 6 **medium potatoes, peeled and diced**
- 2 **stalks celery, diced**
- 1 **small onion, chopped**
- 3 **tablespoons chopped chives**
- 1½ **teaspoons salt**
- ¼ **teaspoon freshly ground black pepper**
- 1 **cup evaporated milk**
- 2 **tablespoons butter**

SPLIT PEA AND TOMATO SOUP

It is hard to imagine that there are people who do not know that split peas are always dried. These peas have a distinct flavor which is enhanced by ham broth. The tomatoes give this recipe a unique freshness.

Rinse and carefully clean the dried peas. Put them in a heavy 3-quart saucepan with the water, onion, ham hock, and salt (when using chopped ham, do not add the salt until later). Simmer on low to medium heat for 1½ hours, stirring with a wooden spoon every 10 minutes to prevent the peas from sticking. Remove the ham hock and cut off all the meat. Chop the meat into bite-size pieces. Puree the peas in a food processor, blender, or food mill. Put the pea puree back in the pan with the milk, tomatoes, pieces of ham, and pepper to taste. Simmer on low heat for 30 minutes, stirring occasionally. Serve with croutons as a garnish.

2 cups dried split peas
6 cups water
¼ cup chopped onion
1 cup chopped smoked ham or a 2-pound smoked ham hock
1 teaspoon salt
1 cup milk
1 cup peeled, seeded, and chopped ripe tomatoes, including their juice
Freshly ground black pepper
Freshly made croutons for garnish

Makes 6 servings

VICHYSSOISE (COLD POTATO SOUP)

Melt butter in heavy soup kettle. Sauté onions till golden and soft. Add potatoes, chicken broth, salt, and pepper. Simmer on low heat till potatoes are very soft, even mushy. Blend or puree mixture in a food processor, or press through sieve with a wooden spoon. Return to kettle. Add light and heavy cream. Over medium heat, stir constantly until mixture begins to boil. Remove and put through sieve or processor again. Cool to room temperature. Cover and chill several hours in refrigerator. Soup should be very cold when served. To serve, pour into chilled bowls and top with chopped chives. In very hot weather, place crushed ice in large bowls and serve soup in cups on top of the ice.

3 tablespoons butter or margarine
2 medium onions, sliced
1½ pounds potatoes, peeled and sliced thinly
2 cups chicken broth
1½ teaspoons salt
◆ Dash pepper
1 cup light cream
2 cups heavy cream
Chopped chives for topping

Serves 6–8

SUMMER BEET SOUP

Put the ham hock in a 6-quart pot with water to cover. Bring to a boil, skim off scum, reduce the heat, and simmer until tender—about 1½ hours. Remove the hock and take off all the meat, cutting it into bite-size pieces. Discard bone. Put meat back in the pan with the cabbage, onions, potatoes, tomatoes, beets, dill, thyme, salt, and pepper. Cook slowly for at least 20 minutes. Remove sprigs of dill and thyme, if used. Add beet tops and cook 2 minutes until wilted. Remove pan from heat and stir in the sour cream and chives just before serving. This is best served in deep soup plates or large bowls.

VARIATION

If you have a garden and grow golden beets, which are not available in the markets, you can use them instead of the red beets and the soup will have a lovely golden tinge.

Makes 6 servings

2 pounds smoked ham hock or ham end
Water to cover ham
1 medium head green cabbage, shredded or diced
2 medium onions, chopped
3 medium potatoes, peeled and diced
2 large ripe tomatoes, peeled, seeded, and diced
1 cup peeled and sliced red beets
3 sprigs fresh or 1 teaspoon dried dill
3 sprigs fresh or ½ teaspoon dried thyme
2 teaspoons salt
¼ teaspoon freshly ground black pepper
1 cup chopped beet tops
½ cup sour cream
2 tablespoons chopped chives

"GOODIES" TO SERVE WITH SOUP

TOASTED CRACKERS

Put plain unsalted crackers on a baking sheet. Sprinkle lightly with grated cheese and paprika. Bake in a preheated 350° F. oven until just browned. Serve at once.

BREAD ALMONDS

Cut dry bread in slices ⅛″ thick. Cut into circles with a tiny round cutter or with a thimble that has been scalded in hot water. With a sharp paring knife, trim the circles to the shape of almonds. Brush with melted butter and bake in a preheated 450° F. oven until delicately browned. Serve with hot soups.

CELERY CURLS AND CARROT STRIPS

Clean carrots and celery. Trim and cut lengthwise in very thin strips. Make 2 to 3 cuts in the end of the celery and place in ice water until curled. Also put carrot strips in ice water to keep crisp. Serve with hot or cold soups.

SPRING IN LANCASTER COUNTY, Watercolor

Typical of the Pennsylvania German garden, each flower
bed is neatly kept in straight rows. Tulips are traditional
spring flowers, which bloom from year to year
announcing the rebirth of spring.

3

MEATS

MEATS

BEEF

Abe's Standing Prime Rib Roast
Beef and Mushrooms in Wine
Barbecued Ribs
Beefsteak Marinade
Creamed Sweet Bologna Gravy
Janet High's Hasty Chili
Hamburg Steak with Herb Cheese
My Special Meat Loaf
Rolled Brisket of Beef with Horseradish Sauce
Sauerbraten
Stuffed Beefsteaks
Swiss Steak with Mushrooms
Baked Fresh Ham with Sherry Baste
Vera Bragg's Beef Pie

LAMB

Charlie's Crown Roast of Lamb with Crème de Menthe

HAM

Baked Home-Cured Ham
Fran Sauder's Ham Loaf
Schnitz und Knepp
Dad's Sausage
Thelma's Ham Roll Surprise
Ham and Corn Pie

PORK

Pork and Sauerkraut with Dumplings
Pork Chops or Cubes, Spring Onions, and Sugar Peas
Breaded Pork Chops
Roast Loin of Pork with Apricot-Pineapple Glaze
Sausage, Corn, and Peppers
Winter Sausage Bake

VEAL

Abe's Roast Round of Veal with Herb Gravy
Wiener Schnitzel

VARIETY MEATS

Panfried Liver and Onions
Braised Beef Heart
Pickled Beef Heart
Sweetbread Croquettes

GAME

Betty's Venison Stew
Fried Rabbit
Hasenpfeffer

ABE'S STANDING PRIME RIB ROAST

Guests marvel that Abe's rib roasts are always moist, yet rare and delicious. Part of the secret is in the roasting, the other in the quality of the beef. We buy only top choice or prime rib, depending on the fat content desired. Abe starts the roast with water in the bottom of the roasting pan, and he tents the roast with foil—never a lid.

1 (6-pound) prime or top choice standing rib roast
1 tablespoon salt
1 teaspoon pepper
1 cup water

Moisten the roast with water so the seasoning will stick. Sprinkle with the salt and pepper. Place in roasting pan. Add the water. Tent the roast loosely with foil. Bake in a preheated 275° F. oven for 4½ hours. To be sure the meat is cooked to your liking, use a meat thermometer. Remove the foil 35 minutes before serving to ensure even browning.

When serving only the eye of the roast, save the rest for barbecued ribs, or to use for a rich stock. Trim the fat and cut each rib away separately for barbecued ribs. Use the sauce recipe for barbecued pork ribs, baking in a shallow pan at 425° F. until crispy. Supergood!

MICROWAVE: Place standing rib roast fat side down on microwave rack in a 9″ x 13″ baking dish. Cover with paper towels. Cook 5 minutes per pound for rare. After 25 minutes remove from microwave, and let stand for 5 minutes. Turn meat fat side up and cover again. Cook 15 minutes longer. Remove from microwave. Cover with aluminum foil and let stand 25 minutes.

Serves 6

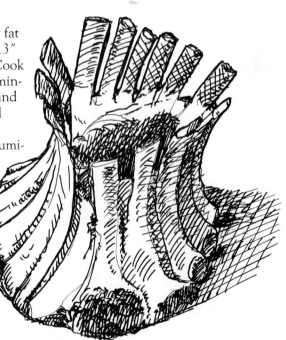

BEEF AND MUSHROOMS IN WINE

An excellent way to use the ends of roast beef left from our dinners in the restaurant.

Bring the broth to a boil in a 6-quart saucepan. Add the wine and allow it to boil for about 2 minutes to cook off the alcohol. In a small bowl, mix the arrowroot and cold water to a smooth paste. Reduce the heat to a simmer and stir in the arrowroot until the broth has thickened. Add the beef and mushrooms and heat thoroughly. Gradually stir in the sour cream, taking care not to boil, or the sour cream will separate. Serve over steamed rice or noodles.

MICROWAVE: Bring broth to boil in a 6-quart covered casserole. Stir in arrowroot, stirring every 30 seconds. Add beef and heat for approximately 4 minutes. Gradually stir in sour cream.

Makes 6 servings

4 cups well-seasoned beef broth
½ cup red or rosé wine
3 tablespoons arrowroot
¼ cup cold water
4 cups rare roast beef, cut in 1″ cubes
1 cup sliced fresh mushrooms
1 cup sour cream

BARBECUED RIBS

Pork Ribs are inexpensive, and delicious served as a main dish or in smaller quantities as an appetizer. The sauce may be made ahead. It is good for beef or pork ribs, and will not spoil for several weeks if it is refrigerated.

Cut the ribs apart and place them in a large baking pan. Sprinkle with salt. Bake in a 450° F. oven for 45 minutes. Spoon the sauce over the ribs and bake for an additional 30 minutes.

Blend thoroughly and use to barbecue the ribs.

Serves 6

3 pounds beef or pork short ribs, cut to make 6 servings
1 teaspoon salt

SAUCE

⅔ cup tomato paste
1 tablespoon Dijon mustard
½ cup brown sugar
½ cup wine, red or white
½ teaspoon salt

BEEFSTEAK MARINADE

Mix and shake all ingredients in a tightly sealed container. Refrigerate 12–16 hours. Reshake before using. Unused marinade will keep indefinitely if refrigerated. To use, put steaks in a container and marinate. Cover with lid and refrigerate overnight before cooking.

1 cup red wine
½ cup olive oil
⅓ cup soy sauce
¼ teaspoon finely ground black pepper
¼ teaspoon dried and crushed rosemary
¼ teaspoon dried and crushed thyme
2 bay leaves, crushed
1 teaspoon ground shallots
1 clove garlic, minced or chopped
◆ Dash Tabasco
¼ teaspoon salt

CREAMED SWEET BOLOGNA GRAVY

On cool evenings during spring plantings and at other busy times, this was a good standby. I was used to creamed dried beef on toast or potato cakes. At Abe's home, his mother used bologna. It became a family favorite.

Melt the butter in a large heavy skillet. Stir in the flour over medium heat until light brown. Add the diced bologna. Stir with a wooden spoon till the meat is well coated and there are no flour lumps. Continue to stir over medium heat till meat edges begin to curl. Gradually add the milk, continuing to stir. Next add the evaporated milk and simmer about 15–20 minutes on low heat until thickened. Serve on whole wheat toast, with potato cakes, or with cooked and peeled sweet potatoes.

Serves 4

3 tablespoons butter or vegetable shortening
3 tablespoons flour
½ pound sliced bologna, diced
¼ teaspoon salt
◆ Dash (or 2) freshly ground pepper
2 cups milk
1 cup evaporated milk

JANET HIGH'S HASTY CHILI

In a large heavy skillet or saucepan, brown the beef in the shortening until it loses its red color. Add the onion and simmer 5 minutes. Add the tomatoes, kidney beans, salt, chili powder, and pepper and simmer for 1 hour on low heat.

This may be prepared in a crockpot.

MICROWAVE: Melt shortening 20 seconds. Crumble ground beef in a 2-quart glass casserole. Stir in onion; cover. Microwave on high for 5 minutes. Add remaining ingredients; re-cover. Microwave on medium for 15 minutes. Let stand, covered for 5 minutes before serving.

Serves 6

1 pound lean ground beef
2 tablespoons vegetable shortening
1 medium onion, diced
2 cups peeled and chopped fresh or canned tomatoes
2 cups canned kidney beans
1 teaspoon salt
2 teaspoons chili powder
1/8 teaspoon cayenne pepper

HAMBURG STEAK WITH HERB CHEESE

Blend beef, salt, pepper, and onions until well mixed. Form into patties about 1″ thick. Fry in a heated, buttered skillet or grill to desired degree of doneness. Top with herb cheese. Serve immediately.

Blend all ingredients thoroughly. Store, covered in the refrigerator. Also delicious as a sandwich spread or as a dip with vegetable sticks.

Serves 4–6

1½ pounds choice ground beef
1 teaspoon salt
¼ teaspoon pepper
1 tablespoon chopped onions, optional

HERB CHEESE

2 tablespoons chopped fresh herbs, such as thyme, chives, dill, and possibly a pinch of lovage or sage (select available herbs and mix to your liking)
8 ounces cream cheese
2 tablespoons sour cream or mayonnaise
½ teaspoon salt (optional)

MY SPECIAL MEAT LOAF

Boil the eggs for 10 minutes. Cool under running water and peel. Set aside. Mix all other ingredients thoroughly and divide in 2 parts. Place first half in baking pan, forming into bottom half of meat loaf. Place hard-boiled eggs end to end in middle. Cover with remaining half. Bake in a 375° F. oven for 1 hour and 15 minutes. Garnish with watercress.

Serves 4–6

- 6 hard-boiled quail or 4 small chicken eggs
- ½ pound hamburger
- ½ pound ground veal
- 2 eggs, beaten
- 1 tablespoon chopped parsley
- ½ cup chopped tomatoes
- 1 teaspoon salt
- ◆ Several dashes freshly ground pepper
- ½ cup milk
- 1 stalk chopped celery
- 1 cup bread crumbs

Watercress for garnish

ROLLED BRISKET OF BEEF WITH HORSERADISH SAUCE

This dish was always served to special guests for summer parties—cold in summer, hot in winter.

Rolled brisket should be served well done, but juicy. Moisten the roast with water. Add salt and pepper. Place in a roaster pan and add the 1½ cups water. Tent with foil and bake in a preheated oven at 300° F. for 4 hours, removing the foil for the last 30 minutes. Save the broth for stock. Serve with Horseradish Sauce. This is delicious served hot or cold and slices nicely for sandwiches.

Mix all ingredients in a bowl until well blended, then whip with whisk until light and airy. Serve with sliced beef.

Serves 8

- 6 pounds rolled brisket of beef
- 2 tablespoons salt
- 1 teaspoon pepper
- 1½ cups water

HORSERADISH SAUCE

- 5 tablespoons grated fresh horseradish
- 3 tablespoons cider vinegar
- 2 tablespoons prepared mustard
- 1 teaspoon salt
- ◆ Dash pepper
- ◆ Dash paprika
- ½ cup sour cream

SAUERBRATEN

This is an old German standby, beloved by many, and an excellent meat to serve with boiled potatoes and a relish. It is not too difficult to make, but when I was first married and wanted to make "sour beef," as it was called in Pennsylvania Dutch Country, it seemed to be a lot of work. It is a variation for a meat that is still reasonably priced.

In a 2-quart saucepan, combine the wine, vinegar, water, onions, salt, and spices. Bring to a boil. Remove from the heat and cool to room temperature. Put the beef in a 1-gallon crockpot or a stainless steel pot. Choose a pot which is not much larger than the roast but leaves enough room for the marinade. Pour the marinade over the roast, and refrigerate for 3 days. Turn the meat twice each day.

When ready to cook the sauerbraten, remove it from the marinade and pat dry with paper towels. Strain the marinade and save it, but discard the onions and spices.

Melt the shortening in a 3-quart saucepot. Brown the sauerbraten on all sides. Remove the meat and sauté the onions, carrots, and celery until the onions are clear. Add the flour and stir until golden brown. Gradually add the marinade and water, and stir until it comes to a boil. Add the meat. Cover and simmer for 1 hour and 15 minutes. (If you prefer the beef pink in the center, cook only 45 minutes.) Serve sliced thin with the marinade gravy. Serve with boiled potato, dumplings, or potato cakes and a relish, or a fresh green salad.

Serves 6

4	**pound roast of top round of beef**
1	**cup dry red wine**
¾	**cup wine vinegar**
1½	**cups water**
1	**medium onion, sliced thin**
1	**teaspoon salt**
8	**whole black peppercorns, broken**
4	**whole cloves**
2	**bay leaves**
¼	**teaspoon ground ginger**
3	**tablespooons vegetable shortening**
½	**cup chopped onions**
½	**cup diced carrots**
½	**cup chopped celery**
3	**tablespoons flour**
⅔	**cup water**

STUFFED BEEFSTEAKS

In a bowl add salt to cooked rice. In a saucepan melt butter and sauté herbs, onions, and pepper for 5 minutes. Add mushrooms and simmer 3 minutes longer. Add rice and stir until well blended. Spoon mixture into the middle of each steak and fold together, keeping as much rice inside as possible. Secure with toothpicks.

Heat butter or oil in large frying pan and add the steaks. Sprinkle lightly with salt and pepper. Brown over medium heat about 5 minutes on each side. Remove steaks from pan and place on a heated platter. To make gravy, dissolve cornstarch in water and wine. Add to beef brownings in pan, stirring constantly till thickened and golden brown. Season to taste. Serve with steaks and rice left from the stuffing mix.

MICROWAVE: To reheat in a microwave oven, splash a little red wine over each steak before reheating.

Serves 4–6

2 pounds beef (top round or sirloin steak) sliced ⅓″ thick
2 tablespoons butter or oil
½ teaspoon salt
◆ Dash pepper
2 tablespoons cornstarch
¾ cup water
¼ cup red or white wine

STUFFING

2 cups cooked rice
1 teaspoon salt
1 tablespoon fresh chives, chopped
1 teaspoon chopped fresh lemon-scented thyme or regular thyme and ½ teaspoon grated lemon rind
½ cup chopped green pepper—about ½ medium-size pepper
½ cup chopped onion
2 tablespoons butter
½ cup sliced mushrooms

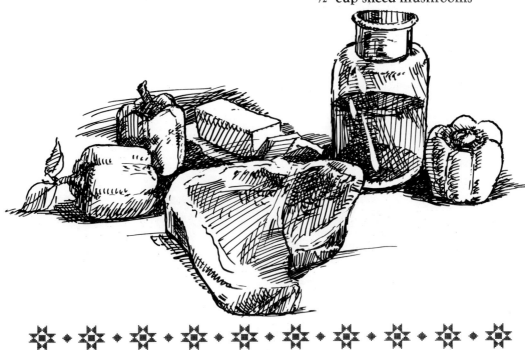

SWISS STEAK WITH MUSHROOMS

In a large heavy skillet, heat the butter. Sauté the onions and mushrooms for approximately 4 minutes. Remove and save. Pound the flour into the steak. Put in heated butter. Add half the salt and pepper and brown thoroughly. Turn and brown, adding the rest of the salt and pepper. When browned add the water, onions and mushrooms and cover. Simmer on low heat for approximately 45 minutes until meat is very tender. Add more water if needed. Check seasonings, adding salt and pepper if needed. There should be about 1 cup gravy to serve with the steak.

Serves 4

3 tablespoons butter or shortening
1 cup sliced fresh mushrooms
2 tablespoons chopped onion
⅓ cup flour
1½ pounds boneless round steak, cut 1" thick
¾ teaspoon salt
¼ teaspoon pepper
1 cup water

BAKED FRESH HAM WITH SHERRY BASTE

Remove rind from ham. Season with salt and pepper. Place in a roaster pan, bone side down, and with a sharp knife score the top in a diamond design. Add the water and tent with heavy foil. Bake at 350° F. in a preheated oven for approximately 4 hours, or until the ham is tender and pulls away from the bone. Every 30 minutes baste the ham with sherry. Save the brownings in the pan for gravy. Deglaze the pan by adding several cups of water and reheating the pan. Thicken by adding a paste of flour, arrowroot, or cornstarch dissolved in cold water. Save any leftover meat as a cold cut, or stir-fry with fresh vegetables.

Serves 8–12

1 fresh ham
2 tablespoons salt
1 teaspoon pepper
3 cups water
2 cups sherry

VERA BRAGG'S BEEF PIE

Vera Bragg is a dear friend and a wonderful cook, and her beef pie is truly special. Everytime Vera goes to Indiana to visit her grandchildren, they ask for this dish. It took a little coaxing to get Vera to measure all the recipe ingredients exactly, but now we can all enjoy her masterpiece. This pie freezes beautifully, baked or unbaked.

Melt the butter in a 3 quart saucepan or a heavy skillet. Sauté the green pepper and onions until the onions are golden. Add the hamburger, salts, and pepper and brown lightly, breaking up the hamburger with a wooden spoon. Cook for about 10 minutes until all traces of red have disappeared from the meat. Add the mushrooms, tomatoes, catsup, and sugar and simmer for 10 minutes. Mix the flour and water to a smooth paste. Stir into the meat mixture. Cook, stirring, for about 5 minutes until thickened. Set aside.

To make the pastry, cut or rub the lard and butter into the flour and salt to make fine crumbs. Moisten the crumbs with the beaten eggs and mix by hand to form a ball of dough. This method makes a much richer, flakier dough than ice water. Turn the dough onto a generously floured pastry board and divide in two. Roll out the crust, rather thicker than for a dessert pie. Use pastry to line the bottom of two deep 10″ pie pans, reserving enough dough for the top crust. Add the meat to the pie shells and moisten edges of pastry with water. Top with the remaining dough and crimp the edges to seal. Make a slash in the top crust to allow steam to escape. Bake in a preheated 350° F. oven for 40 minutes until pie is a light brown.

Makes 6–8 servings or 2 deep 10″ pies

2 tablespoons butter
1 cup finely chopped green bell pepper
1 cup finely chopped onions
1½ pounds lean hamburger
2 teaspoons salt
1 teaspoon Krazy salt
½ teaspoon freshly ground black pepper
2½ cups trimmed and sliced fresh mushrooms
2½ cups peeled, seeded, and diced tomatoes or drained and chopped canned tomatoes
½ cup tomato catsup
1 tablespoon sugar
4 tablespoons flour
½ cup cold water

PASTRY

⅔ cup lard
⅓ cup butter
3 cups all-purpose flour
1 teaspoon salt
3 eggs, beaten

CHARLIE'S CROWN ROAST OF LAMB WITH CRÈME DE MENTHE

While our son Charlie was studying at the Culinary Institute of America he catered many parties for us. It gave him practice in preparation and entertaining and our guests enjoyed watching him. In this particular recipe, we found that if the lamb is basted with crème de menthe the sometimes strong flavor of lanolin quickly vanishes. For special entertaining, the roast can be a showstopper.

Rub lamb with garlic. Season with salt and pepper. Wrap foil around each bone end. Bake at 275° F. for 4 hours. Baste roast with crème de menthe every 20 minutes until all is used. After basting, tent roast with foil till finished. Remove from oven and take foil off bone ends. Place fresh uncooked mushroom cap on each bone end. Fill with baked apple stuffing before serving.

4–5 pound crown roast of lamb (have the butcher cut the joints so it can be fanned into a crown)
1 clove garlic, broken into pieces
2 teaspoons salt (less if desired)
½ teaspoon freshly ground pepper
Foil for wrapping rib bones
½ cup crème de menthe
Fresh mushroom caps (one for each bone end)

APPLE STUFFING

Fry bacon and drain on paper towels. Break into bits. On low heat, sauté celery, onions, and parsley in the bacon fat for 10 minutes. Remove mixture to a large mixing bowl. Add sugar to the remaining fat in the pan; then add apples and raisins. Sauté until apples are golden and almost soft. Put apples, bacon bits, and bread crumbs in the mixing bowl with the celery-onion mixture and toss together until well blended. Bake in 2-quart casserole in a preheated oven at 350° F. for 30 minutes.

Serves 6

6 slices bacon
½ cup chopped celery
⅓ cup chopped onions
¼ cup chopped parsley
½ cup light brown sugar
4 cups apples, peeled, cored, and diced
1 cup raisins
1 cup fresh bread crumbs

✳ ✦ ✳ ✦ ✳ ✦ ✳ ✦ ✳ ✦ ✳ ✦ ✳ ✦ ✳ ✦ ✳ ✦ ✳

BAKED HOME-CURED HAM

Remove the rind from the cured ham and place, bone side down, in a roaster pan. Add water, tent with foil, and bake in a 325° F. preheated oven for 2½ hours. Remove and debone. If the broth seems salty, pour off and add 2 cups fresh water. Put the deboned ham in the water and continue to bake at 325° for another hour. Serve plain or with Wine-Raisin Sauce.

Baking the ham in water keeps it moist and tender. Changing the water is necessary only if the ham is very salty. It will still retain the smoky flavor.

Serves 12

12–14 pound whole smoked, cured ham
4 cups water

FRAN SAUDER'S HAM LOAF

In a large mixing bowl, combine the ham and beef, mixing well with a wooden spoon. Add the remaining ingredients and form into 2 loaves. Place in 2 greased loaf pans or one large baking dish. (Bake one, freeze one). Bake in preheated 350° F. oven for 1 hour or until golden brown and bubbling on top.

MICROWAVE: Microwave ham loaf in a 10–12″ glass casserole for 5 minutes. Rotate dish by half turns and baste with juice for 10 minutes. Let stand 10 minutes before serving.

Serves 8–10

1½ pounds ground cured ham
2 pounds ground beef
1 small onion, diced fine
2 eggs, lightly beaten
½ cup tapioca
½ cup dry bread crumbs
1 cup milk
½ cup water
½ cup white vinegar
¾ cup light brown sugar
1 tablespoon prepared mustard
1 teaspoon salt
½ teaspoon pepper

SCHNITZ UND KNEPP

This traditional dish of the Pennsylvania Dutch was not included in Good Earth and Country Cooking even though it is very popular in this area. The mixture of sweet and salt is not a personal favorite of mine. However, I do love dumplings and Knepp is the Pennsylvania Dutch word for dumplings, while Schnitz is "Dutch" for dried sliced apples.

Put the ham and apples in a heavy 6-quart cooking pot or Dutch oven, with a tight-fitting cover, and add water to cover. Add the brown sugar and, if you like the flavor, cinnamon, or cloves. Bring to a boil. Cover and reduce the heat. Simmer on medium low heat for about 1½ hours until the ham is tender. Precooked ham, of course, will take less time than a smoked ham butt—only about 30 minutes. When tender, remove the ham and debone. Cut the meat into bite-size pieces and return it to the pan. If too much of the ham broth has evaporated in the cooking, add 1 cup hot water. There should be enough liquid to cook the dumplings.

While the ham and apples are cooking, sift the flour with the baking powder and salt into a large bowl. Cut in the butter with a pastry blender or with your fingers. Add the milk and stir vigorously with a wooden spoon until the dough is smooth.

While the liquid is at a simmer, drop in the dumpling dough by tablespoons. Cover the pan with the lid and simmer for 12 minutes, *without peeking.* Remove the dumplings with a slotted spoon and set aside while pouring the ham and apple stew into a pre-heated bowl or deep platter. Arrange the dumplings on top and serve at once.

Makes 6–8 servings

1 (3-pound) smoked ham butt
½ pound sliced dried apples (schnitz)
6 cups water, enough to cover ham and apples
2 tablespoons brown sugar
Cloves or ground cinnamon to taste (optional)

DUMPLING DOUGH
2 cups all-purpose flour
1 tablespoon baking powder
¼ teaspoon salt
2 tablespoons butter, at room temperature
1½ cups milk

DAD'S SAUSAGE

Grind the pork with the salt, pepper, and sugar. Mix well. Form into patties. Fry in heavy skillet until golden brown on each side and fully cooked inside—approximately 12 minutes.

10 pounds

10 pounds pork, coarsely ground
½ cup salt
1¼ tablespoons black pepper
1½ tablespoons sugar

THELMA'S HAM ROLL SURPRISE

Preheat oven to 350° F. In a medium bowl, combine the beef, Russian dressing, bread crumbs, onions, salt, and pepper. Use 2 slices of ham for each roll, placing one above the other. Place ¼ of the beef mixture along the side lengthwise on each of the 4 ham slices. Roll the ham around the meat. Secure each slice with 4 whole cloves. Arrange in a baking dish with the seam side down.

In a small saucepan, melt the butter. Stir in the flour, then the sugar, Russian dressing, orange juice and mustard. Bring to a boil. Pour the sauce over the meat rolls. Bake in a preheated 350° F. oven for 1 hour, basting occasionally. Place the sliced pineapple on top for last 15 minutes of baking.

MICROWAVE: Follow recipe until placing in oven. Place in a covered casserole and bake for approximately 15 minutes, basting every 4 minutes. Place the pineapple on top for last 3 minutes of baking.

Serves 4

¾ pound ground beef
¼ cup Russian dressing
¼ cup dry bread crumbs
¼ cup chopped onions
½ teaspoon salt
◆ Dash pepper
8 thin slices boiled or baked ham
16 whole cloves

SAUCE
2 tablespoons butter
1 tablespoon flour
½ cup light brown sugar
¼ cup Russian dressing
¼ cup orange juice
2 teaspoons prepared mustard
Sliced pineapple for garnish

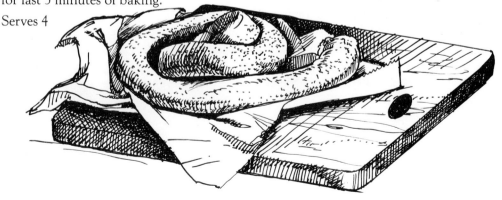

HAM AND CORN PIE

Combine ham, corn, eggs, salt, sugar, pepper, flour, and butter. Pour into pastry-lined pan and cover with top crust. Slit the top crust to let the steam escape. Bake in a preheated oven at 350° F. for 1 hour and 15 minutes. Make 1 to eat and 1 to freeze.

Makes 1 (9″ x 13″) baking dish or 2 (10″) pies

2 cups diced precooked or baked ham
4 cups fresh corn kernels
4 eggs, lightly beaten
1 teaspoon salt
1½ teaspoons sugar
¼ teaspoon freshly ground pepper
2 tablespoons flour
⅓ cup melted butter
Pastry for large baking dish or 2 pie pans; use Meat Pie Pastry recipe (see Index)

PORK AND SAUERKRAUT WITH DUMPLINGS

There are only two ways to enjoy pork and sauerkraut if you are Pennsylvania Dutch. One is with mounds of buttery mashed potatoes; the other is with dumplings. Add a salad and you have a perfect meal. But remember—do not lift the lid for 12 minutes while cooking your dumplings.

Put the pork in a 6-quart Dutch oven or heavy saucepan with a tight-fitting lid. Cover with the water and add the salt and pepper. Bring to a boil, reduce heat, and simmer about 2 hours until tender. Remove the pork and take the meat from the bone. Cut the meat in bite-size pieces and return to the liquid, together with the sauerkraut. Bring the liquid to a simmer. Drop the dumpling dough into the simmering liquid by tablespoons. Immediately cover and simmer for 12 minutes, *without lifting the lid*. Remove the dumplings with a slotted spoon and set aside, while pouring the pork and sauerkraut into a deep platter or large serving dish. Arrange the dumplings on top, and serve at once.

Makes 8–10 servings

1 (4-pound) pork loin roast
3 quarts water
1 tablespoon salt
Freshly ground black pepper to taste
4 cups fresh, or canned sauerkraut, drained
Dumpling dough—see recipe for Schnitz und Knepp (see Index)

PORK CHOPS OR CUBES, SPRING ONIONS, AND SUGAR PEAS

In a wok or heavy skillet, melt butter or oil. When hot, add chops or cubed pork and stir fry until golden brown on all sides. Add onions and peas and stir-fry for 1 minute, stirring constantly. Add salt and pepper and toss in pan. Cover with lid for 1 minute. Serve over noodles or white rice.

VARIATION

Veal may be substituted for the pork, or sliced mushrooms may be added to the peas and onions.

Serves 4

2 tablespoons butter or cooking oil

4 pork chops, deboned, or 2 pounds fresh pork, cut in cubes

12 spring onions, sliced ½" thick, including green tops

1 pound sugar peas or snow peas

1 teaspoon salt

Freshly ground pepper

BREADED PORK CHOPS

Dip the chops in the beaten eggs and season with salt and pepper. Mix the bread and cracker crumbs together. Dip the seasoned chops in the crumbs. Cover well. Melt the shortening in a heavy skillet. Panfry over medium heat for approximately 15 minutes on each side until golden brown, or brown in the oven by placing shortening in the bottom of a pan. Bake in a preheated 375° F. oven for 30 minutes, turning after 15 minutes.

Serves 6

2 pounds fresh pork chops, cut ¾" thick

2 eggs, lightly beaten

1 teaspoon salt

¼ teaspoon pepper

½ cup dry bread crumbs

¼ cup saltine cracker crumbs

Shortening for frying

ROAST LOIN OF PORK WITH APRICOT-PINEAPPLE GLAZE

The loin of pork is a taste treat and often inexpensive. For a different taste, we serve it with a fruit glaze. On one occasion, a guest put the fruit glaze on a broiled fish. Others used it on their roast duck. Everyone was delighted, so do experiment with it.

Season the pork loin with salt and pepper and place it in a small roasting pan. Add the water and cover. Bake in a preheated oven at 375°F. for 3 hours. Remove the cover and pour some of the glaze over the meat. Reduce the heat to 350° and bake for another 30 minutes. Serve the remainder of the glaze with the meat.

MICROWAVE: Microwave in a glass baking dish for 12 minutes per pound (1 hour) on low setting. Cover loin with waxed paper. When finished remove from oven and leave standing for 15 minutes.

Blend all ingredients in a food processor, then bring them to a slow boil in a heavy saucepan. Simmer for 3 minutes, stirring constantly with a wooden spoon. Set aside, and serve hot or cold.

Serves 6

1 (6-pound) loin of pork, with bone
2 teaspoons salt
½ teaspoon pepper
1 cup water

APRICOT-PINEAPPLE GLAZE

½ cup cooked and pitted apricots
½ cup pineapples, cooked
1 tablespoon arrowroot or cornstarch
½ cup red or white wine
¼ cup brown sugar
¼ teaspoon ground cinnamon
¼ teaspoon ground nutmeg
¼ teaspoon ground cloves

SAUSAGE, CORN, AND PEPPERS

Form sausage into bite-size balls. Fry in wok or heavy skillet until golden brown—approximately 8 minutes. Remove all but 2 tablespoons fat, then add corn, peppers, salt, and pepper, and rosemary. Stir-fry until peppers are tender—approximately 5 minutes—covering pan with lid for the last 3 minutes.

Serves 4–6

1½–2 pounds sausage
3 cups corn kernels
3 medium red or green bell peppers, diced
1 teaspoon salt
Freshly ground pepper to taste
Sprig fresh rosemary, chopped fine

WINTER SAUSAGE BAKE

Our children always enjoyed sausage and creamed potatoes, but I found that adding cabbage gave this dish an especially good flavor. Furthermore, this added the vegetable needed to complete a nutritious meal. During the winter, cabbage is inexpensive and it keeps well in the refrigerator. For a stronger flavor and more color, use smoked sausage.

Brown the sausage till golden brown. Place half of it in the bottom of a large 2½-quart oblong baking dish. Add half of the sliced potatoes and sprinkle with half of the flour and salt. Add half the chopped cabbage. Repeat, using the ingredients in the same order. Sprinkle pepper on top. Pour the milk over the dish and bake in a preheated oven at 375° F. for 1 hour. If using a deep baking dish, increase the baking time by approximately 15 minutes.

NOTE: Potatoes may be used peeled or not. Adjust the amount of salt if the sausage is bland.

Serves 4–6

1 pound sausage links, cut in 1″ pieces
6 medium white potatoes, sliced thin
½ medium head cabbage, coarsely chopped
3 tablespoons flour
1½ cups milk
1 teaspoon salt
Freshly ground pepper

ABE'S ROAST ROUND OF VEAL WITH HERB GRAVY

Sprinkle veal with seasonings and place in a small roasting pan. Place bacon strips on top of the seasoned meat. Add 1 cup of the water. Tent with foil and bake in a preheated oven at 300° F. for 3 hours. Before serving, remove meat to a heated platter and deglaze the roasting pan with 1 cup water. Thicken with 1 tablespoon cornstarch or arrowroot dissolved in ¼ cup water. You may add a pinch of thyme and chives to the gravy if you like a combination of herbs.

Serves 6–8

4 pounds fresh veal round or shoulder
2 teaspoons salt, preferably coarse
½ teaspoon coarse pepper
½ teaspoon dried oregano
½ teaspoon dried rosemary
4 slices bacon
2¼ cups water
1 tablespoon arrowroot or cornstarch for sauce (optional)

WIENER SCHNITZEL

Friends often ask why our Wiener Schnitzel is so special. There are two reasons: We do not overcook the veal and the breading is different. The combination of bread and cracker crumbs makes a very fine crust.

With knife, slit edges of cutlets to keep from curling. Pound cutlets till about ¼″ thick. Set aside. Mix flour, salt, and pepper together. Dredge cutlets in this mixture. Combine beaten egg and milk. Dip flour-covered cutlets in egg mixture. Mix bread and cracker crumbs. Coat cutlets. Place cooking oil in heavy skillet and fry cutlets over medium heat till golden brown—approximately 3 minutes on each side. Do not overcook! Garnish with lemon slices and parsley.

Serves 6

2 pounds veal cutlet, cut ½″ thick
½ cup all-purpose flour
1½ teaspoons salt
½ teaspoon freshly ground pepper
2 eggs, lightly beaten
1 tablespoon evaporated or regular milk
1 cup dry bread crumbs
½ cup saltine cracker crumbs, rolled fine
¼ cup cooking oil
Lemon slices
Fresh parsley

PANFRIED LIVER AND ONIONS

In a heavy skillet, melt the butter. Sauté the onions till they are clear and tender; then remove to a heated platter. Heat skillet until it is very hot. Add the liver, pressing it down with a fork to seal in all the juices. Fry until browned, then add salt and pepper. Turn and repeat on other side, about 3 minutes on each side. Return onions to skillet. Cover until onions are hot. Serve as you would steak. Do not be afraid to serve the liver slightly pink in the middle. Liver is tender when not overcooked.

Serves 4

3 tablespoons butter

1 cup sliced onions

1½ pounds fresh calf's liver, sliced 1″ thick, skin removed

¾ teaspoon salt

¼ teaspoon pepper

BRAISED BEEF HEART

Cover with water. Add salt and pepper. Place heart in a 6-quart Dutch oven or heavy pot with lid. Boil on low heat for 2½ hours. Remove heart and trim fat. Cut in half and fill with Bread or Potato Filling. Set each half upside down in a 9″ x 13″ dish, and bake in a preheated oven at 375° F. for 15 minutes. Baste with red wine. Bake 15 minutes longer and serve at once. If you wish to deglaze the pan to make a sauce, quickly add 1 cup hot water and thicken with 2 tablespoons arrowroot dissolved in ¼ cup water. Herbs may be added to this sauce.

Mix all the ingredients together and stuff the heart halves.

Serves 6

3 pounds fresh beef heart, well cleaned

2 quarts water

1 tablespoon salt

¼ teaspoon pepper

Red wine, enough for basting

Bread or Potato Filling (see below)

2 tablespoons arrowroot (optional)

Herbs (optional)

BREAD OR POTATO FILLING

2 cups bread cubes or 2 cups mashed potatoes

2 eggs, lightly beaten

⅓ cup milk

¼ cup very finely chopped onions

¼ cup very finely chopped celery

½ teaspoon salt

Freshly ground pepper

PICKLED BEEF HEART

Beef hearts are inexpensive and so good! I like to prepare the whole heart. I then serve half of it hot with horseradish sauce and pickle the rest. It keeps, refrigerated, for weeks and is a delicious appetizer.

Cut heart in half and remove any large veins. Place in a 5–6-quart Dutch oven or heavy pot. Add the water, salt, and pepper. Next add the onion and pepper, then the thyme. Bring to a rolling boil. Reduce heat to medium and cook, covered, approximately 1 hour until tender. Remove from the pan and remove all fat and veins. When cooked cut the meat in 1″ pieces and put in the pickling syrup.

Mix all the syrup ingredients and bring to a boil in a small saucepan. Cool. This syrup will keep for several weeks.

VARIATION

For a spicy syrup, add 1 tablespoon pickling spices. Stir into the syrup and keep in a sealed jar.

1	(3–4-pound) fresh beef heart
1½	quarts water
2	stems celery, with tops
1	medium onion, quartered
1	green bell pepper, quartered
1	tablespoon salt
½	teaspoon pepper
½	teaspoon fresh or ¼ teaspoon dried thyme

SYRUP

1	cup water
½	cup wine vinegar
½	cup cider vinegar
½	cup sugar

SWEETBREAD CROQUETTES

Mother made this recipe at least six times each winter. She would make quite a few at a time and freeze the majority for later. When Mother served sweetbread croquettes, she fried them as we ate, which kept them moist and juicy. Sweetbread croquettes are an inexpensive main course or, when made smaller, perfect as an appetizer.

Wash the sweetbreads. Put in a 2-quart saucepan with water and 3 teaspoons of the salt. Bring to a boil, reduce the heat, and simmer for 15 minutes. Remove the sweetbreads and place in a bowl of cold water. When cool, dry on paper towels and trim off the covering membrane. Chop the sweetbreads very fine or put them through a grinder or a food processor. There should be 4 cups chopped sweetbreads. Mix the sweetbreads with the celery, onion, 1 teaspoon salt, pepper, eggs, 2 cups of the dry bread crumbs, and the milk until well blended. Form into 6 individual patties and roll in the remaining bread (or cracker) crumbs.

Melt 1 tablespoon butter in a heavy skillet and fry the patties on one side until golden brown. Melt 1 tablespoon butter and fry the croquettes on the second side until golden brown.

NOTE: The sweetbread mixture may also be baked as a loaf, in a greased pan, in a preheated 350° F. oven for 45 minutes.

Makes 6 servings

2 pounds fresh calf's sweetbreads
4 cups water
4 teaspoons salt
1 cup finely chopped celery
1 cup finely chopped onion
¼ teaspoon freshly ground black pepper
3 eggs, lightly beaten
4 cups dry bread crumbs, or 2 cups dry bread crumbs to mix and 2 cups cracker crumbs for coating
1½ cups milk
2 tablespoons butter

BETTY'S VENISON STEW

When Abe and I planned our wedding, we chose November 12 because it fell between small game season—pheasant and rabbit—and deer season. It had to be then, or my dad would not have been there to give me away. Many years later, our sons Charlie, John, and Bob all shared my father's love for game and hunting. John and Bob went archery hunting as well, and John hunted with a restored musket, black gunpowder and all. Needless to say, venison is generally a part of our diet in winter. This recipe for venison is excellent! You can substitute one of the less expensive cuts of beef—with the same tasty results.

Put the venison in a large nonmetallic bowl—glass or pottery is best—with the wine, vinegar, garlic, and caraway seeds. Refrigerate and marinate overnight. For more tender meat, leave the venison in the marinade for up to 2 days; this is especially advisable if the venison meat is from an older animal.

Heat 2 tablespoons of the butter or oil in a large heavy skillet. Remove and dry the meat cubes and brown in the fat, a few at a time, saving the marinade. Heat the remaining 3 tablespoons of butter in a second skillet and sauté the onion and mushrooms until tender and golden. Add the marinade and beef stock. Bring liquid to a boil. Thicken with the cornstarch, mixed to a paste with the water. Reduce to a simmer. Add the browned meat cubes. For a richer flavor and darker color, add ¼ cup of the beef stock to the pan in which the meat was browned. Bring to a boil and scrape the bottom of pan with a wooden spoon to lift the brown glaze, then add to the stew. Cover and simmer at least 30 minutes until meat is thoroughly tender. Serve on rice or noodles. This reheats beautifully.

Makes 6 servings

1½ pounds venison meat, cubed (or substitute beef chuck or top round)
⅔ cup red wine
⅔ cup red wine vinegar
3 cloves garlic, crushed
1 tablespoon caraway seeds
5 tablespoons butter or oil
1 cup chopped onion
1 pound fresh mushrooms, trimmed and sliced
1 cup beef stock
3 tablespoons cornstarch
¼ cup water

FRIED RABBIT

Wash the rabbit. If it was shot, remove all pellets. Marinate in wine for 6–8 hours, refrigerated and covered. Pat dry with paper towels. Combine the flour, salt, pepper, and ginger in a paper or plastic bag. Shake the pieces of rabbit in this until well covered. Heat shortening in heavy skillet. Fry rabbit over medium heat about 15 minutes on each side until golden brown. Cover for the last 10 minutes. For crisper coating, fry a little longer, uncovered.

Serves 4

1 **rabbit, cleaned and cut into serving pieces**
2 **cups dry wine**
½ **cup flour**
1½ **teaspoons salt**
¼ **teaspoon pepper**
¼ **teaspoon ground ginger**
Shortening for frying

HASENPFEFFER

Soak rabbits in wine, covered, for at least 8 hours. Drain and pat dry with paper towels. Place salt, pepper, ginger, and flour in a bag. Shake pieces of rabbit in this mixture until well covered. Put shortening in a heavy skillet. Fry rabbit until golden brown on all sides. Put carrots, potatoes, celery root, onion, and water in a 2-quart saucepan. Add the browned rabbit and bring to a boil. Cover. Reduce heat to low and simmer for approximately 2 hours. Remove rabbit and add the cream. Heat thoroughly. Pour sauce over the rabbit and serve at once.

If you prefer a sweeter taste, add ⅓ cup grape or currant jelly with the cream.

Serves 6

2 **rabbits, cleaned and cut into serving pieces**
3–4 **cups red wine**
½ **teaspoon salt**
¼ **teaspoon pepper**
¼ **teaspoon ground ginger**
½ **cup flour**
3 **tablespoons shortening**
1 **cup diced or thinly sliced carrots**
1 **cup diced potatoes**
½ **cup diced celery root**
½ **cup diced onion**
2 **cups water**
¾ **cup light cream**

FLAT TULIP, Counted Cross Stitch

*The tulip is a floral design which appears on
many American folk art forms. This counted
cross stitch is honoring their beautiful
blaze of color each spring.*

4

POULTRY & STUFFING

POULTRY

CHICKEN

Chicken Breasts with Herb Stuffing
Broil-Fried Chicken with Chives and Lemon
Chicken Pot Pie
Chicken and Waffles
Chicken with Saffron Noodles
Chicken in Patty Shells
Chicken Stoltzfus
Janet High's Baked Chicken Pie
Crispy Fried Chicken
Tarragon Fried Chicken
Roast Chicken with Bread Stuffing
Old Fashioned Chicken Pie

TURKEY

Turkey Croquettes
Roast Turkey
Roast Turkey Breast with Eggplant Stuffing

DUCK

Roast Duck with Orange-Pineapple Glaze

GOOSE

Roast Goose with Potato and Bread Stuffing

GAME

Cornish Game Hens, Barbecued
John's Stuffed Dove Breasts Baked in Clay
Pheasant with Cranberry-Apple Stuffing

STUFFINGS

Cranberry-Apple Stuffing
Chestnut Stuffing
Salsify Stuffing
Herb Stuffing
Potato and Bread Stuffing
Moist Bread Stuffing

CHICKEN BREASTS WITH HERB STUFFING

Split chicken breasts, just enough to fold. Combine flour and seasonings in paper bag. Add chicken and shake. Fill cavity of each chicken breast with herb stuffing.

Thoroughly combine all except last 2 ingredients. Hold stuffing in chicken by skewering breasts with toothpicks. Dip chicken into melted butter. Place in baking dish. Drizzle a little melted butter over each breast. Bake in a preheated slow oven (325° F.) for 45 minutes. Turn. Bake an additional 45 minutes until tender. Sprinkle with chopped parsley. Serve with Mushroom Sauce.

Makes 2½ cups

MICROWAVE: Follow recipe through placing breasts in baking dish. Drizzle with butter. Cover with waxed paper and cook 7 minutes. Turn chicken on other side and cook for 7 minutes. Remove from microwave and let stand 10–15 minutes, covered, before serving.

Serves 4

4 whole boned chicken breasts
¼ cup flour
½ teaspoon salt
¼ teaspoon paprika
◆ Dash pepper
1 Herb Stuffing recipe
½ cup melted butter
About 2 tablespoons chopped fresh parsley
1 recipe Mushroom Sauce (see Index)

HERB STUFFING

2 cups dry bread cubes
1 tablespoon chopped onion
1 teaspoon chopped fresh or ½ teaspoon dried chives
1 teaspoon chopped fresh or ½ teaspoon dried thyme
1 teaspoon chopped fresh or ½ teaspoon dried tarragon
1 teaspoon salt
◆ Dash pepper
2 tablespoons melted butter
½ cup hot milk
2 teaspoons melted butter
Chopped fresh parsley

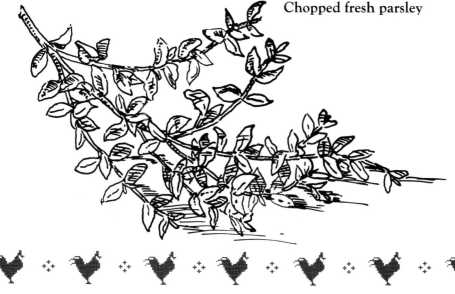

ROAST DUCK WITH ORANGE-PINEAPPLE GLAZE

1 (5–6-pound) duck*
Salt and pepper
2 **cups water**

Wash the duck inside and out. Wash the giblets and place them in the bottom of a roaster pan. Lightly salt and pepper the inside of the duck. Fill with your favorite stuffing, if desired. Salt and pepper the outside generously to ensure proper seasoning through the thick breast meat. Truss the bird. Set in the covered roasting pan with the giblets and water and bake in a preheated 350° F. oven for 4½ hours. Uncover and increase the heat to 375°. Bake 15 minutes longer to brown the skin. Serve with Orange-Pineapple Glaze, substituting oranges for apricots in Apricot-Pineapple Glaze on page 64.

Serves 6

I prefer Peking or Muscovy duck, because of their thick breast.

BROIL-FRIED CHICKEN WITH CHIVES AND LEMON

½ **cup butter**
3 **frying chickens, cut into serving pieces**
2 **teaspoons salt**
½ **teaspoon freshly ground pepper**
2 **tablespoons finely chopped fresh or 1 tablespoon dried chives**
2 **tablespoons freshly grated lemon rind**
Juice of 1 lemon

Melt the butter in a broiler pan after removing the rack. Be sure butter covers every area of the pan. Lay the chicken pieces in the butter with the bone side up. Sprinkle with half the salt and pepper. Broil until golden brown, then turn and sprinkle with the remaining salt and pepper. Then add the chives and lemon rind evenly over each piece. Add the lemon juice last. Broil until golden brown. Reduce oven heat to 350° F. and bake chicken for 15 minutes. Do not baste.

Serves 6

CHICKEN POT PIE

The Pennsylvania Dutch have many unique dishes which are misinterpreted by the rest of the world. When the "Dutch" speak of "pot pie," they are referring to the large squares of noodle dough which are added to the broth of chicken, pork, or beef. The flavor of the pot pie is very delicate. The secret to a successful "slippery pot pie" is to make certain that pieces of the dough are not dropped on top of one another until the broth has boiled up over each layer. The new pasta machines have made it much easier to make this dish. The dough squares may be prepared ahead. Dry them thoroughly. Store in an airtight container in a cool place until ready to use.

Place the chicken in a 4–6-quart Dutch oven or a large heavy pot with a tight-fitting lid. Add the saffron, salt and pepper, and enough water to just cover the bird. Bring to a boil, then reduce the heat and simmer about 1–1¼ hours until the chicken is tender. Remove the chicken from the broth. When cool enough to handle, skin the chicken, take the meat from bones, and cut into large bite-size chunks. Set aside while making Pot Pie Dough.

Mound the flour on a pastry board or marble slab and make a well in the center. Break the eggs into this well. Add the water, butter, and salt. Gradually work the flour into the other ingredients until well blended. Gather into a ball and knead the dough until very tender, smooth and elastic.

Generously flour the board and roll the dough out very thin, no more than ⅛" thick. The thinner it is rolled, the more delicate it will be. When using a pasta machine, roll out strips of the dough. Cut the rolled-out dough into 2-inch squares.

Bring the chicken broth, celery, and potatoes to a boil over high heat. Drop the pot pie squares into the boiling broth in layers, being careful not to put a second layer in the pot until the boiling broth has covered the first one. As the pot is filled, push the squares down with a fork. Cook squares about 10–12 minutes until tender. Add the chicken pieces. Cover and simmer for 5 minutes, until thoroughly heated. Serve pot pie squares, meat, and broth in heated bowls.

Makes 6 servings

1 (4–6-pound) roasting chicken
◆ Pinch powdered saffron
1 tablespoon salt
½ teaspoon freshly ground black pepper
About 2 quarts water
½ cup coarsely chopped celery
2 medium potatoes, peeled and sliced thin

POT PIE DOUGH

2½ cups flour
2 eggs
⅓ cup water
1 tablespoon butter
½ teaspoon salt

CHICKEN AND WAFFLES

Place chicken in a 3-quart covered saucepot. Add salt, pepper, saffron and 1 quart water. Cover and cook approximately 40 minutes over medium heat till leg meat pulls away from the bone. Do not overcook or the meat will fall apart. Remove from heat and cool, saving broth. Debone chicken and remove skin. Cut meat into 1″ chunks. Remove excess fat from chicken broth and heat to boiling. Add chives, and parsley if desired. Thicken broth by adding cornstarch dissolved in ½ cup cold water and boil for 2 minutes. If using cream or milk, add now. Add chunks of chicken, simmering till chicken is hot. Serve over hot waffles. Garnish with sprigs of fresh parsley.

Serves 6

1 (4-pound) roasting chicken
1½ teaspoons salt
½ teaspoon freshly ground pepper
◆ Pinch saffron
Waffles (see Index)
1 quart water
3 tablespoons cornstarch
½ cup cold water
Minced chives and parsley (optional)
½ cup cream or evaporated milk (optional)
Fresh parsley for garnish

CHICKEN WITH SAFFRON NOODLES

This was always served with cold sliced beef or ham for hot summer dinners.

In a 2-quart saucepan heat the chicken stock, saffron, and herbs until boiling. Check for seasoning. Add approximately ½ teaspoon salt and ⅛ teaspoon of pepper if needed. At boiling point add the noodles. Chicken fat will help to keep the noodles from sticking together. If broth is fat-free, add 1 teaspoon butter. Cook over medium heat for 7 minutes. Add the diced chicken and continue to cook until noodles are tender. Serve in heated vegetable dish and top with Browned Butter Crumbs.

Serves 6

3 cups chicken broth, seasoned, including some chicken fat
◆ Pinch saffron
½ teaspoon chopped fresh thyme
1 teaspoon chopped fresh chives
1 teaspoon chopped fresh or pinch dried rosemary
½ pound egg noodles
1 cup diced cooked chicken
Browned Butter Crumbs for topping (see Index)

CHICKEN IN PATTY SHELLS

This was a dish reserved for very special guests.

NOTE: Shells may be made ahead and stored in a sealed container.

Mix salt and flour together. Cut in the lard and butter with a pastry cutter or mix by hand until mixture forms crumbs. Sprinkle ice water over crumbs with one hand while tossing lightly with the other, using only enough water to keep the dough together. Press dough into a ball and place on a lightly floured surface. Divide into 2 parts. Roll into large circles about ⅛″–¼″ thick. Use a round cutter, such as a small saucepan lid, to make circles large enough to fit into a muffin cup. Gently fit dough into cups. Trim and flute the edges. Prick each shell several times with a fork to prevent bubbling while baking. Bake in a preheated oven at 350° F. for 12–15 minutes or until golden.

Put chicken in a large pot and add the water, salt, pepper, and saffron. Bring to a boil and reduce heat to medium. Simmer for 1 hour until chicken is tender and meat pulls away from the leg bone. Remove chicken and cool. Remove excess fat from broth. Reheat broth and thicken to desired consistency. Remove skin and bones from chicken and cut meat into bite-size pieces. Put chicken and chopped parsley into thickened broth and serve in patty shells. Garnish each shell with a sprig of parsley.

Fills 8–10 shells

PASTRY FOR PATTY SHELLS

- ½ cup lard or other shortening
- ¼ cup butter
- 2¼ cups all-purpose flour
- ¾ teaspoon salt
- ⅓ cup ice water

CHICKEN

- 1 (4–5-pound) roasting chicken
- 2 quarts water
- 1 tablespoon salt
- ½ teaspoon pepper
- ◆ Pinch saffron
- ¼ cup cornstarch, dissolved in water to make a thin paste
- 2 tablespoons chopped parsley

Parsley sprigs for garnish

CHICKEN STOLTZFUS

Put the chicken in a 6-quart kettle. Add the water, salt, pepper, and saffron and bring to a boil. Reduce the heat to medium and simmer, partially covered, for 1 hour. Remove the chicken and cool enough to debone. Strain the stock. Reduce the stock to 4 cups. Remove the skin and bones from the chicken and cut the meat into bite-size pieces. Melt the butter in the pot in which the chicken was cooked and mix in the flour. Cook over medium-low heat until golden and bubbling. Add the 4 cups chicken stock and the cream, stirring constantly. Cook over medium-high heat until the sauce comes to a boil. Simmer until thickened and smooth. Reduce heat and add the chicken pieces and chopped parsley. Serve hot over pastry squares. Follow basic pie dough recipe using half butter, half shortening. (see Index)

Serves 6

1 (5-pound) roasting chicken, cleaned, giblets removed
1½ quarts water
1 tablespoon salt
⅓ teaspoon pepper
◆ Pinch saffron
12 tablespoons butter
12 tablespoons flour
1 cup light cream or ½ cup each milk and evaporated milk
¼ cup finely chopped fresh or ⅛ cup dried parsley
Pastry Squares (see basic pie dough, Index)
Parsley for garnish

JANET HIGH'S BAKED CHICKEN PIE

Put the chicken, water, saffron, and salt in a kettle. Cover with the lid and bring to a boil. Reduce heat to medium and cook approximately 35 minutes until the chicken is soft. Remove the chicken and debone. Discard the skin and cut the meat into bite-size pieces. Strain the chicken stock. If necessary, add water to make 2 cups chicken stock.

Sauté the onions in the shortening in a heavy skillet until soft but not brown. Stir in the flour, salt, and pepper. Gradually add the chicken stock. Cook until slightly thickened, stirring constantly. Arrange chunks of chicken and vegetables in a buttered baking dish. Pour the chicken stock evenly on top. Cover with crust from Vera Braggs' Meat Pie. (see Index)

9″ x 13″ baking dish

1	(3½-pound) frying chicken
2½	cups water
◆	Pinch saffron
1	teaspoon salt

¼	cup diced onion
5	tablespoons vegetable shortening or butter
4	tablespoons flour
1	teaspoon salt
⅛	teaspoon pepper
2	cups chicken stock
2–3	cups diced cooked chicken
1	cup cooked peas
1	cup cooked and sliced carrots
2	cups cooked and diced potatoes
1	stalk celery, trimmed and chopped

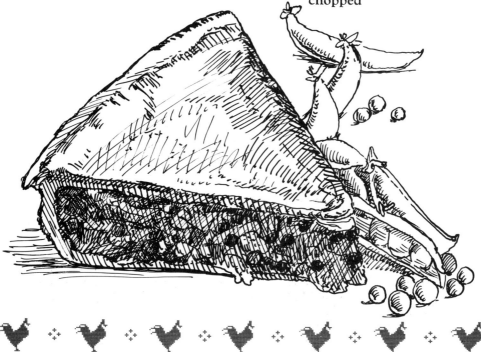

DOROTHY'S CRISPY FRIED CHICKEN

Roll chicken pieces in melted butter. Sprinkle with salt and pepper. Roll in the cornflakes. Place in a foil-lined pan and bake, uncovered, in a preheated 350° F. oven for 1 hour.

Delicious for a picnic!

Serves 4

1 frying chicken, cut into serving pieces
3 tablespoons melted butter
Salt and pepper
2 cups crushed cornflakes

TARRAGON FRIED CHICKEN

Our son John could eat chicken almost every day. He never tired of it, but he liked to vary the preparation. This recipe was his favorite; the chicken stays moist, but the breading is crunchy. This recipe reheats well.

Put the flour, cornmeal, salt, pepper, and tarragon in a paper or plastic bag and mix thoroughly. Dip the chicken pieces in the egg, then put them in the flour mixture and shake until well covered.

Melt the butter and shortening in a heavy skillet or in an electric frypan. Place the chicken in the pan and brown on medium heat. Turn and continue to fry until golden brown. Cover and continue to cook over medium-low heat for approximately 20 minutes, turning occasionally. Remove cover and cook until the crust is crisp.

This recipe is delicious using wild pheasant or Cornish hens, but because these birds are small, reduce the cooking time so the meat does not dry out.

Serves 4–6

¼ cup flour
¼ cup cornmeal
1 teaspoon salt
¼ teaspoon pepper
1 tablespoon finely chopped fresh or dried tarragon
1 frying chicken, cut into pieces
1 egg, lightly beaten
2 tablespoons butter
¼ cup liquid shortening

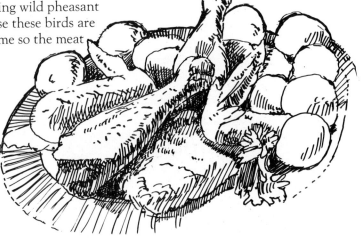

ROAST CHICKEN WITH BREAD STUFFING

This is a basic recipe, but it has to be included because it is requested so often. The carcass and back pieces make excellent soup stock.

Wash and rinse the chicken and sprinkle the inside with the salt and pepper.

Mix all stuffing ingredients together. Stuff the chicken and truss. Salt the outside lightly. Add freshly ground pepper, if desired. Put in a small roasting pan. Add ½ cup water. Tent with foil and roast in a pre-heated oven at 375° F. for 3½ hours. Uncover for last 15 minutes to brown the skin. Place the chicken on a heated platter, removing the stuffing by spoonfuls and placing around bird.

To make gravy, skim the fat from the roasting pan and add 2 cups water. Simmer until the brownings have dissolved. Thicken with 2 tablespoons of cornstarch, which have been dissolved in a ½ cup cold water. Season to taste.

Serves 6

1 (5–6-pound) roasting chicken
½ teaspoon salt
Freshly ground pepper (optional)

STUFFING
4 cups bread cubes
2 eggs, lightly beaten
⅓ cup milk
◆ Dash salt and pepper
½ cup chopped celery
◆ Pinch saffron

GRAVY
2 cups water
2 tablespoons cornstarch
½ cup cold water

OLD-FASHIONED CHICKEN PIE

Pastry crust for individual ramekins for 6, or for large baking pan; use meat pie crust recipe (see Index).

Place chicken in a 4–6 quart Dutch oven or a heavy pot with lid. Add enough water only to cover the chicken, saffron, salt, and pepper. Cover and bring to a brisk boil. Reduce heat and simmer for 1 hour. Remove chicken and debone. Reduce chicken broth to about 2 cups and thicken with arrowroot or cornstarch. Add the chicken, potatoes, peas, celery, and carrots to the broth and pour into unbaked pastry crusts. Cover with crust and slit top to allow for steam to escape. Bake in a preheated oven at 350° F. for 1 hour 15 minutes.

Serves 6–8 or makes 2 (10″-deep) pies

1 (5–6-pound) roasting chicken
2 quarts water
◆ Pinch saffron
1 tablespoon salt
Freshly ground pepper
3 medium potatoes, diced
1 cup fresh or frozen peas
½ cup chopped celery
1 cup diced carrots
2 tablespoons arrowroot or cornstarch dissolved in ¼ cup cold water

TURKEY CROQUETTES

In a large mixing bowl, combine the turkey, celery, celery salt, lemon juice, parsley, white sauce, and salt. Form into cone-shaped croquettes. Roll in crumbs, then dip in beaten eggs and roll in crumbs again. Chill for at least 30 minutes until firm. Fry in deep fat at 375° F. (preheated) until golden brown. Keep warm in a preheated 300° oven until ready to serve. Serve very hot with turkey gravy. Garnish with fresh parsley.

Serves 4

1½ cups diced cooked turkey
¼ cup finely chopped celery
¼ teaspoon celery salt
1 teaspoon lemon juice
1 teaspoon finely chopped parsley
½ cup thick white sauce
½ teaspoon salt
2 cups crumbs (half bread and half saltine crackers)
2 eggs, beaten
Fresh parsley for garnish

ROAST TURKEY

Rinse the turkey. Place the giblets in a small saucepan and cover with water. Add ½ teaspoon salt and a dash of pepper. Cook over medium heat approximately 1 hour until tender.

Lightly salt and pepper the inside of the bird. Use a moist bread stuffing if the turkey is to be stuffed (see Index). Generously salt and pepper the outside of the bird. Put in a roaster pan, breast down. Add water and tent with foil. Bake in a preheated 375° F. oven for 4½ hours, removing foil and turning breast up for the last 30 minutes to brown the skin. If the turkey is not stuffed, reduce the baking time to 4 hours.

To make gravy, use the broth from the cooked giblets to deglaze the roaster pan, by placing the pan over low heat. Stir the broth with a wooden spoon until the brownings are loosened. Thicken by adding 4 tablespoons cornstarch dissolved in ½ cup water to the broth. Stir until smooth and thick. Add cut-up giblets. Serve hot.

Serves 12

1 (15-pound) oven-ready
  turkey
Salt
Freshly ground pepper
2 cups water

GIBLET GRAVY
Broth
4 tablespoons cornstarch
½ cup cold water

ROAST TURKEY BREAST WITH EGGPLANT STUFFING

Turkey breasts are usually reasonably priced and there is little waste. I like a moist stuffing for turkey since white meat has a tendency to be dry. This stuffing is also good with other meats, such as duck, pheasant, or Rock Cornish game hens.

Sprinkle both sides of the turkey breast lightly with salt and pepper. Peel the eggplant and slice ¼″ thick. Put eggplant, salt, onion, and water in a 2-quart saucepan. Cover and simmer about 8 minutes until tender. Drain and mash or puree in a blender. Mix with the 2 tablespoons butter, pepper, eggs, and bread crumbs. Turn into a buttered 1½-quart casserole and sprinkle with the grated cheese, salt, and pepper. Arrange turkey breast on top of stuffing. Bake in a preheated 375° F. oven for 1 hour, basting the breast occasionally with the ¼ cup of melted butter.

Makes 4 servings

1 (2-pound) turkey breast
Salt
Freshly ground black pepper

EGGPLANT STUFFING

- 1 medium eggplant (about 1 pound)
- 1½ teaspoons salt
- 1 tablespoon finely chopped onion
- 1 cup water
- 2 tablespoons melted butter
- ¼ teaspoon freshly ground black pepper
- 2 eggs, beaten
- ½ cup dry bread crumbs
- ¾ cup grated Cheddar cheese
- ¼ cup melted butter for basting

ROAST GOOSE WITH POTATO AND BREAD STUFFING

Wash the goose and sprinkle salt and pepper inside the bird. Fill with Potato and Bread Stuffing. Liberally salt and pepper the outside. After securing the stuffed cavity with skewers, place the bird, breast side down, on a wire rack in a roasting pan. Add the water and cover, or tent with foil. Roast in a preheated 350° F. oven for 5 hours. Remove the cover and turn breast side up, for browning, for the last 30 minutes.

Bake the extra stuffing in a buttered dish for the last 30 minutes of the baking time for the goose.

Make gravy by removing fat, adding 2 cups water to brownings and thickening with 2 tablespoons cornstarch dissolved in ¼ cup water. Stir over low heat until all the brownings have dissolved and the mixture has thickened.

Serves 6

1 (6–8-pound) fresh dressed goose
Salt and pepper
1 recipe Potato and Bread Stuffing (see Index)
2 cups water

GRAVY

2 cups water
2 tablespoons cornstarch
¼ cup cold water

BARBECUED CORNISH GAME HENS

Combine butter, vinegar, salt, pepper, Worcestershire sauce, and chives in a bowl. Place the Cornish hens on a hot outdoor or kitchen grill, skin side up. Baste with the butter mixture. Continue basting each time before turning the hens for approximately 15–20 minutes, until the hens are golden brown and tender.

This recipe may be cooked in a baking dish in the oven, using the oven broiler instead of an outdoor or indoor grill.

Serves 6

½ cup melted butter
2 tablespoons vinegar
1 teaspoon salt
¼ teaspoon freshly ground pepper
1 teaspoon Worcestershire sauce
1 teaspoon finely chopped chives
3 Rock Cornish game hens, cleaned and split in half

JOHN'S STUFFED DOVE BREASTS, BAKED IN CLAY

Our younger son, John, was an enthusiastic hunter, like his father and my father. He loved any excuse to go hunting, and volunteered to provide the game for one of our dinner parties. When he returned, he had masses of tiny doves, which are the hardest birds to hit.

Many people consider pheasant under glass a gourmet delicacy, but dove breasts baked in clay are one of the most elegant and delicious dishes I know. This way of serving these delicate little wild birds keeps the breasts moist, tender, and tasty. For our party, we made an inedible baking clay from flour, salt, and water. We wrapped the breasts in this clay. We then took little strips of the clay and wrote each guest's name on them with a felt-tipped pen. We fastened these strips to the clay covering with 2 cloves. Instead of place cards, each guest had a personally labeled dove breast. We gave our guests crab crackers to break open the hard-baked clay. Of course, this was the talk of the evening, and added a lot of fun to the dinner. If there is a hunter in your family and you enjoy an unusual touch for your dinner, try this. Your guests will be delighted. If doves are unavailable, use the breasts of quail, which are generally available at markets and game farms.

We stuffed the dove breasts with a Chestnut Stuffing. This tends to be a little dry, so we compensated by serving a thickened gravy made from chicken broth. If the Eggplant Stuffing given in the recipe for Roast Turkey Breasts (see Index) is used, there will be no problem and the breasts will stay moist.

Carefully check home-hunted doves for shotgun pellets. Lightly salt the dove breasts. Take one dove breast at a time and press about ½ cup or more of the stuffing onto the bone side. Cover the stuffing with another dove breast, bone side in. Wrap two bacon strips tightly around the breast, and secure the bacon with a toothpick.

Mix the baking clay ingredients together and knead for about 5 minutes until very smooth. Roll out on a board, like pie pastry, and cut into 6 circles, 9″ in diameter, using a 9″ pie plate as a guide. Place a stuffed dove breast in the center of each circle of dough. Fold over all the edges, making a little package. Brush off any excess flour and set, with the sealed edges down, on a baking sheet, not touching. Bake in a preheated 375° F. oven for 1¼ hours.

The clay will become very hard. When serving the breasts, be sure to provide an implement to break the dry shell—lobster crackers, a small hammer, or even the handle of a sturdy knife will do. Have a large bowl or dish on the table for the broken clay.

12 dove or quail breasts
Salt
Chestnut Stuffing (see Index)
12 slices bacon

BAKING CLAY (This is not edible)

4 cups flour
1 cup salt
1½ cups water

The breasts will have steamed in their juices and will take on the flavor of the stuffing. Serve with a rich cream sauce, or with chicken gravy.

VARIATION

Use 3–3½ cups Eggplant Stuffing (see Index) instead of the Chestnut Stuffing.

Makes 6 servings

PHEASANT WITH CRANBERRY-APPLE STUFFING

Pheasants are delicate and plump—nearly all breast meat. This stuffing adds a festive touch to a very elegant bird.

Sprinkle the pheasants inside and out with salt and pepper. In a large mixing bowl, mix the stuffing ingredients. Use ½ cup of the stuffing for each bird. Place the rest of the stuffing in a greased 1-quart casserole. Place the pheasants in a small, deep roaster and add 1 cup of water to the pan. Cover with a lid or with a tent of foil. Bake in a preheated 350° F. oven for 2 hours, or until the meat comes away from base of leg bone. Bake the casserole of stuffing in the same oven for the last 30 minutes.

Makes 4 servings

2 (1½-pound) pheasants, fresh thawed
Salt
Freshly ground black pepper
Cranberry-Apple Stuffing

CRANBERRY-APPLE STUFFING

In a large mixing bowl, mix the cooked rice, celery, apples, and cranberries.

VARIATION

As a substitute for Uncle Ben's seasoned long-grain and wild rice, use 1 cup cooked wild rice and 1½ cups cooked long-grain rice seasoned with salt and pepper to taste, ¼ teaspoon thyme, 1 tablespoon chopped chives, and 1 tablespoon chopped celery leaves.

* If you want it less tart, use 3 cups apples and 1 cup cranberries.

2½ cups cooked Uncle Ben's seasoned long-grain and wild rice
1 cup chopped celery
2 cups chopped apples*
2 cups fresh cranberries, cut in half*

CHESTNUT STUFFING

Chop the chestnuts (this can be done in a blender or food processor) and combine with the butter, cream, cracker crumbs, and salt and pepper to taste.

3 cups boiled or canned chestnuts (not water chestnuts)
½ cup melted butter
¼ cup light cream
½ cup saltine crackers
Salt
Freshly ground black pepper

SALSIFY STUFFING (MOCK OYSTER STUFFING)

Boil washed and scrubbed salsify in salted water in a 2-quart saucepan for approximately 20 minutes until tender. Drain and peel. Cut salsify in ½″ slices. Makes about 4 cups. Boil celery, ½ cup water, and saffron in a small saucepan for 3 minutes. Put bread cubes in a large mixing bowl. Add beaten eggs, milk, salt, pepper, the celery mixture, and the sliced salsify. Toss lightly until thoroughly moistened. To use as a side dish, place in a buttered 2-quart casserole and bake in a preheated oven at 375° F. for 25 minutes, or bake in a buttered covered electric skillet at the same temperature setting.

Delicious served with poultry dishes.

Serves 6

2 pounds fresh salsify (oyster plant)
1 teaspoon salt
1 quart water
⅓ cup chopped celery
½ cup water
◆ Pinch saffron
3 cups day-old bread cubes
2 eggs, beaten
½ cup milk
1 teaspoon salt
½ teaspoon freshly ground pepper

HERB STUFFING

Thoroughly combine all ingredients.

2 cups dry bread cubes
1 tablespoon chopped onion
1 teaspoon chopped fresh or ½ teaspoon dried chives
1 teaspoon chopped fresh or ½ teaspoon dried thyme
1 teaspoon chopped fresh or ½ teaspoon dried tarragon
1 teaspoon salt
◆ Dash pepper
2 tablespoons melted butter
½ cup hot milk
2 teaspoons melted butter
Chopped fresh parsley

POTATO AND BREAD STUFFING

Put the water in a 1-quart saucepan and bring to a boil. Add the celery, onion, salt, pepper, parsley, and saffron. Boil approximately 7 minutes until the celery is clear. Lightly mix the celery mixture with the potatoes, beaten egg, bread crumbs, and milk in a large bowl. If used as a side dish, bake in a preheated 350° F. oven for 30 minutes.

- ½ cup water
- ½ cup chopped celery with leaves
- ¼ cup chopped onion
- 1 teaspoon salt
- ¼ teaspoon ground pepper
- 1 tablespoon chopped parsley
- ◆ Pinch saffron
- 2 cups mashed potatoes
- 3 eggs, lightly beaten
- 2 cups fresh bread cubes
- 1 cup milk

MOIST BREAD STUFFING

Put bread cubes in a large bowl. Add beaten eggs, celery, saffron, milk, salt, pepper, and onion. Toss lightly as for a salad. Do not press the filling or it may become heavy. Spoon into a generously buttered 2-quart baking dish and dot with the butter. Bake in a preheated 350° F. oven for 30–40 minutes. When done, the tops of the cubes should be golden brown. Cover with foil to keep very hot until served.

Use to stuff birds, pork chops, or beef hearts, or just bake in a pan and serve as an accompaniment to the main dish.

Serves 6

- 6 cups bread cubes
- 3 eggs, lightly beaten
- ½ cup chopped celery
- ◆ Pinch saffron
- ⅔ cup milk
- 1 teaspoon salt
- ¼ teaspoon pepper
- ¼ medium onion, chopped fine (optional)
- 4 tablespoons butter

THE FAMILY

Then world has found the way to the Groff's Farm Restaurant where the heavy black register of dinner guests, their comments and home addresses reads like an atlas.

Signers on just one page, from California, Massachusetts, American Samoa, Britain, Michigan, Canada, Germany, Kentucky and Indiana had all managed to find their way to the bustling farm-turned-three-star-restaurant on Pinkerton Road. Clearly, the farm in the middle of nowhere has become a tourist attraction in its own right.

Eddie Albert, star of the old television show "Green Acres" about a man who gave up a successful career in the city for the country life, actually visited the farm and told Betty and Abe he envied their success at having a business at home. "Green Acres" apparently wasn't just another role he played.

Because of the farm's proximity to the nation's capital, New York City, Philadelphia and Baltimore, many a famous person has dined at its tables.

Senators and congressmen, sports stars, actors and astronauts have all come to the Groffs' door, but Betty refuses to dwell on the famous names. She declares, "I've always stressed to our staff that when you are here, you are to be treated like family and are our most important guest." She adds with a touch of country wisdom, "There's nothing as fleeting as fame!"

The Groffs cater to families touring Pennsylvania Dutch country, but the farm meals also appeal to people old enough to have certain "taste memories" they're trying to re-create and those who yearn for good home cookin' when home is hundreds or thousands of miles away. (One particular group of students from nearby Franklin and Marshall College marks the conclusion of every final exam period with a hearty, farm-style meal of prime rib and Chicken Stoltzfus with all the trimmings. Their theory is that a meal here even can make failing an exam forgettable!)

Visitors expect to meet the Groffs because that's what makes eating at the farm an experience rather than just a good meal. Charlie and Cindy are on hand practically every day the farm is open. Betty and Abe, whenever they're in town, also make it a point to greet each guest.

In the early days, when Abe still did the farming, he preferred to stay out of the limelight and left much of the "entertaining" of guests to Betty. But once a few writers talked with and included Abe in articles they wrote about the farm, his days in the barn and fields were over. He was as much in demand for his knowledge of the land, farming and politics as Betty was for her ability to field questions about Lancaster County history, food, family life and culture.

But don't get the idea these two are stuffy old professors of Pennsylvania Dutch lore. Because they're walking contradictions of one's mental picture of a farm husband and wife, they're all the more interesting.

Although the pair routinely will joke about rarely leaving the farm since the horse went lame, they regularly cover ground with more horsepower under the hood than could ever be found on four hooves in an Amishman's barn. "I love fast cars, fast boats and fast horses!" admits Betty. And Abe? Well, he's happiest water skiing and riding snowmobile trails with Charlie.

Be on guard for teasing when you meet Betty. A guest who asked her, "Is it possible to meet Mrs. Groff?" was stunned with the result. Betty answered, "Oh, sure. I'll get her for you." She walked into the kitchen and then returned to carry on a conversation. This sort of incident is to be expected from a woman who once spent a morning cooking up an April Fool's Day recipe for chocolate-covered wax ice cubes containing water. When a person bit into one of the lovely-looking confections, water gushed out. When one thinks of it, such a feat was no small trick—but that's another story.

The Groffs married on November 12, 1955, took up residence at the farm in July of 1956 and, for the next four years, busied themselves as farmer and wife. The 96 acres were planted with tobacco, tomatoes, hay, wheat and corn. Abe also managed a dairy herd.

Betty admits, however, "By 1960, I was becoming a little restless. When I was growing up on my family's Strasburg farm, with a father whose butcher shop business attracted customers to the farm both day and night, and an uncle who was a prominent minister, there was plenty of contact with the 'outside world.' But life on the Mount Joy farm was more isolated.

During that time, I did get a kick out of driving the tractor—something that Charlie learned first-hand. Whether I was planting tobacco or pulling the wagon to pick up basket after basket of juicy red tomatoes, one-year-old Charlie rode at my side in a specially adapted car seat. The rhythmic click of the planter each time a seed went into the ground was his special lullaby. He'd fall asleep in minutes."

Of course, the Groffs' younger son John narrowly escaped having an even earlier introduction to farming. His mother continued driving the tractor throughout her pregnancy (with the doctor's permission and Abe's help in getting up and down from the equipment). One afternoon, she was totally oblivious of an approaching thunderstorm that quickly turned the tobacco field they were planting into a sea of mud. The tractor became mired and Betty, giggling as only she would in such a predicament, plodded through the quagmire on foot to make her way home. The next day Johnny was born.

When farming began losing its fascination, she toyed with making chocolates to sell and even bought the equipment at a candy shop that was going out of business. But her father and common sense prevailed. She noted, "You can work for weeks and have only a few hundred pounds to sell. And my Dad asked me, 'What makes you think you'll succeed in the same area where a good shop failed?'

"It was my mother who came up with the perfect idea to keep me on the farm but happy, too," Betty said.

Her mother had heard of a restaurant owner who was looking for a local woman to prepare true home-style meals for groups of Pennsylvania Dutch country visitors. Because Betty had just succeeded in serving a well-received meal to 35 of the world's toughest food critics—her relatives—she and her mother decided she was capable of

the task. With Abe's blessing and the agreement that the plan wouldn't interfere with his farm work, Betty readied the menu and the house for her first visitors.

Because shoo-fly pie is one of the best-known Pennsylvania Dutch specialties (though not a Groff family favorite), she knew guests would expect a good one. After baking what seemed to be hundreds and having the pie-loving Abe sample every one, she found the "right" one and Abe pronounced it, "Superb." Betty admits, though, that she still wonders if Abe really liked it or whether he was just saying that so she finally would make another flavor.

Out came the fine linens, silver, crystal and even the 36 place settings of wedding china. Two friends were hired to help on the big night, and Betty plotted her strategy for cooking for 36 on an ordinary kitchen stove.

How did she do it? The ham was roasted in the oven; the biggest pot was reserved for pot pie. Mashed potatoes occupied another burner. Sugar peas and fresh corn cut from the cob were stacked, one on top of the other, for a double-boiler effect. Chocolate cake and cracker pudding, made in advance, were served at the beginning of the meal. (Although the custom sounds peculiar, the budding restaurateur decided she wanted her guests to taste these dishes while they still had the room to enjoy them.) Pie and ice cream rounded out the meal.

The night of the big event, Betty wore a long pink dress so no one would see how badly her knees were shaking!

The guests, members of the Internal Revenue Service's Camera Club for retirees, were greeted at the door by young Charlie and the family dog. They raved about the farm's beauty and the aromas coming from the kitchen. Betty relaxed and the evening went perfectly. To this day, she maintains a pleasant, non-audit correspondence with some members of the group. And her profit—$60 after expenses—was used to buy a row of red rose bushes to climb the white board fence between the garage and pond. Two of the bushes still flourish.

Craig Claiborne, brought to the farm by Lancaster County friends, gave the fledgling business a major boost. He dined anonymously, though he made no secret of taking notes during the meal and asking questions. When he was finished, Claiborne said, "You know, I'd really like to write about your wonderful place, but you must promise you will begin accepting parties of fewer than 12."

Betty said, "When I told him I couldn't break even with 12, let alone smaller numbers of diners, the gentleman identified himself and said, "I want to tell the world about you. This is the kind of place everyone is hunting for. Don't ever change. Keep the quality you now have and be yourself. If you have prices that are too low, it is much better to raise them than lower the quality."

After Claiborne's full-page feature story about Groffs' Farm appeared in The New York Times, it seemed everyone in the world wanted to taste Pennsylvania Dutch food. Betty suddenly found herself with a full house on a nightly basis.

The late James Beard, who also visited and wrote about the farm several times, is remembered by the Groffs as a warm and friendly person who could talk on any subject. "We were in awe of him because he was so well known. And yet, he was so friendly and outgoing. There was no dish that didn't suit him and he wanted to know the history and preparation of each one," Betty commented. Before leaving, Beard tucked a copy of an 1856 Philadelphia cookbook under his pillow as a gift for his hosts.

For the first 10 years, the farm restaurant also continued to serve as the Groffs' home—a situation that sometimes gave rise to interesting incidents.

The family's furnishings, including a delicate and beautiful Victorian sofa, routinely were used by the guests. But after the sofa had been repaired a second time, Betty gave four-year-old Charlie some special instructions: "Make sure no more than two people sit on the sofa. If it looks as if a third person is going to sit down, you hop on between the other two and strike up a conversation."

The system worked for several weeks until one day Charlie either missed his cue or three women were too quick to sit down. Panic-stricken, he blurted out, "My mommy doesn't want three fat ladies on the sofa!" He knew he'd said something wrong and tearfully reported to his mother who was still in the kitchen. Fortunately, each lady had a weighty sense of humor.

Because guests were curious about the 231-year-old farmhouse's construction, Betty's father cut out a floor board so the home's mud straw cement (used for insulation, sound and fire-proofing in colonial times) was readily visible. One evening, Betty heard guests laughing when they gazed at the cut out, rather than expressing amazement, and discovered that the boys had filled the hole with Matchbox toys and marbles.

Besides learning a bit about the home, there was at least one more unexpected bonus for a guest whose coat had been left near an aquarium filled with tadpoles about to undergo metamorphosis. "When the evening was over," Betty commented, "we noticed that the plastic wrap over the top of the jar was out of place and at least one new frog had gone AWOL." Apparently, however, the person who found it in a pocket wasn't hopping mad because the Groffs heard no repercussions from the incident.

Visitors also were able to wander through the remainder of the farmhouse's rooms in the early years. Because of their explorations, Abe wound up hiding in a closet for 30 minutes when he should have been downstairs greeting guests. Several very proper ladies had approached the bedroom while he was changing and he had to duck out of sight. While he listened from behind a closed door, the ladies happily continued their conversation and straightened up for Mrs. Groff because, as one said, "I'll bet she doesn't know this room was left in such a mess, with all the drawers left open." (It was Abe's custom to leave them open until he finished dressing and then he'd close them all at once.)

From time to time, guests who were unaware that the family still lived in the house, surprised Betty while she was dressing for dinner, too.

But nothing was done about the problem until one night when Betty was late going upstairs to check on the boys, tuck them in and hear their prayers. When she opened the door to Johnny's room and discovered him trying to sleep between the fur coats that mistakenly had been piled on his bed (rather than on the bed across the hall), she leaned her head against the door casing and cried. "We had done what we feared most—put the business before our children." After that, family bedrooms were off-limits and the couple decided to look for another house to call home.

Abe found a rambling brick home in downtown Mount Joy that was equidistant from the farm restaurant and from the Cameron Estate Inn and with its purchase, the family's life on the farm ended.

Betty commented, "Life was simple in the early days though the frustrations of crop failure, weather, economics and disease gave farming its set of worries. Today, we worry about accounting, new restaurant rulings, liability and competition.

"As stimulating as farming was, I don't miss it because we worked so hard that we never had the chance to realize how beautiful the farm was. Now when we drive in to do a day's work, I can really appreciate the treasure we have."

Bless those who enter and leave this home. Keep them warm and protected from hunger, filling all their earthly needs.

DECORATIVE CERTIFICATE, BLESSING FRAKTUR

*Celebrating the giving and sharing with those who
have touched our lives, the Blessing Fraktur is a
prayer for their continued safety
and welcomed return.*

5

FISH & SHELLFISH

FISH & SHELLFISH

Batter-Dipped Fish or Shrimp
Charlie's Clam Casino
Corn'n Salmon Skillet
Milk-Baked Fish
Grilled Salmon
Baked Cod with Grapefruit
Poached Fish with Horseradish Sauce
Martha Barr's Crab Cutlets
Panfried Trout or Whiting
Salmon Cakes
Smoked Trout
Troupe Hershey's Crab Meat Casserole

BATTER-DIPPED FISH OR SHRIMP

Check fish and remove any small bones. If using shrimp, devein. Pat dry and dip in the batter. Drop several pieces at a time in shortening that has been heated to 375° F., and fry until golden brown. Drain on paper towels. Do not place too many pieces in the fryer at one time or they will stick together.

Serves 6

1½ pounds fresh or frozen whitefish fillets, or peeled shrimp
Beer Batter for coating (see Index)
Liquid shortening for frying

CHARLIE'S CLAM CASINO

The idea of making the seasoned butter ahead of time and freezing it was brought to us by Charlie while he was at the Culinary Institute of America. These clams are delicious and easy to make and they are always received enthusiastically.

SEASONED BUTTER

Blend the Seasoned Butter ingredients. Spoon onto several small sheets of aluminum foil. Roll up until the butter is approximately the size of a silver dollar in diameter. Chill until solid.

When ready to serve, set the clams in their half shells on a baking dish (if you fill the dish with rock salt, they will balance more firmly). Slice the chilled butter to the thickness of a quarter. Put 1 piece on top of each clam. Top with a square of bacon. Broil in a preheated broiler until the bacon curls crisply. Serve immediately.

Makes 6 servings

½ pound butter
½ green bell pepper, chopped fine
2 tablespoons chopped pimento
Juice 1 lemon
2 tablespoons chopped parsley
◆ Pinch salt
18 cherrystone clams on the half shell
4 bacon slices, cut in pieces about 1" square

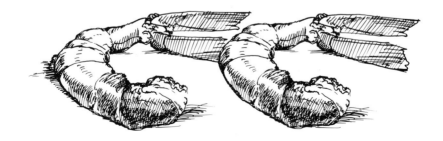

CORN'N SALMON SKILLET

Low calorie dish.

Spray vegetable oil in a medium nonstick skillet and cook cucumber, onion and dill weed till clear, approx. 5 minutes. Stir in salmon, corn and half of the yogurt. Cook over low heat, stirring until mixture is hot but not boiling. Spoon mixture into a heated serving dish and top with remaining yogurt and a dash of paprika.

Serves 4

2 cups cucumbers, thinly sliced

4 ounces onion, chopped

1 teaspoon dill weed

1½ cup canned salmon, drained and flaked

2 cups canned cream-style corn

1 cup plain unflavored yogurt, divided in half

Paprika

MILK-BAKED FISH

Arrange fish in greased baking dish. Add butter to milk. Add salt (celery salt, onion or garlic salt could be substituted), pepper and parsley. Pour carefully around the fish. Top with crumbs and dot with butter. Bake in preheated 350° F. oven for approx. 30 minutes or until milk is nearly absorbed. Serve without additional sauce.

Serves 4–6

2 pounds fish, strong flavored such as shad or cod (steaks or fillets)

1 cup milk, heated

2 teaspoons butter or margarine

¼ teaspoon each of salt, pepper and parsley flakes

1 cup crumbled corn flakes, chips or cracker crumbs

3 tablespoons butter or margarine (optional)

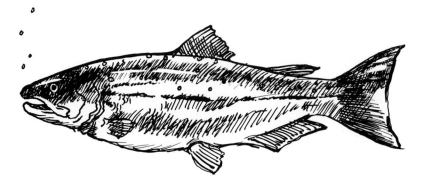

GRILLED SALMON

Bob Adam's specialty, it is simply scrumptious!

Place salmon in heavy foil. Add butter and seasonings. Place lemon slices in decorative design. Sprinkle with paprika. Fold foil tightly and tuck in the ends, folding toward top. Bake on covered gas grill. Start on high for 10 minutes. Turn heat to low and bake 10 minutes more. Check for doneness. If it is clear in center, turn heat off and leave salmon on grill for another 10 minutes. Never overcook. As soon as fish flakes when touched with fork, remove and serve.

NOTE: When using a charcoal grill with a rack which cannot be adjusted, cooking time may increase by 5 or 10 minutes.

Serves 15

- 10 **pounds fresh salmon, filleted**
- ¼ **cup butter or oil**
- 1 **teaspoon dill weed**
- 1 **teaspoon salt**
- 1 **teaspoon freshly ground pepper**
- 2 **fresh lemons, thinly sliced**

Paprika

BAKED COD WITH GRAPEFRUIT

Preheat oven to 350° F. Section grapefruit, squeezing a few sections to collect juice. Brush cod fillets generously with grapefruit juice. Sprinkle with salt and pepper and place in 12″ x 8″ baking pan. In a small bowl, combine bread crumbs, melted butter and thyme. Sprinkle over fish. Arrange the remaining grapefruit sections over bread crumbs. Bake 25 to 30 minutes or until fish flakes easily.

MICROWAVE: Bake, covered with plastic wrap, for 12 minutes.

Serves 6 to 8

- 2 **pounds cod fillets, fresh or frozen**
- 1 **cup grapefruit sections, fresh, membranes removed or canned sections**
- ¾ **teaspoon salt**
- ⅛ **teaspoon pepper**
- 1 **cup bread crumbs**
- ¼ **cup butter or margarine, melted**
- ½ **teaspoon thyme leaves**

POACHED FISH WITH HORSERADISH SAUCE

Place fish in an 8″ fry pan or poaching pan. Add water, lemon juice, and salt. Cover and simmer for 5 to 10 minutes or until fish flakes easily when tested with a fork. Remove fish to a heated platter. Sprinkle with paprika and serve with horseradish sauce.

1 pound Flounder fillets, fresh or frozen
3 cups water
2 tablespoons lemon juice
½ teaspoon salt
◆ Dash of paprika
Horseradish sauce (see Index)

MARTHA BARR'S CRAB CUTLETS

Melt the butter over medium heat in a heavy 2-quart saucepan. Add the parsley, onion, and flour, blending until smooth. Next add the cream, salt, paprika, and dry mustard, stirring constantly. Add the crab meat. Bring to the boiling point. Immediately remove from the heat and pour into a large platter to cool. Shape into individual-size cones or into cutlets of rectangles, rounds, or squares. Dip in beaten egg and roll in bread crumbs. Fry in hot (390° F.) fat until golden brown. Drain on paper towels. Crab cutlets may be placed in a preheated 250° oven after frying until ready to serve— up to 30 minutes. If left in the oven too long, the coating will split.

Serves 4–6

2 tablespoons butter
1 tablespoon minced fresh parsley
¼ teaspoon onion juice or 1 teaspoon minced onion
4 tablespoons flour
⅔ cup light cream
½ teaspoon salt
¼ teaspoon paprika
¼ teaspoon dry mustard
2 cups lump crab meat, carefully cleaned
⅓ cup flour
1 egg lightly beaten
½ cup fine dry bread crumbs
Shortening for frying
Fresh parsley for garnish
Lemon slices for garnish

PANFRIED TROUT OR WHITING

Whiting is available in all fish markets and reasonably priced. The flavor is similar to trout. I always fry my fish whole, with the heads, fins, etc. on, then fillet after cooking.

Clean the fish, removing the eyes. Lightly salt the inside of each fish. Place flour, salt, seafood seasoning, and pepper in a plastic bag. Shake each fish in the flour mixture.

In a large heavy skillet heat the butter. Add fish, frying until golden brown—approximately 6 minutes on each side. Place whole fish on heated platter. Put fresh parsley in eye sockets of fish., Arrange a slice or two of lemon on each fish.

To fillet, gently lift up the head of the fish. Place a fork behind the gill and center backbone. Pull the head back toward the tail. The whole backbone will come away from the fish, leaving the bottom fillet on the platter. Turn the fish. The spine with all the bones intact will lift out easily.

Serves 4

4 fresh whitings
½ cup flour
½ teaspoon salt
½ teaspoon seafood seasoning
◆ Dash pepper
About 4 tablespoons butter for frying
Lemon and parsley for garnish

SALMON CAKES

Remove any skin or small bones from salmon. Flake the fish with a fork. Combine salmon, onions, dill, basil, salt, milk, beaten eggs, butter, and bread crumbs. Cover with plastic wrap and refrigerate for 30 minutes. Form into balls, patties, or cakes and roll in bread crumbs. Fry in preheated shortening in a deep-fat fryer at 375° F. (or in heavy skillet) until golden brown on both sides. Serve with Lemon Sauce and dill pickles.

NOTE: An excellent appetizer! If used this way, make balls smaller and serve on fancy picks. Makes 14 small balls.

Serves 4

1 pound fresh salmon, filleted and poached (canned salmon may be substituted)
2 tablespoons finely chopped onion
1 tablespoon fresh minced or ½ tablespoon dried dill
1 teaspoon fresh minced ½ teaspoon dried basil
1 teaspoon seasoned salt
¼ cup evaporated milk or regular milk
3 eggs, beaten
2 tablespoons melted butter
1 cup fresh bread crumbs
½ cup bread crumbs for coating
Shortening

SMOKED TROUT

Blend the horseradish and sour cream in a small bowl. Arrange the smoked trout on a platter with a bowl of this horseradish sauce, or on individual salad plates.

Serves 6

1 **pound smoked trout, skinned and filleted**
⅓ **cup prepared horseradish**
1 **cup sour cream**

TROUPE HERSHEY'S CRAB MEAT CASSEROLE

Troupe is very organized and talented and entertains beautifully. Since she works, she prepares as much of her food the day before her party as possible, so that the last-minute details will not fluster her. This recipe, which she shared with me, is rich and elegant. It looks beautiful, served in a silver casserole.

Mix all ingredients gently in a large bowl. Cover and refrigerate overnight. Remove from the refrigerator several hours before serving. Place in a greased 2-quart casserole or baking dish, and bake in a preheated 350° F. oven for 20 minutes.

Makes 6 servings

2 **cups fresh lump crab meat**
1 **cup fine bread crumbs**
1 **cup light cream**
1½ **cups mayonnaise**
6 **hard-boiled eggs, chopped fine**
1 **tablespoon finely chopped parsley**
1 **tablespoon finely chopped onion**
½ **teaspoon salt**
Freshly ground black pepper to taste

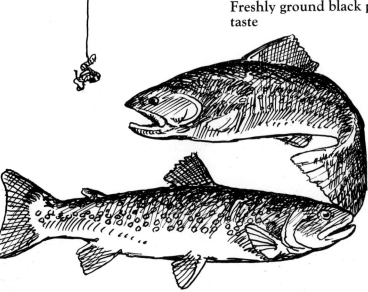

SUMMER IN LANCASTER COUNTY, Watercolor

*The warmth of Summer in Lancaster County is seen in the
wealth of vegetables and flowers that grow in abundance.
Forget-Me-Nots are tiny five petal flowers which appear
first in spring and bloom into mid-summer.*

6

EGGS, CHEESE, RICE, & NOODLES

EGGS

Armenian Easter Omelets
Charlie's Eggs Benedict
Deviled Eggs
Zucchini Omelet

CHEESE

Chived Egg Cheese
Herb Cheese
Janet High's Cheese Roll

RICE

Buttery Rice
Rice Stuffing

NOODLES

Betty's Special Noodles with Cream and Cheese
Noodles
Green (Spinach) Noodles
Saffron Noodles

ARMENIAN EASTER OMELETS

This recipe is from Pat Powell of Columbus, Ohio, and is served only at Eastertime. It is an Armenian recipe passed down from generation to generation. It is pretty and green and with only a mild onion flavor. Very unusual, it is worth making; you will be delighted with the results.

Combine the parsley, scallions, beaten eggs, salt, pepper, and garlic in a large bowl. Place a generous amount of olive oil in a heavy skillet and heat. Drop the mixture by tablespoonful into the hot fat. Fry approximately 4 minutes on each side until golden brown. Remove the omelets from the heat and put on paper towels to cool. Continue to make omelets, adding more olive oil as needed. Serve cold on a fancy platter or dish.

16 small (2″–3″) omelets

- 4 **cups finely chopped parsley**
- 4 **cups finely chopped scallions**
- 4 **eggs, lightly beaten**
- 1½ **teaspoons salt**
- ◆ **Several dashes freshly gound pepper**
- 1 **clove garlic, crushed and minced**
- 1 **cup olive oil for frying**

CHARLIE'S EGGS BENEDICT

Poach eggs in vinegar water, using 1 tablespoon vinegar and ½ teaspoon salt per pan. Prepare Hollandaise Sauce (see Index).

TO ASSEMBLE

Drain eggs very thoroughly. Put a slice of ham on 1 half of each muffin. Add 1 egg. Pour sauce on top. Slip under the broiler for a few minutes to brown sauce (optional) and decorate with sliced truffle or olive before serving.

Serves 4

Poached eggs
½ **English muffin for each egg, toasted and buttered**
Slice of baked ham for each egg
Hollandaise Sauce
Truffle or slice of black olive for garnish

DEVILED EGGS

Cut eggs in half lengthwise and remove yolks, being careful not to break the whites. Put yolks, mustard, mayonnaise, salt, and pepper in a blender or food processor or beat with a mixer until smooth and creamy. Check and add more salt if needed. Fill the egg whites with the yolk mixture, using a cake decorator tube or teaspoon. Sprinkle with paprika immediately before serving. Garnish each egg half with a sprig of parsley or a slice of olive.

Serves 8

6–8 hard-boiled eggs
  1 tablespoon Dijon mustard
  2 tablespoons mayonnaise
 ½ teaspoon salt
 ¼ teaspoon pepper
Paprika
Parsley or olive slices for garnish

ZUCCHINI OMELET

What to do when the garden seems full of zucchini? This omelet recipe was given to me by a dear Italian friend, Lou Silvi. His mother called them frittatas. *We have made them often; they are tasty at a brunch during the hot summer days when you don't want to spend a lot of time in the kitchen.*

Melt butter in a small skillet. Sauté onion and zucchini until clear. Pour beaten eggs on top of zucchini. Cook over medium heat until the edges can be easily lifted from the sides of the skillet. Season with salt and pepper. Turn and cook on the other side for only 1 minute. Serve at once on heated plates.

Serves 2

1½ tablespoons butter
  2 tablespoons coarsely chopped onion
 ½ cup unpeeled but very thinly sliced zucchini
  3 eggs, slightly beaten
Salt and freshly ground pepper

CHIVED EGG CHEESE

After Good Earth and Country Cooking *was published, one of the dishes I demonstrated most often at shows to promote the book was the egg cheese. People liked to see a cheese being made while they watched. When they tasted it, many offered serving suggestions—chives or onions—but making it without is good also. Adding a dash of freshly grated nutmeg can be interesting. Try it this way when serving the cheese with fresh fruits, such as strawberries or peaches.*

Warm the milk in a saucepan. Beat the eggs in a bowl until light and fluffy, then mix in the buttermilk, sugar, and salt. Beat slightly, then pour slowly into the warm milk. Cover the saucepan and leave it for several minutes on medium to low heat, stirring occasionally. Lightly mix in the fresh or dried chives.

Remove the lid. Watch the mixture until the curds and whey (the liquid part) separate. Immediately spoon the curds carefully into a pierced mold, such as a coeur à la crème mold, using a slotted spoon. Allow to cool and drain. Place the mold on another bowl or pan to enable the liquid to drip through. Be sure to spoon the curds lightly into the mold. If the curds are drained in a sieve, they become solid and heavy. Unmold the cold drained egg cheese onto a dish and serve with bread or crackers.

2	quarts sweet milk
6	large eggs
2	cups buttermilk
2	teaspoons sugar
1	teaspoon salt
3	tablespoons chopped fresh or 2 tablespoons dried chives

VARIATION

Do not add chives to the cheese. Instead unmold, and grate nutmeg over the top. Serve with fresh fruit.

Makes 8 servings

HERB CHEESE

Blend all ingredients thoroughly. Store, covered, in the refrigerator. Also delicious as a sandwich spread, or as a dip with vegetable sticks.

2	tablespoons chopped fresh herbs (such as thyme, chives, dill, and possibly a pinch of lovage or sage—select available herbs and mix to your liking)
8	ounces cream cheese
2	tablespoons sour cream or mayonnaise
½	teaspoon salt (optional)

JANET HIGH'S CHEESE ROLL

In a food grinder or processor, mince the cheese, olives, pickles, onion, peppers, and egg together until well blended. Add bread crumbs and mayonnaise. Mix well and form into a roll. Coat the outside with chopped nuts. Wrap in plastic and refrigerate overnight. Serve with crackers.

Serves 12–15

1 pound sharp cheese at room temperature
8 stuffed medium or 12 small olives
5 medium-size sweet pickles
2 tablespoons chopped onions
2 tablespoons chopped green peppers
1 hard-boiled egg
½ cup dry bread crumbs
4 tablespoons mayonnaise
½ cup finely chopped nuts (optional)

BUTTERY RICE

Cook rice according to package directions. Each type of rice is a little different, some being precooked (these take only a minute). When cooked, add 1 tablespoon butter per serving and season with salt and pepper. Toss until well blended. Serve steaming hot.

RICE STUFFING

In a bowl, add salt to cooked rice. In a saucepan, melt butter and sauté chives, herbs, onions, and peppers for 5 minutes. Add mushrooms and simmer 3 minutes longer. Add rice and stir until well blended.

1 teaspoon salt
2 cups cooked rice
2 tablespoons butter
1 tablespoon chopped fresh chives
1 teaspoon chopped fresh lemon-scented thyme, or 1 teaspoon fresh regular thyme and ½ teaspoon grated lemon rind
½ cup chopped onion
½ cup chopped green peppers (about ½ of a medium pepper)
½ cup sliced mushrooms

BETTY'S SPECIAL NOODLES WITH CREAM AND CHEESE

When I was a child, my Mother used to say that she thought I could live on noodles and potatoes. She taught me how to make noodles. It is time-consuming but enjoyable, and with the new noodle machines, the work is really simple now. Here is my version of a "noodle feast." They are so rich you can use them as a main course, complementing them with a crisp green salad.

Bring water to a boil. Add butter, saffron, and salt. Add noodles and boil approximately 10 minutes on medium heat until tender. Drain and put in a heated serving bowl. Melt butter in a 1-quart saucepan and add seasoning. Whip egg yolks with a fork and blend with cream. Pour into melted butter. Keep on very low heat while adding the grated cheese, stirring gently till well mixed. Do not bring to a boil. When very warm, pour over noodles and toss until thoroughly mixed. Top with Browned Butter Crumbs or freshly ground pepper.

Serves 4–6

½ pound egg noodles
4 cups water
1 tablespoon butter or oil
◆ Pinch saffron
1 teaspoon salt
2 egg yolks
3 tablespoons butter
½ teaspoon garlic salt or regular salt with a small clove of garlic, crushed
⅓ cup light cream
¼ cup grated Parmesan cheese
Browned Butter Crumbs (optional; see Index)
◆ **Few dashes freshly ground pepper (optional)**

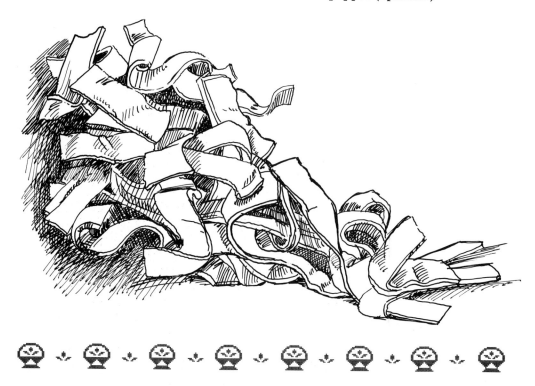

NOODLES

Put 2 cups of the flour and the salt in a
large mixing bowl. Make a well in the center,
and add the egg yolks and water. Stir until
well blended. A food processor does this very
quickly. Mix until you can work the dough
into a ball, kneading to make smooth. Cover
with plastic wrap and let stand for at least 30
minutes. If using a pasta machine, cut dough
according to directions. If rolling by hand,
divide dough in thirds. Dust a generous
amount of flour on top and bottom of each
piece. Roll the dough as thin as you like the
noodles, and flour both sides generously.
Trim the edges, so that the dough is a neat
square or rectangle. Starting at the one end,
roll the dough into a very tight roll, as for a
jelly roll. Using a sharp butcher knife, cut
the roll into thin slices, approximately ¼"
wide. As the slices fall onto the cutting
board, toss them lightly with your hands so
they do not stick together. Place on clean
towels or a tablecloth to dry before cooking.
Do not let them stick together.

Noodles, after being thoroughly dried,
may be stored in an airtight container for
weeks. They also store well in the refrigerator
or freezer.

Cook as for Saffron Noodles (see Index).

Serves 6–8

2½ cups all-purpose flour
½ teaspoon salt
4 egg yolks
¼ cup cold water

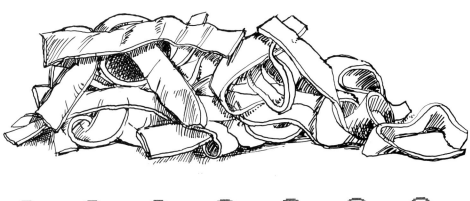

GREEN (SPINACH) NOODLES

Put 2½ cups of the flour and the salt in a large mixing bowl. Make a well in the center and add the egg yolks, spinach, and water. Stir until well blended. Knead for several minutes until spinach and dough are well mixed. A food processor does this very quickly. Work dough into a ball until it is smooth. Cover with plastic wrap and let stand for at least 30 minutes. If using a pasta machine, cut dough according to directions, using the flour remaining to dust the noodles. If rolling by hand, divide dough in 3 parts. Dust a generous amount of flour on top and bottom of each piece. Roll the dough as thin as you like the noodles, and flour both sides generously. Trim the edges so that the dough is a neat square or rectangle. Starting at one end, roll the dough into a tight roll, as for a jelly roll. Using a sharp butcher knife, cut the roll into thin slices, approximately ¼" wide. As the slices fall onto the cutting board, toss them lightly with your hands so they do not stick together. Place on clean towels or a tablecloth to dry before cooking. Do not let them stick together.

Noodles, after being thoroughly dried, may be stored in an airtight container for weeks. They also store well in the refrigerator or freezer.

Cook as for Saffron Noodles.

Serves 12

- 3 cups all-purpose flour
- 1 teaspoon salt
- 5 egg yolks
- 1 cup finely chopped fresh spinach or ½ cup thawed frozen spinach, drained
- ¼ cup cold water

SAFFRON NOODLES

Put the salt, saffron, butter, and water in a 2-quart saucepan. Bring to a boil and add the noodles. Reduce heat to medium and boil, stirring occasionally, for approximately 12 minutes until tender. Place noodles in a heated serving dish and top with Browned Butter Crumbs.

Serves 6

1½ teaspoons salt
◆ Pinch saffron
1 tablespoon butter or oil
1 quart water
3 cups noodles
Browned Butter Crumbs (see Index)

FORGET-ME-NOT, Counted Cross Stitch

Rows of baskets highlight one of the most delicate garden flowers. The Forget-Me-Not, with its beautiful blue flower, appears early in spring and welcomes in the warmth of summer.

7

VEGETABLES

VEGETABLES

Alma Bobb's Tomato Pudding
Asparagus with Hollandaise Sauce
Baked Lima Beans in Sour Cream
Baked Dried Corn Pudding
Baked Potatoes
Baked Sweet Potatoes
Batter-Dipped Eggplant
Bettie Stewart's Squash and Cranberries
Betty's Baked Corn and Broccoli Pudding
Black Walnut Sweet Potatoes
Carrots with Nutmeg
Broiled Tomatoes
Brussels Sprouts and Water Chestnuts
Buttered Beets
Buttered Carrots
Celeriac With Browned Butter Crumbs
Charlie's Lima Beans
Corn Fritters with Sweet Basil
Corn on the Cob
Creamed Onions
Danish Brown Potatoes
Dried Green and Yellow Beans with Ham Hock
Dried Corn
French-Fried Zucchini
Fresh Garden Peas with Browned Butter
Fresh Lima Beans in Thyme
Fresh Steamed Spinach with Browned Butter

Thelma's Asparagus Supreme
The Late Dr. Babcock's Fried Green Beans
Kohlrabi, Rutabaga, and Turnips
Marian Kreider's Carrot Loaf
Marian's Cream or Cheese Potatoes
Mary's Onion Rings
Mashed Potatoes
Mavis's Asparagus and Water Chestnuts
Italian Green Beans with Water Chestnuts
Ruth's Tomato Casserole
Parsleyed Potatoes
Pattypan Squash in Chive Butter
Potato Cakes
Potato Dumplings
Potatoes in Jackets
Potato Pancakes
Potato Puffs
Poulticed Potatoes
Shirley Wagner's Eggplant Casserole
Sweet-Sour Red Cabbage
Scalloped Salsify
Red Cabbage with Plums and Bacon
Scalloped Potatoes with Bacon, Chives, and Celery
Scalloped Potatoes with Sharp Cheese
Sour Cream-Potato Casserole
Special Lima Beans
Stir-Fried Corn and Lima Beans
Stir-Fried Green Beans and Onions with Bacon
Superb Sweet Potatoes
Puffed Potatoes
Swiss-Style Green Beans
Whole Browned Potatoes
Tomato and Eggplant Casserole
Tomato Sauce
Fried Corn and Red Peppers in Bacon
Whole Scraped Potatoes with Browned Butter
Whole Tiny Buttered Beets

ALMA BOBB'S TOMATO PUDDING

Put the bread cubes in a 9″ x 13″ baking dish. Pour melted butter on top. Toss gently. Mix the tomato puree, water, and sugar together in a 1-quart saucepan. Simmer over medium heat for 5 minutes. Pour over the buttered bread cubes and mix thoroughly. Set the baking dish in pan of hot water. Bake in a preheated 375° F. oven for 45–50 minutes.

This may be prepared the day before serving and refrigerated unbaked.

MICROWAVE: Bake in a covered casserole for 12 minutes. Let stand for 5 minutes after removing from oven.

Serves 8

4 cups fresh bread cubes
1 cup melted butter
2 cups canned tomato puree
½ cup water
½ cup light brown sugar

ASPARAGUS WITH HOLLANDAISE SAUCE

Wash and trim the asparagus by snapping each stalk; it snaps where the tender part begins. Discard the lower portion. To cook, lay the spears in a flat pan and add the water, salt, and sugar. Bring to a boil over medium heat. Boil for only 4 minutes. If asparagus is not tender enough, remove the pan from the heat and cover until ready to serve. Spears should not be limp. Remove from the water with a slotted spoon or forks, and place in a heated vegetable dish. Serve with Hollandaise Sauce or Browned Butter.

Serves 6

2 pounds fresh asparagus
1 cup water
1½ teaspoons salt
1 teaspoon sugar
Hollandaise Sauce (see Index)
or Browned Butter (see Index)

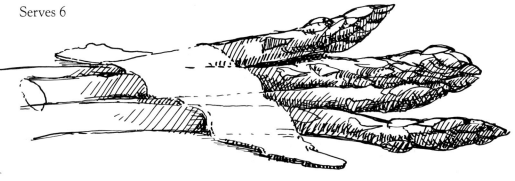

BAKED LIMA BEANS IN SOUR CREAM

Wash beans and soak in water in a bowl overnight. Drain. Put in a saucepan. Cover with water and cook approximately 40 minutes until tender. Drain and rinse. In a small bowl mix remaining ingredients until well blended. Add to the beans. Pour into a buttered 2-quart baking dish. Bake in a preheated oven at 350° F. for 1 hour.

MICROWAVE: Microwave in a covered casserole for 20 minutes, stirring every 5 minutes. Let stand for 5 minutes before serving.

Serves 4–6

1 pound dried lima beans
1 quart water
3 teaspoons salt
¼ pound or ½ cup butter, melted
¾ cup light brown sugar
1 tablespoon dry mustard
1 tablespoon molasses
1 cup sour cream

BAKED DRIED CORN PUDDING

Put the dried corn and milk in a quart bowl. Cover with a lid or plastic wrap and refrigerate overnight. Next day, put the sugar, salt, pepper, and melted butter in a small bowl. Slowly add the flour to make a smooth paste. Add the eggs. Combine the mixture with the corn and milk. The milk should be almost completely absorbed by the corn. Pour into a buttered 1½- quart baking dish, and bake in a preheated 350° F. oven for 45 minutes.

MICROWAVE: Pour into the buttered 1½-quart baking dish, cover, and microwave on high for 12 minutes. Let stand 3–5 minutes before serving.

Serves 6

1 cup dried corn
3 cups milk
1 tablespoon sugar
1½ teaspoons salt
♦ Several dashes freshly ground pepper
2½ tablespoons melted butter
1½ tablespoons flour
3 eggs, beaten

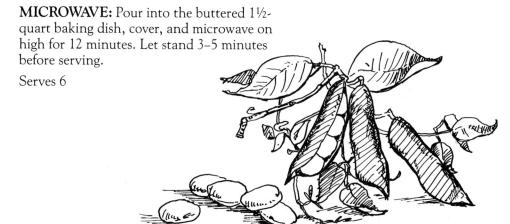

BAKED POTATOES

Choose a mealy potato for baking. Some varieties tend to become watery. I prefer the Idaho, Irish Cobbler, or Maine baking potato. Scrub potatoes thoroughly and prick the skin twice to keep them from exploding in the oven. Bake potatoes in pre-heated oven at 375° F. for 1 hour. Serve with fresh butter, salt, and pepper. Many people enjoy sour cream and chives with their baked potatoes. Chives should be added to the sour cream before serving. The baked skin is so crisp and should be eaten with butter, salt, and pepper. I do not like a baked potato that has been wrapped in foil. When using foil, the skin is soft, and not to my liking.

MICROWAVE: Potatoes are easy to bake in a microwave oven. Be sure to place them in a circle, leaving 1 inch between them, and pierce the skins with a fork. Each (medium size) potato takes approximately 4 minutes on high. Halfway through the cooking time turn them over. I always place mine on a paper towel and when they are finished let them stand for 10 minutes, wrapped in a terry towel to keep hot.

VARIATION

Follow recipe for Baked Potatoes, but instead of serving butter or sour cream with chives, serve with Herb Cheese (see Index).

1 per person

BAKED SWEET POTATOES

Scrub and trim potatoes. Place in a pre-heated 375° F. oven and bake approximately 45 minutes until tender, testing with a fork. If potatoes are very large, bake at least 60 minutes.

Baked sweet potatoes are perfect when the skin begins to puff. Remove from oven directly to a serving plate and make a 2″ slit in the top. Add the butter, salt, and pepper, or serve butter separately.

MICROWAVE: One medium potato takes approximately 4 minutes. Add 3–4 minutes for each additional potato. Place in a circle with 1″ between and pierce the skin with a fork. Halfway during the cooking time turn them over. I always place mine on a paper towel and when they are finished let them stand for 10 minutes, wrapped in a terry towel to keep hot.

Makes 1 per person

1 firm sweet potato per person
Fresh sweet butter or herb butter
Salt and pepper to taste

BATTER-DIPPED EGGPLANT

Peel eggplant and cut as for french fries, or in ¼″ slices. Layer in a large bowl, sprinkling salt on each layer. Let stand for at least 30 minutes and then drain off the liquid. (The salt draws out the excess water.) Pat dry with paper towels and dip in batter.

Mix all batter ingredients in a blender or mixer, and chill, covered, for at least 30 minutes, or until needed.

Coat only enough eggplant in the batter to fry at one time. Fry in preheated deep fat at 375° F. until golden brown.

NOTE: Some people like fried eggplant served with catsup, but recently I have been told that it is delicious with applesauce too.

Serves 6

2 medium eggplants
2 tablespoons salt

BATTER

1¼ cups all-purpose flour
½ teaspoon salt
1 tablespoon baking powder
¼ cup milk
8 ounces beer
1 egg
◆ Dash pepper

BETTIE STEWART'S SQUASH AND CRANBERRIES

New recipes for hard-shell winter squash are always welcome, since the vegetable is available in prolific quantities during its winter season. This recipe is unusual and colorful. Furthermore, the casserole can be frozen after baking. Serve it with your Thanksgiving turkey, or with roast pork or chicken.

Peel the squash and cut into cubes. Cook in lightly salted water until tender. Drain well, then puree by putting through a food mill. There should be about 4 cups. Mix well with the eggs, butter, sugar, salt, pepper, and cranberries. Put in a buttered 1½-quart casserole. Grate nutmeg over the top. Bake in a preheated 350° F. oven for 45 minutes.

Makes 8 servings

2 pounds butternut squash
Salt
2 cups water
2 eggs, beaten
⅓ cup melted butter
¼ cup light brown sugar, firmly packed
1 teaspoon salt
Freshly ground black pepper to taste
1½ cups raw cranberries, halved
Freshly grated nutmeg

BETTY'S BAKED CORN AND BROCCOLI PUDDING

This is easy, delicious, and pretty served in the baking dish. The first evening we served it, our guests all asked for seconds. The recipe has a custard-like consistency. It is quite different from the better-known baked corn. It can also be prepared in an electric skillet for an outdoor party.

Use 1 tablespoon of the butter to butter a 9″ x 13″ baking dish. Arrange the broccoli buds at each end of the dish. Put the corn in the center. Sprinkle the lemon zest over the broccoli, and grind pepper over the corn.

In a bowl, combine the flour, salt, sugar, and remaining butter. Gradually add the eggs and mix well. Stir in the milk to make a thin batter. Pour over the vegetables. Bake in a preheated 350° F. oven for 1 hour until the egg mixture is set and firm. Bake longer, if needed. To test the pudding, insert a silver knife in the center. It is ready when the knife comes out clean. We used to test this recipe with a broom straw, but who has a broom anymore?

MICROWAVE: Follow this recipe through the entire preparation. Cook in a covered baking dish using waxed paper or plastic wrap covering for 15 minutes, until the egg mixture is set and firm. You can test in your microwave as indicated above. Let stand 3–5 minutes before serving.

Makes 6 servings

4   tablespoons butter
4   cups broccoli buds
4   cups corn kernels
Grated zest of 1 lemon (yellow part only)
Freshly ground black pepper
⅓   cup flour
2   teaspoons salt
1   teaspoon sugar
4   eggs
1   cup milk

BLACK WALNUT SWEET POTATOES

Cover the sweet potatoes with hot salted water. Boil approximately 15 minutes until tender. Peel and quarter potatoes. Place in a 1-quart buttered baking dish and baste with melted butter. Sprinkle with brown sugar and walnuts. Bake in a preheated oven at about 350° F. for approximately 30 minutes until golden brown.

Serves 4

1   pound yellow sweet potatoes
Water to cover
1   teaspoon salt
2½   tablespoons butter, melted
¼   cup light brown sugar
½   cup broken or coarsely chopped black walnuts (English walnuts may be used)

CARROTS WITH NUTMEG

Cut carrots in large chunks, approximately 1½"–2" long. Carrots seem much more flavorful when prepared in larger pieces. Put the water, salt, sugar, nutmeg, and butter in a 1½-quart saucepan with lid. Bring to a boil. Add carrots. Cover and reduce heat to medium. Simmer approximately 12–15 minutes, depending on the thickness of the carrots, until tender. Remove with a slotted spoon to a preheated serving dish. Top with Browned Butter. Save carrot broth for soup stock.

MICROWAVE: Place carrots in a 2-quart casserole with only ¼ cup water, salt, and sugar. Microwave on high for 7–10 minutes.

Serves 4–6

1	pound carrots, peeled or scraped
1	cup water
1½	teaspoons salt
1½	teaspoons sugar
¼	teaspoon ground nutmeg
1	tablespoon butter
1	tablespoon Browned Butter for topping (see Index)

BROILED TOMATOES

Peel the tomatoes and cut in half horizontally. Put flour in a shallow bowl and roll each tomato half in the flour. Dip in the butter and sprinkle top with brown sugar, tarragon, salt, and pepper. Place in a baking dish and broil approximately 5 minutes until golden brown.

Serves 4–6

3	large tomatoes, peeled
⅓	cup flour
4	tablespoons melted butter
3	tablespoons light brown sugar
2	teaspoons chopped fresh tarragon
1	teaspoon salt
	Freshly ground pepper

BRUSSEL SPROUTS AND WATER CHESTNUTS

Put the sprouts, water, and salt in a 2-quart covered saucepan. Bring to a boil and cover. Reduce heat to medium and cook approximately 6 minutes until sprouts are tender. Drain. In a heavy skillet, melt the butter and add the sliced chestnuts. Sauté on medium heat until the edges turn golden. Add the sprouts and stir until heated thoroughly. Serve in a heated dish, topping with Browned Butter.

Serves 6

- 1 **quart brussel sprouts, cleaned and trimmed**
- 2 **cups water**
- 1 **teaspoon salt**
- 3 **tablespoons butter**
- 1 **cup water chestnuts, sliced and drained**
- 2 **tablespoons Browned Butter (see Index)**

BUTTTERED BEETS

Scrub the beets and place in a large saucepan with lid. Cover with water and add salt. Cook over medium heat approximately 30 minutes until tender. Drain and cool slightly. Remove the peels and cut into thin slices. Put beets in a 1-quart saucepan and add butter. On very low heat simmer for approximately 10 minutes until heated through. Check for seasonings, adding more salt if desired. Sprinkle with pepper and serve piping hot.

Leftover beets are delicious in vegetable salad.

MICROWAVE: Place scrubbed beets in a 2-quart casserole with ½ cup water; microwave on high for 15 minutes. Remove peels and slice. Place butter in casserole with sliced beets for 4 minutes. Let stand for 3–5 minutes before serving.

Serves 6

- 2 **pounds small fresh beets**
- **Water to cover**
- 1½ **teaspoons salt**
- 2 **tablespoons butter**
- ◆ **Dash freshly ground pepper**

BUTTERED CARROTS

Follow same recipe as for Carrrots with Nutmeg (see Index) omitting the nutmeg. You may wish to add more Browned Butter (see Index), according to taste.

CELERIAC WITH BROWNED BUTTER CRUMBS

You may not recognize this winter vegetable in the markets, and you may wonder how to serve it. Celeriac, or celery root, is a large knobby beige-brown vegetable which looks much like a puffy turnip with little roots at the bottom. It is not related to regular celery; the flavor is different and very subtle. We use it in beef vegetable soup or potato soup. It may be cooked and pureed and mixed in equal parts with mashed potatoes. We especially enjoy celeriac served with browned butter crumbs. In French restaurants, celeriac is served as an hors d'oeuvre as Céleri Rémoulade. In that recipe, very thin strips of celery root are served either raw or slightly blanched, mixed with rémoulade sauce, a crisp and crunchy first course. Top with Browned Butter Crumbs (see Index).

Cook the sliced celeriac and salt in the water about 20 minutes until tender. Drain well and put in a vegetable dish. Meanwhile, heat the butter in a heavy skillet until golden brown. Stir in the bread crumbs. Sprinkle the crumbs over the celeriac. Serve at once. Delicious with rich meat or roast duck.

Makes 4–6 servings

2 large celeriac, peeled and sliced thin
1 cup water
1 teaspoon salt
¼ cup salted butter
⅓ cup dried or ½ cup fresh bread crumbs

CHARLIE'S LIMA BEANS

Put the water, salt, sugar, and butter in a 2-quart covered saucepan. Bring to a boil and add the lima beans. Cover and reduce heat to medium. Simmer approximately 5 minutes if frozen, 6 minutes if fresh, until tender. Meanwhile put the flour in a small bowl. Gradually combine with milk to make a thin paste. Add this and the evaporated milk to the lima beans. Simmer for 3 minutes until slightly thickened to the consistency of cream. Serve in a heated dish topped with Browned Butter or a chunk of fresh butter.

Serves 6

½ cup water
1 teaspoon salt
1 teaspoon sugar
1 tablespoon butter
1 quart fresh or frozen lima beans
1 tablespoon flour
½ cup milk
½ cup evaporated milk
Browned Butter (see Index) or fresh butter (optional)

CORN FRITTERS WITH SWEET BASIL

Thoroughly mix corn, egg, salt, sugar, pepper, flour, and basil in a bowl, blender, or food processor. Heat the butter or shortening in a heavy skillet. Drop the corn mixture by tablespoons into the hot fat. Fry on each side until golden brown. Delicious made in an electric skillet, tableside, and served as soon as they are made. Tasty with powdered sugar or syrup.

NOTE: Corn kernels put through a blender may be substituted for the grated corn. Do not use canned creamed corn, as it is too liquid.

Serves 4

1 cup grated uncooked corn
1 egg, beaten
½ teaspoon salt
¼ teaspoon sugar
◆ Dash freshly ground pepper
1 tablespoon flour
1 teaspoon fresh finely chopped or ½ teaspoon dried sweet basil
2 tablespoons butter or shortening
Powdered sugar (optional)
Syrup (optional)

CORN ON THE COB

Corn should not be overcooked. Fill a large kettle half full with water and bring to a boil. Drop the corn into the boiling water. When the water comes to a boil again, remove the corn and serve. If you are preparing the corn ahead of time, add 1 teaspoon salt and 1 tablespoon sugar to the water and let the corn stay in the water until ready to serve. Excellent for large parties.

MICROWAVE: Wrap each ear of corn in waxed paper or plastic wrap, allowing 2 minutes per ear. Do not do more than 6 at one time—allow space between the ears in oven.

VARIATION

MICROWAVE: Clean corn and gently pull back the husks. Remove silk and sprinkle with a few drops of water. Place a few husks back on each cob and cook approximately 3 minutes per ear, leaving space between each one.

1 or 2 ears per person, silked and cleaned
Water to cover

CREAMED ONIONS

Although this is a very basic recipe, I am including it because we are often complimented on our creamed onions at the restaurant. It is probably the browned butter which makes the difference in the flavor. Most people feel that this dish should be made only with tiny white onions, but I prefer big sweet onions quartered. Someone once told me an interesting fact about onions. It seems the drier the climate during the year the onions are grown, the stronger the flavor will be.

Peel the onions. Cook in the water with the salt for about 15 minutes until tender. Drain well, and combine with the white sauce. Top with the Browned Butter.

Makes 6 servings

1 **pound tiny white onions, or large sweet onions, cut in quarters**
1 **cup water**
2 **teaspoons salt**
1 **cup thin white sauce**
3 **tablespoons Browned Butter (see Index)**

DANISH BROWN POTATOES

Kirsten Rosenthal Bishop says that in Denmark they often served these with another type of potato dish at the same meal. Kirsten came here as an American Field Service student from Copenhagen, Denmark, and lived with our family for about a year. After finishing school, she returned annually and finally married Ned Bishop from Landisville. She is now an American citizen and with her husband attends all our family functions, since we are her adopted "American" family. We also enjoy seeing Kirsten's parents on their visits to the United States.

In a 2-quart covered saucepan, in salted water, cook the scrubbed potatoes in their skins. Drain and peel. Cut into 1″ cubes. Melt the sugar in a heavy pan. Just as the sugar begins to brown, stir in the butter to make a smooth mixture. Turn heat to very low. Place the potatoes in this sauce and turn occasionally as they brown on all sides.

Serves 6

1½ **pounds white potatoes, preferably small**
1 **teaspoon salt**
4 **cups water**
3 **tablespoons white sugar**
3 **tablespoons butter or margarine**

DRIED GREEN AND YELLOW BEANS WITH HAM HOCK

Arlene Kenworthy, of Atglen, Pennsylvania, shared this marvelous recipe with me several years ago. We've held a very deep regard for her and her late husband, Dr. William Kenworthy. He was my doctor when I had a serious fall from our horse during my childhood, and we've cherished our friendship since then.

Place ham hock and water in 4-quart Dutch oven with lid. Cover and bring to a boil. Add dried beans. Cook until meat and beans are tender—approximately 45 minutes to 1 hour. Remove hock and cut meat into bite-size pieces. Return meat to the beans and broth and add Great Northern beans, salt, and pepper to taste. Add milk or water as desired.

NOTE: This dish is also delicious reheated the next day. Here are several successful suggestions for drying beans: To dry fresh beans, use needle and heavy thread. String beans whole, inserting the string through the center of each bean. Hang in a dust-free place until beans are very dry.

Or: Parboil beans for 5 minutes. Spread on paper towel or cookie sheets and place in warm oven. Dry in oven for 60 minutes at lowest heat. Leave oven door ajar as for broiling while the beans are drying. Set on a sunny windowsill until completely dry.

Put beans between linen tea towels and place in a microwave oven for 10 minutes. Remove and set in a sunny window until dry. Do not package for several days, or beans will mold.

Serves 6

1 smoked ham hock
2 cups dried green and yellow beans, preferably whole
2 cups canned Great Northern or marrow beans
6 cups water
Salt and pepper to taste
1 cup milk (water may be substituted)

DRIED CORN

Put the dried corn and milk in a quart bowl. Cover with a lid or plastic wrap, and refrigerate overnight. Thirty to 45 minutes before serving time place soaked corn, salt, sugar, and light cream in a heavy 2-quart covered pan. Bring to a boil and reduce heat to low. Simmer for about 30 minutes. Pour into a heated serving dish and top with butter. This recipe reheats beautifully.

Serves 4–6

1	cup dried corn
1½	cups milk
1½	teaspoons salt
2	teaspoons sugar
¾	cup light cream
2	tablespoons butter

FRENCH-FRIED ZUCCHINI

While I was visiting on the West Coast, I was delighted to find that the fish restaurant on the wharf in San Francisco served french-fried zucchini, french fries, and batter-fried fish. Since childhood, I have enjoyed french-fried food. Naturally this zucchini recipe appealed to me. You may use this batter equally well for other vegetables.

Make the batter several hours ahead. Stir the egg yolks, salt, oil and beer into the flour, beating until smooth with a wire whisk or electric hand beater, or use a blender. Cover the bowl with plastic wrap. Allow the batter to stand for several hours, overnight if possible, so that the gluten in the flour will expand.

Trim the ends from the zucchini. Slice lengthwise, then cut as for french fries. Place in a colander and sprinkle with salt. Let stand 30 minutes to remove some of the liquid from the vegetable. Drain, rinse, and pat dry on paper towels. When ready to fry the zucchini, beat the egg whites until stiff but not dry. Stir the batter, which will have become thick, and fold in the beaten egg whites.

Heat oil in a deep fryer to 375° F. Dip the zucchini sticks in the batter. Fry, a few at a time, so as not to lower the temperature of the oil, for about 2 minutes until golden brown. When cooked, remove to paper towels to drain. Keep the zucchini warm in a low oven. When all are cooked, serve at once.

BATTER

2	eggs, separated
1½	teaspoons salt
2	tablespoons salad oil
¾	cup beer, at room temperature
¾	cup flour
6–8	medium zucchini
	Salt
	Oil for deep frying

Makes 6 servings

FRESH GARDEN PEAS WITH BROWNED BUTTER

Put peas, onions, salt, sugar, butter, and water in a 1½-quart saucepan. Bring to a boil. Reduce heat to medium. Boil for approximately 3 minutes until tender. If using frozen peas, 2 minutes is adequate. Drain and serve in heated serving dish, topped with Browned Butter.

Serves 6

3 cups shelled fresh green peas (frozen may be substituted)

½ cup spring onions cut in ½" pieces

1 teaspoon salt

1 teaspoon sugar

1 tablespoon butter

½ cup water

2 tablespoons Browned Butter (see Index)

FRESH LIMA BEANS IN THYME

Put the water, salt, sugar, thyme,* and butter in a 2-quart covered saucepan. Bring to a boil and add the lima beans. Cover and reduce heat to medium. Boil approximately 6 minutes until tender. Place in heated dish and top with Browned Butter.

*NOTE: If you love the taste of thyme, chop it fine and add to the lima beans. If you only want the flavor, do not chop it, but add the sprigs to the boiling beans and remove before serving.

MICROWAVE: Place ¼ cup water in a 2-quart casserole with limas, salt, sugar, thyme, and butter. Microwave on high for 6–8 minutes.

Serves 4

1 quart fresh young lima beans, shelled and washed

½ cup water

1 teaspoon salt

½ teaspoon sugar

1 tablespoon fresh or ⅓ teaspoon dried thyme

1 tablespoon butter

1 tablespoon Browned Butter (see Index)

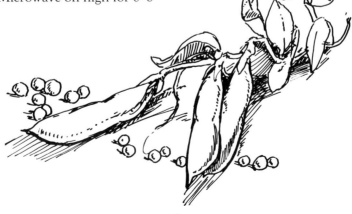

FRESH STEAMED SPINACH WITH BROWNED BUTTER

Wash spinach at least 3 times to remove all the sand. Trim the bottoms and run under cold water. Shake off the water, leaving any on the leaves for steaming. Place the spinach in a 2-quart saucepan and cover. Bring to a boil and turn off the heat. (The water on the leaves and the spinach itself will provide all the moisture needed to come to a boil.) Do not overcook. Drain and serve, topped with browned butter.

Serves 4

1 pound fresh spinach
1 teaspoon salt
2 tablespoons Browned Butter (see Index)

THELMA'S ASPARAGUS SUPREME

Put asparagus in a saucepan and add water and salt. Bring to a boil and cook for 3 minutes. Drain. In a 1-quart saucepan, melt the butter and stir in the flour. Gradually add the milk, continuing to stir until thickened. Put half the asparagus, cooked eggs, and pimientos in a greased 1½-quart baking dish. Pour half of the white sauce over the asparagus. Repeat, using the remainder of the ingredients. Top with the grated cheese and crumbs. Bake in a 350° F. oven for 40 minutes.

MICROWAVE: Place asparagus in a covered casserole dish with ¼ cup water and cook on high in microwave for 7–10 minutes. Drain. Continue recipe. Microwave in a covered casserole for 12 minutes. Let stand 5 minutes before serving.

Serves 6

1½ pounds fresh asparagus, cleaned and cut into bite-size pieces
2 cups water
1 teaspoon salt
4 hard-boiled eggs, sliced
¼ cup chopped pimentos
2 tablespoons butter
2 tablespoons flour
1 cup milk
1 cup grated sharp cheese
1 cup fresh bread crumbs

THE LATE DR. BABCOCK'S FRIED GREEN BEANS

In central Pennsylvania, people talk about eating fried green beans when they were children, but few seem to have a recipe to prepare it. Apparently it was served when they went to visit Grandmother. This particular recipe was given to me by the late Jessie Babcock, the wife of a Methodist minister and the mother of one of our dearest friends, Dr. J. Reed Babcock, of Bellefonte, Pennsylvania. Mrs. Babcock made it in a heavy skillet, But I prefer a wok. The recipe was changed according to the season and Mrs. Babcock's mood. Sometimes it was topped with sliced fresh tomatoes, and, on occasion, sweet potatoes were used instead of white ones. We make it quite often and fully understand its popular appeal.

Fry the bacon in a heavy skillet until crisp. Remove and drain on paper towels. Add the beans, potatoes, corn, and pepper to the fat in the pan. Stir and fry until golden brown. Add the milk and evaporated milk, cover with a lid, and simmer on low heat for 10 minutes. Serve garnished with the crumbled crisp bacon.

Makes 6 servings

½ **pound bacon**
1 **pound green beans, trimmed and cut in pieces**
3 **medium potatoes, peeled and sliced thin**
1 **cup sweet corn kernels (about 3 ears, kernels cut off)**
1½ **teaspoons freshly ground black pepper**
½ **cup milk**
¼ **cup evaporated milk**

KOHLRABI, RUTABAGA, AND TURNIPS

All of these vegetables are reasonably priced in season, yet seldom used. I hope this recipe will encourage you to try them. All of these vegetables retain their colors well when they are cooked, and are pleasing to the eye when sliced, diced, and cubed.

Put the vegetables and beef stock in a 3-quart saucepan, cover, and cook about 25 minutes over medium heat until tender. Check for seasoning, and add salt and freshly ground pepper as needed, depending on the seasoning in the beef stock. An excellent vegetable to serve with beef or pork.

VARIATION

Use ham stock in place of beef.

Makes 6 servings

1 **pound kohlrabi, peeled and cubed**
1 **pound rutabaga, peeled and sliced**
½ **pound white turnips, peeled and diced**
2 **cups beef stock**
Salt
Freshly ground pepper

MARIAN KREIDER'S CARROT LOAF

In a heavy skillet, sauté the onions in the butter. Put the mashed carrots, eggs, milk, bread crumbs, and buttered onions in a large bowl. Mix and then add the celery and salt, continuing to mix. Put in a greased 1½-quart ring mold or loaf pan, and bake in a preheated 350° F. oven for 40 minutes. Turn upside down on a platter. Surround the outside or, if using ring mold, the center, with the buttered peas.

MICROWAVE: Put into a greased Bundt pan and bake for 10 minutes. Let stand for 3–5 minutes before serving

Serves 6

2 tablespoons butter
1 medium onion, minced
3 cups carrots, cooked and mashed
2 eggs, slightly beaten
1 cup milk
1½ cups dry bread crumbs
½ cup finely diced celery
1½ teaspoons salt
Fresh garden peas, cooked and seasoned (see Index)

MARIAN'S CREAM OR CHEESE POTATOES

Put the mashed potatoes, butter, sour cream or cream cheese, milk, and salt in a mixing bowl. Beat well. Fold in the eggs. Pour into a 2-quart buttered casserole. Bake in a preheated 350° F. oven for 1 hour until golden brown on top.

You can make this a day ahead and store in the refrigerator overnight before baking. Add 15 minutes to the baking time if the dish has been refrigerated.

MICROWAVE: Microwave in covered casserole for 12 minutes, rotating the dish every 3 minutes. Let stand 3–5 minutes before serving.

Serves 6–8

12 medium white potatoes, cooked and mashed
6 tablespoons butter or margarine
8 ounces sour cream or cream cheese
1¼ cups milk
¾ teaspoon salt
2 eggs, well beaten

MARY'S ONION RINGS

Cut the onions in ⅓″ slices and separate into rings.

Mix all ingredients except onions in blender or mixing bowl. Dip the onion rings in this batter, draining off all excess. Fry in preheated deep fat at 375° F. for 2 minutes until golden brown.

VARIATION

This batter can also be used to fry chicken.

Serves 6–8

2 large onions

BATTER

1 cup flour
½ teaspoon baking soda
½ teaspoon salt
1 egg, lightly beaten
1 cup buttermilk or 1 cup milk plus 1 tablespoon vinegar

MASHED POTATOES

Put the potatoes in a large covered kettle. Add the salt and water and cook approximately 30 minutes until soft. Remove potatoes with slotted spoon and put in a large mixing bowl. Slowly add the evaporated milk, heated milk, and butter. Whip until very fluffy. Check for seasoning, adding more pepper and salt if needed. Serve in heated dish, topping with Browned Butter.

If the potatoes are mealy, they become fluffier. A baking potato is fine too, but do not use new potatoes, as they tend to be lumpy. We use Kennebec, Idaho, or Irish Cobbler varieties. Katahdin potatoes are firm and look nice when served whole, but they are inclined to be watery and are unsuitable for mashing.

Serves 6

1½ pounds white potatoes, peeled and quartered
1½ teaspoons salt
1 quart water
⅓ cup evaporated milk
⅓ cup milk, heated
4–6 tablespoons butter
Freshly ground pepper
Browned Butter (see Index) for topping

MAVIS'S ASPARAGUS AND WATER CHESTNUTS

Mavis, a friend from California, was the first to introduce me to the taste of stir-fried asparagus. The Chinese trick of cutting it diagonally is very important; it stays so crunchy and green. The bacon is my way of making it taste more Pennsylvania Dutch and it also provides enough meat flavor to make it perfect as a main course. Abe and I often eat a full recipe for lunch, with nothing but a good relish.

Cut the asparagus in 1½″ diagonal slices as follows: start at the tip and cut toward the bottom stem until it feels tough. Either throw away the tough part or use it for Cream of Asparagus Soup. A few tough ends will ruin this dish.

Fry the bacon in a wok or heavy skillet until crisp. Remove and drain on paper towels. Add the asparagus and garlic to the hot bacon fat and stir. Cover for 1 minute. Add the water chestnuts and stir-fry about 1 minute until edges are golden. Check for seasoning and add salt, if needed. Garnish with crumbled bacon and serve at once.

VARIATION

For a more Oriental flavor, add ½ teaspoon chopped fresh ginger with the garlic.

MICROWAVE: Lay spears evenly in a flat casserole with lid, adding only ¼ cup water, salt, and sugar. Microwave for 8 minutes.

Makes 4 servings

1 **pound fresh asparagus**
4 **slices bacon**
1 **clove garlic, crushed or sliced thin**
2 **cups water chestnuts, drained and sliced**
½ **teaspoon salt**

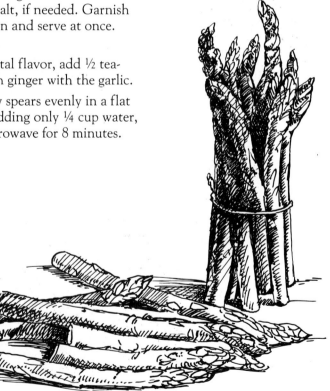

ITALIAN GREEN BEANS WITH WATER CHESTNUTS

Wash and cut the beans diagonally into bite-size pieces. Fry the bacon in a wok or heavy skillet until crisp. Remove and drain on paper towels. Add the beans and garlic to the hot bacon fat and stir-fry for 1 minute. Cover with lid and fry for another minute until beans are bright and green and slightly golden around edges. Add the sliced water chestnuts and stir-fry approximately 1 minute until their edges are also golden brown. Sprinkle with salt and pepper, and check for seasoning. Serve at once, garnishing top with crumbled bacon.

Serves 4

1 pound fresh Italian or regular green beans
4 slices bacon
1 clove garlic, crushed or thinly sliced
1 cup drained sliced water chestnuts
½ teaspoon salt
◆ Dash freshly ground pepper

RUTH'S TOMATO CASSEROLE

In a heavy skillet, fry the bacon and onion until golden brown. Add the tomatoes, bread cubes, sugar, and salt and mix until well blended. Pour into a buttered 2-quart casserole and bake in a preheated 350° F. oven for 30 minutes. Garnish with buttered croutons and slices of hard-boiled egg.

MICROWAVE: In a covered glass casserole fry bacon, roughly 35 seconds per slice, along with onion to cook. Follow above recipe; microwave in a buttered 2-quart covered casserole for 8 minutes, turning every 2 minutes. Let stand 3–5 minutes before serving.

Serves 4–6

4 slices bacon, cut in 1" pieces
¼ cup chopped onion
2 cups peeled and chopped fresh or canned tomatoes
2 cups bread cubes
3 tablespoons light brown sugar
½ teaspoon salt
1 hard-boiled egg, sliced, for garnish
Croutons for garnish

PARSLEYED POTATOES

Scrub and peel the potatoes, cutting in half if they are very large. Place potatoes, water, salt, and pepper in a 2-quart covered saucepan. Bring to a boil and simmer approximately 30 minutes until soft. Drain and add milk or cream. Reheat to almost boiling. Add the parsley and serve very hot. Top with a pat of butter if desired.

MICROWAVE: Place potatoes in a 2-quart casserole with ½ cup water. Microwave for 10 minutes. Add cream and heat for 1–2 minutes.

Serves 4

1 pound white potatoes, peeled
2 cups water
1½ teaspoons salt
◆ Dash pepper
½ cup milk or cream
2 tablespoons chopped parsley
Butter (optional)

PATTYPAN SQUASH IN CHIVE BUTTER

During the few weeks in early fall when tiny baby pattypan squash are available in the local markets, they are a rare delicacy. They are tender and bright green and look almost too good to eat. Enjoy them, even though they may be a trifle expensive, for in only a short time, each tiny squash would make a nice big squash, which would be more profitable for the grower.

Put squash, salt, and water in a 3-quart covered saucepan. Bring to a boil. Reduce heat to medium. Cook approximately 3 minutes until tender. Pour off water. Add butter and chives. Simmer on low heat for 2 minutes. Serve in heated dish.

Serves 6

2 quarts tiny pattypan squash (no larger than 2" across)
1 teaspoon salt
1 cup water
¼ cup butter
¼ cup chopped fresh or ⅛ cup dried chives

POTATO CAKES

In a large mixing bowl combine potatoes, beaten eggs, and parsley. Stir in onion salt or onion, if desired. Form into patties and dredge in flour. Melt shortening in heavy skillet and fry potatoes until golden brown on each side.

Serves 6

4 **cups mashed potatoes, seasoned with salt and pepper**

2 **eggs, beaten**

1 **tablespoon chopped parsley**

⅓ **cup all-purpose flour**

◆ **Shortening for frying**

½ **teaspoon onion salt or 1 tablespoon chopped onion (optional)**

POTATO DUMPLINGS

Cook cleaned unpeeled potatoes in boiling water about 30 minutes until tender. Drain, cool slightly, and peel. Put the potatoes through a food mill or ricer. Place in a large bowl and gently stir in the salt and pepper. Make a well in the center and add eggs. Sift ½ cup of the flour over the eggs. Add the bread crumbs, nutmeg, and parsley. Mix until it is smooth and holds together. Shape into egg-size balls. Roll in the remaining flour. Meanwhile, bring about 2 quarts lightly salted water to boiling point in large saucepan. Reduce heat to medium. Drop in potato balls, 1 at a time, just enough to fit comfortably in the pan. Boil gently, uncovered, for 2 minutes after they rise to the surface. With a slotted spoon, transfer dumplings to paper towels to drain. Serve hot.

Serves 6

2 **pounds white potatoes**

2 **teaspoons salt**

¼ **teaspoon pepper**

2 **eggs**

⅔ **cup all-purpose flour**

⅓ **cup dry bread crumbs**

◆ **Dash freshly grated nutmeg**

3 **tablespoons chopped parsley**

POTATOES IN JACKETS

Choose medium potatoes and scrub thoroughly. Place in a covered saucepan, adding 1 teaspoon salt per 4 potatoes. Cover with water and bring to a boil. Reduce heat to medium and cook approximately 35 minutes until tender. Serve very hot. When eating potatoes, cut in half and mash with a fork. Add lots of butter, salt, and pepper to taste.

Leftovers may be used for home fries or whole browned potatoes, etc.

1 potato per person

POTATO PANCAKES

Louis Graybill of Denver, Colorado, was one of our son Charlie's roommates at the Culinary Institute of America. When he came to our house for the weekend, Louis would make these potato pancakes. They are different from the Pennsylvania Dutch because we use mashed potatoes, but they are delicious. These pancakes are especially good served with sauerbraten, cooked beef tongue, or hot beef heart. In the spring, try them with cold sliced ham, asparagus with water chestnuts, and a relish.

In a large bowl mix the potatoes, onion, eggs, flour, and salt until well blended. Fry immediately in preheated hot oil or butter at 375° F. in an electric skillet or a heavy frying pan. Drop by large serving spoonfuls into the oil and fry until golden brown on each side. Serve immediately.

VARIATION

Sprinkle grated cheese or paprika on top when serving.

Serves 6

4 medium potatoes, coarsely grated
1 medium onion, coarsely grated
2 eggs, slightly beaten
¼ cup flour
1 teaspoon salt
◆ Dash freshly ground pepper
¼ cup oil or butter for frying
Grated cheese or paprika (optional)

POTATO PUFFS

For a specially rich dish, add 1 beaten egg to the mashed potatoes.

Form the mashed potatoes into egg-size balls. Cut cheese into ½" squares. Press a hole in middle of each potato ball and add a square of cheese. Form into balls again, trying to keep the cheese as near to the center of the ball as possible. Dip each ball in whipped egg and roll in bread crumbs and parsley. Refrigerate for 1 hour. Fry in preheated deep fat at 375° F. until golden brown, then place in preheated oven at 250° until ready to serve. Potato puffs may be kept in the oven for about 20 minutes. Excellent when made ahead of time and frozen. Increase oven time to 45 minutes if taken directly from the freezer.

When prepared properly, the cheese should ooze out as you cut the puff.

Serves 8

4   cups mashed potatoes, seasoned to taste
½   pound Velveeta cheese
2   eggs, whipped
1   cup bread crumbs
2   tablespoons chopped parsley
Oil for frying

POULTICED POTATOES

These potatoes were always served on a cool evening when we needed something to warm us up. They are a little spicy because of the amount of pepper used.

Peel potatoes and slice very thin. Place the sliced potatoes, salt, pepper, and water in a 1½-quart saucepan. Bring to a boil, cover, and reduce the heat to medium low. Simmer for approximately 30 minutes until most of the water has evaporated. Stir occasionally to prevent sticking. Serve very hot with a pat of butter on top.

Serves 6

1   pound white potatoes, peeled
1   teaspoon salt
½   teaspoon pepper
1   cup water
Butter pat for topping

SHIRLEY WAGNER'S EGGPLANT CASSEROLE

We have cooked this recipe many times for our Wednesday-night dinners. The crackers absorb the moisture from the eggplant. It gives the dish a nice crunchy texture, and it is truly simple to make. Delicious served with cold meat or poultry for a summer luncheon!

Put the vegetables, water, and salt in a 3-quart saucepan and cook, uncovered, about 5 minutes until eggplant is transparent, stirring constantly with a wooden spoon to prevent sticking. Drain well. Butter a 2-quart baking dish and put in a layer of the vegetables, a layer of cheese, and a layer of crackers. Sprinkle with pepper and dot with butter. Bake in a preheated 350° F. oven for 30 minutes.

MICROWAVE: Cook, covered, for 12 minutes in your microwave. Let stand 3–5 minutes before serving.

Makes 6–8 servings

1½ 2	large eggplants, peeled and cubed—about 8 cups
1	green bell pepper, diced
1	medium onion, diced
½	cup water
2	teaspoons salt
1½	cups grated Cheddar Cheese
12	saltine crackers, broken up
½	teaspoon freshly ground black pepper
4	tablespoons butter, cut in small pieces

SWEET-SOUR RED CABBAGE

Shred cabbage. Mix sugar, salt, water, and vinegar in 3-quart saucepan; cover. Boil 1 minute, then add cabbage. Simmer for 30 minutes until tender. Delicious served with any pork dish.

Serves 6

8	cups shredded red cabbage
½	cup sugar
2	tablespoons salt
½	cup water
½	cup cider vinegar

SCALLOPED SALSIFY

Abe's mother always makes the best use of winter vegetables. She and Dad have a marvelous winter garden. Nothing is wasted! Salsify keeps well into spring, so Abe's mother stores it to use throughout the winter. Salsify looks like a long thin parsnip. It is generally called "oyster plant," as it tastes much like oysters—and can be used like oysters, too.

1	pound salsify (oyster plant)
2	cups water
1½	teaspoons salt
2	cups oyster crackers
6	tablespoons melted butter
	Freshly ground black pepper to taste
1	cup light cream

Boil the salsify, unpeeled, in the water with 1 teaspoon of the salt until just tender when pierced with a knifepoint. Drain and peel, then slice ½″ thick. Butter a 9″ pie pan or 1-quart casserole. Put in a layer of 1 cup oyster crackers. Top with the sliced salsify. Pour the melted butter over the salsify. Sprinkle with the remaining ½ teaspoon salt and the pepper. Top with the rest of the crackers. Pour the light cream on top. Bake in a preheated 375° F. oven for 25 minutes. Serve hot as a vegetable dish with turkey or roast poultry.

Makes 4–6 servings

RED CABBAGE WITH PLUMS AND BACON

One of our guests, after eating this recipe, said, "Wow, that really gives red cabbage class!" Very true, and it is beautiful besides.

¼	pound bacon
1	medium head red cabbage, coarsely shredded
1½	teaspoons salt
	Freshly ground black pepper, to taste
2	tablespoons brown sugar
1	tablespoon vinegar
12	damson, or Italian prune plums, pitted and chopped

Fry the bacon in a large heavy skillet until crisp. Remove and drain on paper towels. Fry the cabbage in the bacon fat for 3 minutes, stirring constantly. Add the salt, pepper, sugar, and vinegar and cover. Reduce the heat to medium low and simmer 5 minutes, then stir and add the plums. Cover again. Reduce the heat to low and simmer for 20 minutes. Garnish with the crumbled bacon and serve. Good with roast pork, goose, or pheasant.

VARIATION

Use chopped apples instead of plums.

Makes 6 servings

SCALLOPED POTATOES WITH BACON, CHIVES, AND CELERY

Peel the potatoes and slice about ⅛″ thick— a food processor works fine for this. Meanwhile, put the bacon in the 2-quart baking dish to be used later for the potatoes and bake, uncovered, in a preheated 375° F. oven until the bacon is crisp. Remove bacon and drain on paper towels. Put the potatoes, chives, celery, flour, salt, and pepper in a large mixing bowl and toss until well blended. Add ½ the potatoes to the remaining bacon fat in the pan, dot with butter, and add the rest of the potatoes. Add the milk and bake in a 350° oven for 1 hour.

MICROWAVE: Microwave on high in a covered casserole dish for 15 minutes, turning ¼ turn approximately every 4 minutes. Let stand 3–5 minutes before serving.

Serves 6

1½ pounds white potatoes
6 slices bacon
¼ cup chopped fresh or 1/8 cup dried chives
½ cup chopped celery
4 tablespoons flour
1½ teaspoons salt
♦ Several dashes freshly ground pepper
2 tablespoons butter
1¼ cups milk

SCALLOPED POTATOES WITH SHARP CHEESE

Peel the potatoes and slice about ⅛″ thick. Mix with flour, salt, and pepper. Place half of the potatoes in bottom of a buttered 2-quart baking dish. Dot with ½ the butter, and sprinkle with ½ the grated cheese. Add the rest of the potatoes and repeat with remaining butter and cheese. Pour milk over the potatoes and bake in a preheated 350° F. oven for 1 hour.

MICROWAVE: Microwave in a covered casserole for 12 minutes, rotating the dish every 4 minutes. Let stand 3–5 minutes before serving.

Serves 6

1½ pounds white potatoes
4 tablespoons flour
1½ teaspoons salt
♦ Several dashes freshly ground pepper
3 tablespoons butter
½ cup grated sharp or Cheddar cheese
1¼ cups milk

SOUR CREAM-POTATO CASSEROLE

Melt the butter in a heavy skillet and sauté the onion until golden, but not brown. Place sliced potatoes in buttered 1½-quart casserole and sprinkle with the cooked onions, bread crumbs, and cheese. In a bowl combine the eggs, sour cream, salt, pepper, and milk until blended. Pour over the potatoes. Sprinkle with the cheese if desired. Bake in a preheated oven at 350° F. for 20 minutes.

NOTE: If you are not serving the potatoes immediately, add extra milk to keep from baking dry.

MICROWAVE: Microwave on high for 6–8 minutes. Use a covered casserole. Let stand 5 minutes before serving.

Serves 6

- 2 tablespoons butter
- ½ cup finely chopped onion
- 4 cups sliced cooked potatoes
- ¼ cup dry bread crumbs
- ¼ cup grated American cheese
- 2 eggs, well beaten
- 1 cup sour cream
- 1 teaspoon salt
- ◆ Dash pepper
- ½ cup milk
- Freshly grated cheese (optional)

SPECIAL LIMA BEANS

Fry bacon in a small skillet. Remove when crisp and drain on paper towels. Put the bacon fat, water, garlic, oregano, salt, and pepper in a 1½-quart saucepan with a lid and bring to a boil. Simmer one minute. Add the lima beans. Cover and cook on medium heat approximately 6 minutes if fresh, 5 minutes if frozen, until tender. Do not overcook. Serve in heated dish, topped with the grated cheese.

Serves 4–6

- 4 slices bacon
- ½ cup water
- 1 clove garlic, chopped or crushed (optional)
- 1″ sprig fresh or ⅛ teaspoon dried oregano
- 1 teaspoon salt
- ¼ teaspoon freshly ground pepper
- 1 quart fresh or frozen lima beans
- ¼ cup grated cheese

STIR-FRIED CORN AND LIMA BEANS

It seems everyone dislikes certain vegetables from childhood, and succotash was the one I hated most. Possibly it was because this dish is generally made of leftovers and always seemed tasteless. When the vegetables are stir-fried, the flavor is fresh and the appearance is as good as it tastes. Now this recipe is one of my favorites.

Fry the bacon in a wok or heavy skillet until crisp. Remove and drain on paper towels. Put the lima beans in a heated pan and stir-fry for 1 minute. Remove and place in heated dish. Add the corn and salt to the heated pan and stir-fry for approximately 1–2½ minutes until golden. Add the lima beans and cover. Steam for 4 minutes on low heat. Add pepper if desired. Serve in heated dish, crumbling the bacon over the top before serving.

Serves 6

4 slices bacon
1 cup fresh or frozen lima beans
2 cups corn kernels (about 3 ears, kernels cut off)
½ teaspoon salt
◆ Dash pepper (optional)

STIR-FRIED GREEN BEANS AND ONIONS WITH BACON

Fry the bacon until crisp in a wok or heavy skillet. Remove the bacon and drain on paper towels. Toss in the cut green beans, garlic, and onions. Stir-fry for 1 minute. Add water and cover with lid. Cook on medium heat for 3–5 minutes until desired softness is reached. I like the beans crisp. Serve piping hot with crumbled bacon on top.

Serves 4

4 slices bacon
1 pound green beans, cleaned and cut diagonally into bite-size pieces
1 small clove garlic, thinly sliced
1 medium onion, chopped
1 teaspoon salt
¼ teaspoon freshly ground pepper
1½ tablespoons water

SUPERB SWEET POTATOES

Next to plain buttered sweet potatoes, this recipe is the best! So often, sweet potatoes are ruined when the cook uses too much sugar, pineapple, and marshmallows. Folding in the whipped cream makes the sweet potatoes light and fluffy without being overpowering. This recipe blends well with any meal, and the topping adds a special touch.

Wash the unpeeled sweet potatoes. Cook in a large saucepan in the water with 1 teaspoon salt for about 20 minutes until tender but not mushy. Drain, peel, and mash to a puree. This may be done in a food processor, blender, or electric mixer. Add the remaining salt, butter, pepper and milk. For white sweet potatoes, which are drier, you will need ½ cup milk, but if you use the moist orange type, often sold as yams, (which they are not, just another type of sweet potato) use only ¼ cup. Beat until smooth and fluffy. Whip the chilled cream in a chilled bowl (this helps it to thicken faster). Fold half of the whipped cream gently into the potato mixture, and put in a buttered 1½–2-quart casserole. Top with the rest of the cream and sprinkle with the brown sugar. Bake in a preheated 375° F. oven for 20–25 minutes until golden brown.

Makes 6 servings

2 pounds (about 6 medium) sweet potatoes, orange, yellow, or white
4 cups water
2 teaspoons salt
2 tablespoons butter
Freshly ground black pepper to taste
¼–½ cup scalded milk, depending on type of sweet potatoes used
1 cup heavy cream
¼ cup brown sugar

PUFFED POTATOES

Puffed potatoes are old favorites of Kitty and John Brown and our family. We love the crisp skins, and the addition of Herb Cheese is interesting.

Scrub the potatoes and cut them lengthwise in slices about 1″ thick, leaving the skins on. Place on clean center rack of a preheated 450° F. oven, not using a pan or foil. Bake approximately 20 minutes. Potatoes should blister on top. This will enable you to prick the blisters and make room for the butter or Herb Cheese. Salt and pepper to taste. Serve piping hot. Excellent as snacks, too.

Serves 4–6

4–6 large baking potatoes
Salt and pepper to taste
Lots of butter or Herb Cheese (see Index)

SWISS-STYLE GREEN BEANS

In a 2-quart saucepan, bring beans, onion, and water to a boil for 10 minutes. Drain. Put beans and onions in a buttered 1½-quart casserole. In a 1-quart saucepan, melt the butter. Blend in the flour until smooth. Gradually add sour cream and salt, stirring constantly with wire whip. Fold in the grated cheese. Pour cheese sauce over beans. Top with almonds and bake in a preheated oven at 350° F. for 40 minutes.

This dish is very rich. For a milder flavor, use white American cheese.

MICROWAVE: In a 2-quart covered glass casserole bring beans, onions, and ¼ cup water to a boil for about 7 minutes. Drain and place beans and onions in a buttered casserole. Cover. Bake on high in the microwave oven for 14 minutes. Let stand 3–5 minutes before serving.

Serves 6

* When using frozen beans, cut the baking time to 20 minutes

4 cups fresh or frozen* cut green beans
1 medium onion, finely chopped
1 cup water
2 tablespoons butter or shortening
3 tablespoons all-purpose flour
2 cups sour cream
1½ teaspoons salt
6 ounces Swiss or white American cheese, grated
½ cup slivered almonds

WHOLE BROWNED POTATOES

Sprinkle the potatoes lightly with salt and pepper. Put next to beef or other roast for the last 45 minutes of the baking time. Alternatively, put butter in a heavy skillet. Brown the potatoes over medium heat until golden brown and heated through.

Serves 6

6 medium white potatoes, cooked and peeled
Salt and pepper
Butter

TOMATO AND EGGPLANT CASSEROLE

One winter, Abe and I took a Caribbean vacation at the Golden Lemon on St. Kitts, owned by our good friend Arthur Leaman. We spent our time eating and relaxing—wonderful, when someone else is cooking. Arthur's cook put freshly grated nutmeg on top of this casserole, giving it another flavor entirely. Tomato and eggplant make a delicate and delicious combination. I have made this recipe without tomatoes and used it as eggplant stuffing for turkey. Turkey tends to be dry, but the eggplant adds a lovely moistness. There are many ways to use a good recipe!

Peel the eggplant and slice ¼" thick. Put in a saucepan with the onion, salt, and ½" boiling water. Cover and simmer about 10 minutes until tender. Drain well and mash. Blend in the butter, eggs, pepper, oregano, and bread crumbs. Turn into a buttered 1½-quart casserole. Cover with the tomato slices. Sprinkle with the cheese and salt and pepper. Bake in a preheated 375° F. oven for 25 minutes until lightly browned.

MICROWAVE: Microwave on high in a covered, buttered 1½-quart casserole for 8 minutes, moving ¼ turn every 2 minutes. Let stand 3–5 minutes before serving.

Makes 6 servings

1	medium eggplant
1	tablespoon finely chopped onion
1½	teaspoons salt
2	tablespoons butter
2	eggs, beaten
¼	teaspoon freshly ground black pepper
½	teaspoon oregano
½	cup dry bread crumbs
1	large tomato, cored and cut into 6 medium-thick slices
½	cup grated cheese

TOMATO SAUCE

Drain the juice of tomatoes into a 2-quart saucepan. Add the salt, sugar, onion, pepper, and cornstarch and stir until cornstarch is dissolved. Bring to a boil on medium heat, stirring constantly. Simmer for 1 minute and add the tomatoes. Check for seasonings, adding more sugar or salt as desired. Serve in heated serving dish. Top with Browned Butter.

NOTE: ½ cup diced green peppers may be added to the recipe for variety. You may want to garnish this with slices of hard boiled egg, croutons, or watercress.

Serves 6

4 cups tomatoes, peeled, quartered, and with juice
1 teaspoon salt
1 tablespoon sugar
½ medium onion, finely chopped
◆ Dash freshly ground pepper
2 tablespoons cornstarch
2 tablespoons Browned Butter (see Index)

FRIED CORN AND RED PEPPERS IN BACON

Fry bacon in a wok or heavy skillet until crisp. Drain on paper towels. Add the corn and peppers to the hot bacon fat and stir-fry for approximately 3 minutes. Season with salt and pepper. Cover and steam for 1 minute longer. Serve immediately, topped with slices of bacon.

Serves 6

6 slices bacon
4 cups corn kernels (about 6 ears, kernels cut off)
2 medium red bell peppers, diced
½ teaspoon salt
◆ Dash freshly ground pepper

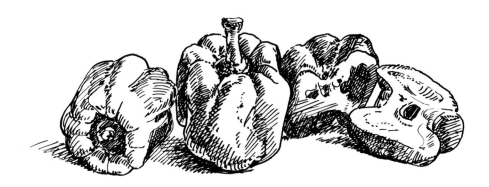

WHOLE SCRAPED POTATOES WITH BROWNED BUTTER

Freshly dug potatoes are exceptionally flavorful, almost sweet, and should be enjoyed to their fullest. If you are uncertain about freshness, check whether the skin can be easily removed. If it can, they will be great for scraping. The flavor of these potatoes is well worth the time it takes to prepare them—usually 1 hour to serve 6–8. You can scrape these potatoes and store them in fresh cold water until ready to use. Be sure to prepare plenty, as your guests will generally eat several.

To scrape this type of potato, dip it in cold water and hold it in one hand. With a sharp paring knife, scrape the potato until all the skin is removed, but do not peel it, as that removes too much of the outside layer of vitamins and flavor.

Bring the salted water to a boil in a covered saucepan, using 1 teaspoon salt per 6 medium potatoes. Boil over medium heat approximately 35 minutes until soft but not falling apart. The new potatoes will burst around the edges, but that is part of their beauty and they will soak in the delicious Browned Butter (see Index) used when serving this dish. I use approximately 3 tablespoons of Browned Butter when I serve these potatoes, but you can select your own garnish. A sprig of parsley in the center of the serving dish is an added touch.

WHOLE TINY BUTTERED BEETS

Remove the tops from beets and wash thoroughly. Place in a saucepan with salt, pepper, and water. Bring to a boil and cover. Cook over low heat for approximately 30 minutes until the beets are tender. Remove the beets and cool enough to peel. Peel and put in a heated serving dish. Top with butter. If too cool, reheat the beets in the liquid in which they were cooked.

MICROWAVE: Place in a casserole with ½ cup water and microwave for 12–14 minutes. Continue to follow recipe.

Serves 6

18 **fresh tiny beets**
 1 **teaspoon salt**
    Freshly ground pepper to taste
 2 **cups water**
 2 **tablespoons butter**

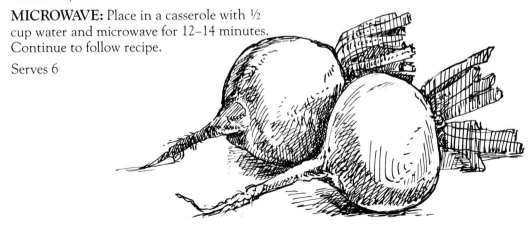

DECORATIVE CERTIFICATE, GRANDPARENT FRAKTUR

*Grandparents are very special people. To many they are deeply loved
and to those of us who look forward to becoming grandparents,
a grandchild is a gift sent from God. The Grandparent
Fraktur records this joyous event.*

8

SALADS & SALAD DRESSINGS

SALADS

Banana-Nut Salad
Cabbage Salad
Caesar Salad
Fresh Cutting Lettuce with Dressing
Cherry Salad
Chicken Salad
Cucumbers and Onions in Marinade
Cole Slaw
German Hot Potato Salad
Macaroni Salad
Marinated Tomatoes and Onions
Mother's Potato Salad
Ham Salad
Waldorf Salad
Polish Potato and Apple Salad
Spinach Salad
Sunburst Salad
Celery and Cauliflower Salad with Mustard Dressing
Garden Greens with Eggs and Creamy Sweet-Sour Dressing
Tossed Garden Salad

SALAD DRESSINGS

Hot Bacon Dressing
Mary Sweigart's Sweet-Sour Dressing
Mother's Mayonnaise
Mustard Dressing
Boiled Salad Dressing
Creamy Sweet-Sour Dressing

BANANA-NUT SALAD

Peel and cut the bananas in half, then split lengthwise. Dip the cut side of the banana in the chopped nuts. Arrange 2 slices on fresh lettuce leaves. Place 1 tablespoon of the mayonnaise to one side of the salad. If the nuts will not stick to the banana, spread with a little mayonnaise, then sprinkle with nuts. Serve chilled.

Serves 6

3 **large bananas**
½ **cup salted peanuts, chopped**
Fresh lettuce leaves
¼ **cup Mother's Mayonnaise (see Index)**

CABBAGE SALAD

Grate cabbage into a large mixing bowl. Clean peppers, dice, and add to the cabbage. Peel and grate the carrots, clean and slice the radishes, chop the celery, and add all to the cabbage. Toss lightly. Make syrup of sugar, vinegar, wine, salt, celery seed, and mustard seed, stirring together until the sugar is dissolved. Pour this syrup over the salad and toss. Cover with plastic wrap and refrigerate for several hours or overnight. Serve with sandwiches or cold meats.

Serves 6

1 **firm head cabbage**
2 **medium sweet bell peppers (1 red and 1 green if available)**
2 **carrots**
8 **radishes**
4 **stems celery**
2 **cups sugar**
½ **cup herb or cider vinegar**
¼ **cup white wine**
2 **teaspoons salt**
1 **teaspoon celery seed**
1 **teaspoon mustard seed**

CAESAR SALAD

Wash the romaine thoroughly and drain as much as possible. Break into bite-size pieces and refrigerate. Sauté the garlic in the salad oil in a heavy skillet until golden brown. Remove the garlic. Add the bread cubes, stirring until they are golden brown and crisp. Drain the cubes on paper towels and keep warm. In a small bowl, blend the olive oil, lemon juice, salt, and pepper. Add the oil from the anchovies and shake until thoroughly blended. Place the romaine in a large salad bowl and add the beaten egg. Toss lightly. Add the cheese and toss again. Place the romaine on individual serving plates and add the croutons and anchovies. Pour olive oil dressing over each salad. Serve chilled.

Serves 6

- 2 **heads fresh romaine lettuce, or use part Bibb**
- 2 **or 3 cloves garlic, chopped**
- 4 **tablespoons salad oil**
- 2 **cups white bread cubes**
- ½ **cup good olive oil**
- 2 **tablespoons lemon juice**
- 1 **teaspoon salt**
- ◆ **Several dashes freshly ground pepper**
- 1 **large egg, lightly beaten**
- 1 **tin of 10–12 anchovy fillets**
- ½ **cup freshly grated Parmesan cheese**

FRESH CUTTING LETTUCE WITH DRESSING

Use oak leaf lettuce or spring garden lettuce. Cut the tender lettuce leaves and gently wash in cold water. Drain and place in individual salad bowls or in 1 large salad bowl. Use Boiled Salad Dressing (see Index), adding ½ cup chopped dill or sweet pickles, ¼ cup chopped pimento, ¼ cup chopped celery and ¼ cup chopped nuts. Serve dressing in a separate bowl.

CHERRY SALAD

Remove the seeds from the cherries and fill with the hazelnuts. Arrange on crisp lettuce and serve with Boiled Salad Dressing (see Index). If too thick, thin with sour cream, milk, or yogurt to desired consistency.

Serves 6

2 cups Queen Anne cherries, pitted
½ cup hazelnuts
Lettuce for 6
½ cup Boiled Salad Dressing

CHICKEN SALAD

Blend all ingredients in a large bowl and refrigerate, covered, until ready to serve. Serve on crisp lettuce leaves.

If using as a sandwich spread, blend everything in food processor.

VARIATION

Turkey is excellent, too.

Serves 6

2 cups diced cooked chicken
1 cup chopped celery
4 hard-boiled eggs, chopped
1 teaspoon celery seed
1 tablespoon chopped parsley
¼ teaspoon freshly ground pepper
1 cup mayonnaise

CUCUMBERS AND ONIONS IN MARINADE

Wash the cucumbers and slice about ¼″ thick. Slice the onions the same thickness. Place in a large bowl and sprinkle herbs on top. In a small bowl, blend the remaining ingredients with a wire whisk until all the sugar is dissolved. Pour over cucumbers and onions. Cover with plastic wrap and refrigerate for several hours.

Serves 6

6 **large cucumbers**
2 **medium onions**
2 **tablespoons each chopped dill, chives, oregano, parsley, and thyme**
½ **cup salad oil**
½ **cup wine vinegar**
¼ **cup white wine**
¼ **cup granulated sugar**
½ **teaspoon salt**
½ **teaspoon celery seed**

COLE SLAW

Put the cabbage, peppers, and carrots in a large mixing bowl and add the remaining ingredients. Press with your hands until all the sugar is dissolved and everything is well blended. Chill in the refrigerator for several hours before serving.

Serves 6

1 **firm head cabbage, finely shredded**
½ **cup chopped green bell pepper**
½ **cup chopped red bell pepper**
2 **carrots, grated**
¾ **cup sugar**
⅓ **cup cider vinegar**
½ **teaspoon salt**
½ **teaspoon celery seed**

GERMAN HOT POTATO SALAD

While our son Charlie studied at the Culinary Institute, they chartered a plane for the students and fellows to attend the Culinary Olympics in Frankfurt, Germany. I reconstructed this recipe after eating in a quaint little restaurant in Saxenhausen, a delightful area, renowned for its charming eating places. I was interested in eating only typically German dishes, and selected a veal hock, cooked on a rotisserie, while Abe enjoyed roast duck. Each meal was served with sweet-and-sour cabbage and this hot potato salad.

Fry the bacon in a large heavy skillet until crisp. Remove the bacon and drain on paper towels. Sauté the onion and celery in the bacon fat about 5 minutes until the onions are translucent. Add salt, sugar, pepper, and the cornstarch dissolved in water. Next add the vinegar and boil for 2 minutes. Finally add the hot potatoes and the crumbled bacon. Stir gently. Serve hot, garnished with sliced stuffed olives.

NOTE: To make 6 cups diced potatoes, cook 8 medium potatoes in salted water for 30 minutes, or until just soft. Drain, peel, and dice while hot.

Makes 6–8 servings

6 slices bacon
1 cup chopped onion
¾ cup diced celery
2 teaspoons salt
1 teaspoon sugar
⅛ teaspoon freshly ground pepper
2 tablespoons cornstarch, dissolved in ¼ cup water
½ cup cider vinegar
6 cups waxy potatoes, cooked, peeled, diced, and hot
6 large pimento-stuffed green olives or 12 small green olives, sliced

MACARONI SALAD

Place cooked macaroni in a large mixing bowl. Add diced eggs, celery, olives, and salad dressing. Stir gently until blended. Check for seasoning, adding more salt and pepper if desired. Arrange fresh lettuce on individual salad plates or in a large bowl. Spoon the salad on top. Garnish with the sliced olives. Serve chilled.

Serves 6

2 cups cooked macaroni

3 hard-boiled eggs, peeled and diced

½ cup chopped celery

⅓ cup sliced olives, saving a few for garnish

¾ cup Boiled Salad Dressing (see Index)

Crisp lettuce leaves

MARINATED TOMATOES AND ONIONS

Put the tomatoes in a large bowl. Place the onions on top. Sprinkle the herbs on top. In a small bowl, blend the oil, vinegar, wine, sugar, salt, and pepper with a wire whisk until all the sugar is dissolved. Pour over the tomatoes and onions. Cover with plastic wrap and refrigerate for several hours. Serve chilled, garnished with fresh parsley.

Serves 6

2 pounds firm tomatoes, cored and sliced

2 medium onions, sliced

2 tablespoons chopped herbs (dill, chives, oregano, parsley, thyme, etc.)

½ cup salad oil

½ cup cider vinegar

¼ cup white wine

¼ cup granulated sugar

½ teaspoon salt

◆ Several dashes freshly ground pepper

Fresh parsley for garnish

MOTHER'S POTATO SALAD

This is a simple potato salad, but Mother's Mayonnaise and the celery leaves and celery seed make it a little different. Incidentally, I have found that potatoes used for potato salad must be cooked in well-salted water. Otherwise salt will have to be added to the salad several times to keep it tasty and flavorsome.

Combine the first five ingredients in a bowl. In another bowl, combine the mayonnaise and yogurt and add to the salad. Refrigerate several hours or overnight.

VARIATION

Add chopped olives to the salad, or slice olives and arrange on top.

Makes about 3 cups

2 cups cooked and diced potatoes

½ teaspoon dried or 1 tablespoon chopped fresh celery leaves

2 hard-boiled eggs, chopped

½ teaspoon dried or 1 tablespoon finely chopped fresh onion

½ teaspoon celery seed

½ cup Mother's Mayonnaise (see Index)

½ cup plain yogurt

HAM SALAD

Blend all ingredients thoroughly in a large bowl. Refrigerate, covered, until ready to serve. Serve on crisp lettuce leaves.

Serves 6

2½ cups baked or cooked ham, chopped

1 cup finely diced celery

¼ cup finely diced sweet pickles

4 hard-boiled eggs, chopped

1 teaspoon Worcestershire sauce

◆ Dash Tabasco sauce

1¼ cups mayonnaise

WALDORF SALAD

Combine the apples, celery, nuts, and mayonnaise gently in a large bowl. Chill in the refrigerator until ready to serve. Serve on crisp lettuce leaves. Garnish with nut halves or maraschino cherries.

Serves 6

2 cups whole red apples, diced
1 cup chopped celery
½ cup broken nuts
½ cup Mother's Mayonnaise (see Index)
Fresh lettuce leaves
Nut halves or maraschino cherries for garnish

POLISH POTATO AND APPLE SALAD

Cube or dice the potatoes and put in a large salad bowl. Add the onion, celery, parsley, salt, capers, and dill seed. Toss or stir gently. Add pepper, lemon juice, beaten egg, diced hard-boiled eggs, sour cream, and diced apple. Again mix gently but thoroughly to avoid breaking up the potatoes and eggs. Cover with plastic wrap and refrigerate for several hours. Serve on crisp salad greens.

Serves 6

3 cups cold cooked potatoes
1 small onion, diced
½ cup chopped celery
1 tablespoon minced parsley
2 teaspoons salt
½ teaspoon chopped capers
¼ teaspoon dill seed
¼ teaspoon ground pepper
1 tablespoon lemon juice
1 large egg, lightly beaten
2 hard-boiled eggs, peeled and diced
½ cup sour cream
1 large unpeeled apple, cored and diced
Crisp salad greens

SPINACH SALAD

Tear spinach and put in a large bowl or individual serving bowls. Arrange egg slices on top and serve with Hot Bacon Dressing, using the bacon bits for garnish.

Serves 6

6 cups fresh spinach, trimmed, cleaned, and washed
4 hard-boiled eggs, peeled and sliced
Hot Bacon Dressing (see Index)
Bacon bits

SUNBURST SALAD

Wash and crisp the lettuce leaves. Arrange on individual salad dishes. Place a whole slice of pineapple on the lettuce. Place the apricot in the center of the slice of pineapple. Place spoonful of dressing to one side of the lettuce. Serve chilled.

Serves 6

Iceberg lettuce for 6
6 slices pineapple, drained
6 apricots, seeded
Mother's Mayonnaise (see Index) or Boiled Salad Dressing (see Index)

CELERY AND CAULIFLOWER SALAD WITH MUSTARD DRESSING

This salad has a very snappy taste. The mustard dressing will give any salad zest.

Combine celery, cauliflower, and olives in a large mixing bowl. Add Mustard Dressing. Refrigerate for 1 hour. To serve, put on crisp lettuce leaves and garnish with a light dash each of paprika and celery seed.

NOTE: When trimming cauliflower, cut very close to the top so the little buds will separate easily.

Makes 6–8 servings

3 cups celery sliced ¼" thick
3 cups cauliflower flowerets
¼ cup sliced stuffed green olives
Mustard Dressing (see Index)
Lettuce leaves
◆ **Dash paprika**
◆ **Dash celery seed**

GARDEN GREENS WITH EGGS AND CREAMY SWEET-SOUR DRESSING

Wash the greens and tear as for salad. Refrigerate the greens to ensure crispness. Add the dressing, cover, and refrigerate for 30 minutes.

When serving, arrange greens in individual serving bowls and place sliced eggs on top. Serve dressing separately.

Serves 6

Greens for 6 servings
3 hard-boiled eggs, sliced
Creamy Sweet-Sour Dressing (see Index)

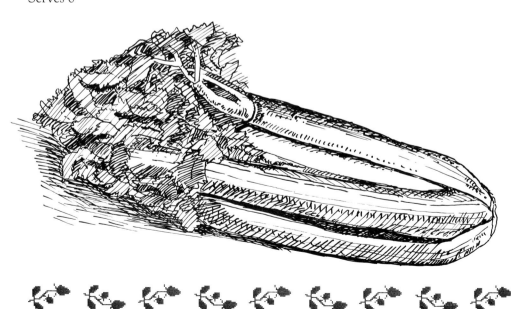

TOSSED GARDEN SALAD

Wash the lettuce, drain, and break into bite-size pieces. Put in a large salad bowl. Add the radishes, pepper, cucumber, onion, and carrot. Toss and serve with salad dressing.

Serves 6

1 head lettuce
12 red radishes, sliced
1 green bell pepper, sliced or chopped
1 cucumber, sliced
1 onion, sliced, or several spring onions (optional)
1 carrot, grated or sliced
Salad dressing of your choice

HOT BACON DRESSING

In a deep skillet, fry the bacon until crisp. Remove and drain on paper towels. In a small bowl combine the cornstarch, salt, and sugar. Add the eggs, stirring with a whisk until smooth, then slowly add the vinegar. Blend milk with egg mixture and slowly add to the bacon fat in the skillet. Return skillet to the stove and place on low to medium heat, stirring constantly. Bring to a boil and continue to boil for 1 minute, stirring with whisk continually. Break the bacon into bits and add half of the bacon to the dressing. Save the rest for garnishing salads.

This dressing may be served cold, but it is tastier when hot or warm. It reheats nicely in a microwave oven.

Makes 2½ cups

½ pound bacon
2 tablespoons cornstarch
1½ teaspoons salt
3 tablespoons granulated sugar
2 eggs, slightly beaten
⅓ cup cider vinegar
2 cups milk

MARY SWEIGART'S SWEET-SOUR DRESSING

Blend all the ingredients in a blender or mix well in a bowl. Refrigerate in a sealed jar, shaking well before using.

Makes about 2 cups

⅔ cup sugar
¾ teaspoon paprika
1 teaspoon celery seed
⅓ cup honey
¼ teaspoon salt
1 tablespoon lemon juice
1 cup salad oil
5 tablespoons vinegar
1 teaspoon prepared mustard
1 tablespoon grated onion

MOTHER'S MAYONNAISE

I constantly use my mother's mayonnaise recipe for chicken salad, potato salad, even on garden vege-tables. Our guests love it, because it contains no oil or egg yolks, and it is low in cholesterol. This mayonnaise is simple to make and keeps almost indefinitely in the refrigerator. Mix it with ground ham for a delicious ham salad or sandwich filling. Because this recipe is very concentrated, I have lately cut the potency with sour cream or, yogurt. Turmeric adds the yellow tinge we all associate with mayonnaise. For fewer calories, use a sugar substitute.

Blend the vinegar, 1 cup of the water, the sugar, salt, pepper, and turmeric in a small heavy saucepan, and bring to a boil. Mix the cornstarch to a paste with the remaining ¼ cup water and add to the pan, stirring over low heat until thick. Remove from heat and cool. Mix in the mustard and imitation mayonnaise.

Makes 3 cups

1	cup vinegar
1¼	cups water
2	cups sugar
¼	teaspoon salt
⅛	teaspoon freshly ground black pepper
¼	teaspoon turmeric
⅓	cup cornstarch
2	tablespoons prepared mustard
½	cup commercial imitation mayonnaise

MUSTARD DRESSING

In a small bowl, combine all ingredients. Beat with wire whip until smooth and creamy. Let stand in refrigerator for 1 hour.

½	cup sour cream
1	teaspoon dry mustard
1	tablespoon mayonnaise
½	teaspoon salt
½	teaspoon Krazy Salt
2	teaspoons white wine

BOILED SALAD DRESSING

Using the top pan of the double boiler, beat the egg yolks until frothy. Add the vinegar. In a small bowl, carefully mix the salt, mustard, sugar, paprika, and flour. Slowly add the water, stirring constantly, to make a smooth paste. Pour into the yolks and vinegar, mixing until well blended. Place in double boiler over boiling water and cook approximately 12 minutes until thick and creamy. Thin to desired consistency with sour cream, milk, or yogurt.

Makes 1½ cups

4 egg yolks
½ cup cider vinegar
1 teaspoon salt
1 teaspoon dry mustard
4 tablespoons sugar
¼ teaspoon paprika
2 tablespoons flour
½ cup water
Sour cream, milk, or yogurt

CREAMY SWEET-SOUR DRESSING

Blend the vinegar, sugar, milk, salt, pepper, celery seed, and herbs in a small bowl until all the sugar is dissolved. Cover and refrigerate for 30 minutes.

½ cup cider vinegar or wine vinegar
⅔ cup sugar
¾ cup evaporated milk
½ teaspoon salt
◆ Several dashes freshly ground pepper
½ teaspoon celery seed
1 tablespoon chopped fresh herbs (thyme, rosemary, chives, etc.)

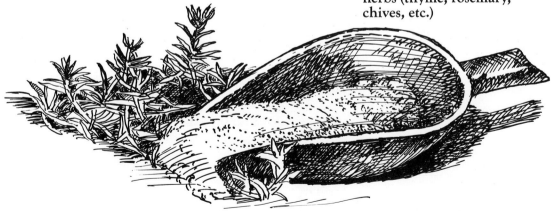

FALL IN LANCASTER COUNTY, Watercolor

*Fall in Lancaster County is many things: the cool crisp air of early
morning, the frost across the fields, the withered corn stalks ready
for autumn harvest, while in the air hundreds of trumpet
swans cry as they announce their winter arrival.*

9

SAUCES & BUTTERS

SAUCES

Barbecue Sauce
Cheese Sauce
Hollandaise Sauce
Horseradish Sauce
Hot Sauce
Lemon-Rum Sauce
Lemon Sauce
Mushroom Sauce
Rémoulade Sauce
Vanilla Sauce
Chocolate Sauce
Wine-Raisin Sauce
Orange Sauce
White Sauces

BUTTERS

Browned Butter
Browned Butter Crumbs
Herb Butter

GLAZES

Apricot or Orange-Pineapple Glaze

BARBECUE SAUCE

Blend thoroughly and pour over ribs 20 minutes before they are done.

⅔ cup tomato paste (6-ounce can)
1 tablespoon Dijon mustard
½ cup brown sugar
½ cup wine
½ teaspoon salt

CHEESE SAUCE

Melt the butter in a heavy 1-quart saucepan. Slowly add the flour and simmer until well blended. Very gradually add the milk and simmer until sauce has thickened. Add the grated cheese and stir until sauce is smooth and the cheese has melted.

MICROWAVE: Soften butter in a cup 5 seconds, stir in flour to make paste. Heat milk in a measuring cup for 2 minutes. Mix together with cheese, then cook for 2 minutes longer. Stir once during this time.

2 tablespoons butter
2 tablespoons flour
1½ cups milk
¼ pound grated White American cheese

BROWNED BUTTER

Melt the butter in a large pan over medium-low heat. After it has melted, stir occasionally until the butter begins to brown. Be sure to remove from the heat before it burns, or it will lose its flavor. It should be a rich nut-brown color.

½ pound butter

BROWNED BUTTER CRUMBS

Follow recipe for browned butter, adding 2 cups dry bread crumbs.

HOLLANDAISE SAUCE

Put the egg yolks and water in the top of double boiler and whip with a wire whisk. Place over boiling water, making sure that water does not touch the bottom of the pan. Whip the egg yolks lightly until cooked to a soft peak. Slowly pour the hot butter into the eggs, whipping lightly to blend. Beat in the lemon juice, pepper, and salt. Do not reheat this sauce. It may be kept warm up to 1½ hours but cannot be refrigerated or reheated.

4 egg yolks
1 tablespoon water
¾ pound butter, melted and clear
Juice of 1 small or ½ large lemon
◆ Dash pepper
⅓ teaspoon salt

HORSERADISH SAUCE

Mix all ingredients in a bowl until well blended, then whip with whisk until light and airy.

5 tablespoons grated fresh horseradish
3 tablespoons cider vinegar
2 tablespoons prepared mustard
1 teaspoon salt
◆ Dash pepper
◆ Dash paprika
½ cup sour cream

HOT SAUCE

Blend all the ingredients thoroughly. Refrigerate in a covered container. This sauce will keep for weeks, refrigerated.

1 cup catsup
¼ cup grated horseradish
1 tablespoon lemon juice
1 teaspoon Worcestershire sauce
¼ teaspoon salt
◆ Dash Tabasco

LEMON-RUM SAUCE

In a heavy 2-quart saucepan, mix the sugar, salt, flour, and cornstarch. Slowly add the water until smooth. Place over medium heat and bring to a boil, stirring constantly. Add the grated lemon rind. Reduce heat to low and simmer for 7 minutes. Add butter, lemon juice, and rum, and stir once more. Serve hot.

This sauce reheats well in a microwave oven.

Makes 12 servings

1 cup sugar
¼ teaspoon salt
1 tablespoon flour
2½ tablespoons cornstarch
2 cups water
Grated rind of 1 lemon
2 tablespoons butter
4 tablespoons lemon juice
1 cup rum

LEMON SAUCE FOR SALMON CAKES OR ASPARAGUS

In a 1-quart saucepan combine cream, butter, mint, and salt. Heat over low to medium heat until the butter is melted and the mixture is hot. In a small bowl, beat the egg yolks. Spoon about ½ cup of the heated mixture into the beaten yolks. Add to the remaining cream mixture in saucepan. Cook over low heat, stirring constantly with wooden spoon, for approximately 2 minutes, until thickened. Do not overcook, as sauce will curdle. Remove from heat, then add lemon juice and rind. Serve warm. Delicious on salmon, asparagus, or broccoli.

Serves 4–6

1 cup light cream
3 tablespoons butter
1 teaspoon chopped mint leaves
½ teaspoon salt
2 egg yolks, lightly beaten
2 tablespoons lemon juice
½ teaspoon grated lemon rind

MUSHROOM SAUCE

Sauté mushrooms and onion in butter until tender but not brown. Cover and cook 5 minutes over low heat. Push mushrooms to one side of pan and stir flour into the butter. Add heavy cream, sour cream, and seasonings. Heat slowly, stirring constantly, almost to boiling point. Do not boil.

Makes 1½ cups

½ pound fresh mushrooms, cut in half
¼ cup minced onion
2 tablespoons butter
2 tablespoons flour
½ cup heavy cream
½ cup sour cream
½ teaspoon salt
¼ teaspoon pepper

RÉMOULADE SAUCE

Combine all ingredients in a small bowl. Blend well and let stand for several hours before using.

Serves 6–8

1 cup mayonnaise
1 small clove garlic, finely chopped
½ teaspoon lemon juice
1 sweet pickle, finely chopped
1 tablespoon chopped parsley
1 tablespoon chopped tarragon
1 tablespoon dry mustard
◆ Dash paprika
◆ Dash pepper

VANILLA SAUCE

In a heavy 1-quart saucepan, thoroughly mix the sugar, flour, and salt. Gradually add the water, stirring to make a smooth sauce. Bring to a boil over medium heat, stirring constantly, and simmer for 2 minutes. Remove from heat and add the vanilla, lemon extract, and butter. Whip with a wire whisk until well blended. Serve hot. For a thinner sauce, add a little hot water and stir until smooth.

⅔ cup sugar
3 tablespoons flour
¼ teaspoon salt
1½ cups water
1 teaspoon vanilla extract
½ teaspoon lemon extract
1 tablespoon butter

CHOCOLATE SAUCE

In a heavy 1-quart saucepan, thoroughly mix the sugar, flour, and salt. Gradually add the water stirring to make a smooth sauce. Add the chocolate and bring to a boil over medium heat. Reduce heat and simmer approximately 2 minutes until the chocolate is melted. Remove from heat and add the vanilla. Serve hot. If sauce becomes too thick, add a little hot water and stir until smooth.

½ cup granulated sugar
2 tablespoons flour
⅛ teaspoon salt
1 cup water
1 square unsweetened chocolate
¼ teaspoon vanilla extract

WINE-RAISIN SAUCE

In a 2-quart saucepan, stir the wine, sugar, mustard, and salt with a wire whip until well mixed. Add the raisins. Simmer on low heat for 30 minutes. Add the dissolved arrowroot to the sauce. Return to a boil and simmer 1 minute until thickened.

Makes about 12 servings

2½ cups dry red or white wine
1 cup sugar
2 tablespoons prepared mustard
½ teaspoon salt
1 cup raisins
2 tablespoons arrowroot dissolved in ¼ cup water

ORANGE SAUCE

In the top of double boiler combine the egg yolks, rind and juice of orange, and sugar. Beat until well mixed. Place over boiling water and bring to a boil. Simmer approximately 6 minutes until mixture forms a custard. Remove from heat and cool. In a bowl, whip the cream to soft peaks and fold into the custard. Chill. Serve on angel food cake or chiffon cake.

4 egg yolks
Grated rind and juice of 1 orange
⅔ cup sugar
1 cup whipping cream

HERB BUTTER

Place butter in bowl to soften at room temperature. When soft, mix in the herbs until thoroughly blended. Wrap in waxed paper and refrigerate.

½ pound butter
⅓ cup chopped herbs, including parsley and chives, with small amounts of thyme, dill, basil, oregano, or rosemary.

APRICOT OR ORANGE-PINEAPPLE GLAZE

If using fresh fruit, cook with ¼ cup water till soft—about 12 minutes. Blend all ingredients in food processor. Bring to slow boil in heavy saucepan. Simmer 3 minutes, stirring constantly with a wooden spoon. Set aside and serve hot or cold.

½ cup cooked apricots (pits removed)
½ cup cooked pineapple
1 tablespoon arrowroot or cornstarch
½ cup red or white wine
¼ cup brown sugar
¼ teaspoon ground cinnamon
¼ teaspoon grated nutmeg
¼ teaspoon ground cloves

WHITE SAUCES

In a 1-quart saucepan, heat the shortening. Gradually add flour, stirring with whisk, until it becomes a smooth paste. Gradually add the milk, stirring constantly, until thickened. Add salt and pepper and reduce heat to very low. Stir for at least a minute before adding to prepared dish.

Makes 1 cup

THIN
- 1 tablespoon shortening
- 1 tablespoon flour
- 1 cup milk
- ¼ teaspoon salt
- ◆ Dash freshly ground pepper

MEDIUM
- 2 tablespoons shortening
- 2 tablespoons flour
- 1 cup milk
- ¼ teaspoon salt
- ◆ Dash freshly ground pepper

THICK
- 3 tablespoons shortening
- 3 tablespoons flour
- 1 cup milk
- ¼ teaspoon salt
- ◆ Dash freshly ground pepper

TRUMPET SWANS, Paper Quilt
*In the fall, all along the Susquehanna River, flocks of trumpet
swans gather announcing the approach of winter. Sleek
and white, they grace our chilling winter air
with their refined natural beauty.*

10

BREADS

BREADS

Apfel Kuchen
Apple Muffins
Blueberry Muffins
Basic Sweet Dough
Basic White Bread
Basic Whole Wheat Bread
Croutons
Cheese Biscuits
Corn Bread Muffins
Hungarian Coffee Cake
Garlic and Cheese Bread
Dill Bread
Jennifer Harris's Methodist Muffins
Oatmeal Bread
Pflatzlings
Spicy Popovers
Moravian Coffee Cake
Sticky Buns
Swedish Tea Ring
Bread Turtle
Waffles
Beer Batter

APFEL KUCHEN

After the second rising of the sweet dough, divide it in half. Roll each half out on a lightly floured board, making a circle a bit larger than the pan. Pat the dough into greased pans, with a ¾″ ridge around the edges of the pans. In a small bowl, combine the sugar, cinnamon, nutmeg, and soft butter. Arrange the apple slices in the center of the dough. Sprinkle with the sugar mixture, saving ¼ cup. Cover, and set in a warm place to rise for 30 minutes. Bake in a preheated 375° F. oven for 35 minutes. Sprinkle remaining sugar mixture on top of the cakes as soon as they are taken out of the oven. Serve warm or cold.

Makes 2 pans, each 9″ round

Basic Sweet Dough (see Index)
½ cup granulated sugar
½ teaspoon ground cinnamon
¼ teaspoon grated nutmeg
2 tablespoons soft butter
2 cups peeled and sliced apples

APPLE OR BLUEBERRY MUFFINS

In a large mixing bowl sift the flour, baking powder, salt, and sugar. Add the eggs, milk, and melted butter all at once and stir until well moistened. Do not overbeat—the batter should be lumpy and rough. Fold in the apples or blueberries and the cinnamon and pour into buttered muffin pans. Fill only ⅔ full to allow for baking expansion. Sprinkle cinnamon sugar on top of each muffin and bake in a preheated 400° F. oven for 20–25 minutes. Serve hot with lots of butter or jam.

Makes 20–24 muffins

2 cups sifted flour
2 teaspoons baking powder
½ teaspoon salt
3 tablespoons granulated sugar
2 eggs
¾ cup cold milk
¼ cup melted butter
¾ cup peeled and finely chopped apples or blueberries
½ teaspoon cinnamon or nutmeg
3 tablespoons granulated sugar mixed with 1 teaspoon ground cinnamon for topping
Butter or jam (optional)

BASIC SWEET DOUGH

Put the milk, sugar, and salt in a large bowl and stir until the sugar is dissolved. Put the yeast in a small bowl and add the lukewarm water. Add the pinch of sugar on top and let stand for 5 minutes. If it rises, the yeast is working. Stir the yeast and add to the milk mixture. Stir in the eggs and shortening. Gradually add the flour, first mixing with a wooden spoon, then by hand, or with kneading hook on an electric mixer. Add only enough flour to make it easy to handle, almost sticky, but dry enough to work and shape. When using a kneading hook, knead for approximately 4 minutes. When kneading by hand, turn dough onto a lightly floured board and knead by folding dough toward you, then pressing down and away from you with the heel of your hand. Keep turning dough as you knead for approximately 5 minutes, continuing until it is smooth and elastic. Dough should not stick to the board. If it does, sprinkle more flour on top of the dough and on the board and continue to knead. Place dough in a large greased bowl. Turn the dough to bring the greased side on top. This will prevent the dough from drying out. Cover with a clean damp cloth. Let rise for approximately 1½ hours in a warm draft-free place until double in size. When double, knead with the kneading hook for 1 minute, or by hand, punching in the center, then working the dough to remove all large air bubbles. When smooth, cover again and let rise approximately 30–40 minutes until *almost* double. Shape as desired and bake according to directions for the type of bread being prepared (see following recipes).

Makes 1 coffee cake or large pan of rolls

¾ cup lukewarm milk
½ cup granulated sugar
1 teaspoon salt
2 packages dry granular yeast
½ cup lukewarm water
◆ Pinch granulated sugar
2 eggs, lightly beaten
¼ cup butter
¼ cup margarine
5 cups sifted flour

BASIC WHITE BREAD

Cool the milk. When it is lukewarm, add the sugar, salt, and butter. Let the yeast proof (form tiny bubbles on the surface, which shows it is active) and add it to the milk. Combine with the flour and mix thoroughly. Knead vigorously on a lightly floured surface or in an electric mixer with a dough hook, until the dough is smooth and elastic to the touch. Put the dough in a greased bowl, turning it so it is oily on all sides. Cover with a damp cloth and let it rise in a warm, draft-free spot until double in bulk. Cut or punch the dough and knead a little more. Divide the dough into 3 parts. Shape each piece into a smooth loaf and place in a greased loaf pan. Cover with a cloth. Let the dough rise in a warm place until doubled in bulk. Bake in a preheated 350° F. oven for 45 minutes until the bread pulls away from the sides of the pan. Brush the top of the loaves with the melted butter.

3 loaves, 5" x 11" each

2 cups scalded milk
3 tablespoons granulated sugar
1¼ tablespoons salt
3 tablespoons butter
2 packages dry granular yeast or 2 yeast cakes dissolved in ¼ cup lukewarm water (110° F.)
7 cups sifted all-purpose flour, or stone ground flour, if available
Melted butter

BASIC WHOLE WHEAT BREAD

Use Basic White Bread recipe, substituting whole wheat flour for ½ of the white flour. Add ¼ cup honey to the milk mixture.

CROUTONS

It seems hard to understand why people buy boxes of croutons when they are so easy to make. Cut thick slices of day-old white bread into ½″ squares. Place in a well-buttered baking dish or on a buttered baking sheet. Sprinkle with Krazy Salt or a seasoned salt of your choice. Dot with bits of butter, and bake in a preheated 350° F. oven until light brown and crisp. These keep well in an airtight container.

CHEESE BISCUITS

Sift the flour, baking powder, salt, and red pepper or paprika into a mixing bowl. Cut in the butter with your hands or with a pastry blender. Add the milk, stirring lightly. Be sure not to overbeat. Fold in the cheese and Worcestershire sauce. When completely blended, turn onto a well-floured board. Roll out to ½″ thickness. Cut with a floured cutter, or with a floured knife. Brush tops with beaten egg and place on buttered baking sheet. Bake in a preheated 450° F. oven for 14 minutes until golden brown.

These keep well for several days stored in the refrigerator in an airtight container.

VARIATION

Sprinkle poppy seeds, celery seeds, or sesame seeds on top.

Makes 36 (1″) biscuits or 18 (2″) biscuits

3 cups flour, sifted before measuring
5 teaspoons baking powder
1 teaspoon salt
¼ teaspoon ground red pepper or paprika
3 tablespoons butter
1 cup milk
1 cup grated Cheddar cheese
1 teaspoon Worcestershire sauce
1 egg, well beaten
Poppy, celery, or sesame seeds (optional)

CORN BREAD MUFFINS

Sift the cornmeal, flour, sugar, salt, and baking powder together in a bowl. In another bowl, cream the butter. Beat in the eggs. Combine the sifted dry ingredients and the creamed butter-and-egg mixture alternately with the milk. Stir only until the dry ingredients are blended. Do not overbeat. Pour into greased muffin tins. Bake in a preheated 375° F. oven for 30 minutes until they pull away from the sides of the tins. Serve warm with butter and jam, if desired.

Makes 24 muffins

1½ cups yellow cornmeal
1¼ cups all-purpose flour
⅓ cup granulated sugar
1 teaspoon salt
1 tablespoon baking powder
⅔ cup butter
2 eggs
1½ cups milk
Butter or jam (optional)

HUNGARIAN COFFEE CAKE

After the second rising of the dough, cut the dough into small pieces, 1"–1½" squares. Roll into balls. In a bowl, combine the sugar, cinnamon, and nuts. Roll each ball in the melted butter, then roll them in the cinnamon mixture. Place 1 layer of the balls in a well-buttered 9" tube pan, being careful not to crowd. Sprinkle with ½ the raisins. Place the remaining balls of dough on top to make the second layer. Sprinkle with the rest of the raisins. Press the raisins lightly into the dough. Let rise for 45 minutes. Bake in a preheated 375° F. oven for 40 minutes. Loosen from pan. Place a large serving dish on top of the pan. Invert carefully so the butter-and-sugar mixture runs around the sides of the cake. Use a fork to remove the first round "ball" from the pan. The remainder will follow easily.

9" tube pan

Basic Sweet Dough (see Index)
½ cup melted butter
¾ cup granulated sugar
1 teaspoon ground cinnamon
½ cup finely chopped nuts
½ cup raisins

GARLIC AND CHEESE BREAD

Generously butter slices of bread, preferably homemade bread. Sprinkle with garlic salt and Parmesan cheese. Put under the broiler until the edges are golden brown and the bread is hot. Serve immediately.

DILL BREAD

After scalding the milk, let it cool to luke-warm. Add the sugar, salt, dill, and butter. When the dissolved yeast proofs (tiny bubbles will appear on the surface), add it to the lukewarm milk mixture. Combine with the flour in a large bowl and mix thoroughly. Then turn out onto a lightly floured surface and knead vigorously until smooth and elastic (if you have an electric mixer with a dough hook, you can mix and knead the bread with this). Put dough in a greased bowl, turning so it is greased on all sides. Cover with a moist tea towel and let rise in a warm, draft-free place until double in bulk. Punch down the risen dough, turn out of the bowl, and knead a little more. Then divide into 4 equal parts, shape each part into a loaf and place in four greased bread pans, 5″ x 9⅛″ size. Cover with a cloth and let rise in a warm place until double in bulk. Bake in a preheated 350° F. oven for 35 minutes.

Makes 4 loaves

2 cups scalded milk
2 tablespoons granulated sugar
1 tablespoon salt
1 tablespoon chopped fresh or dried dillweed
2 tablespoons butter
2 packages active dry yeast dissolved in ¼ cup luke-warm water (110°–115° F.)
7 cups sifted all-purpose flour

JENNIFER HARRIS'S METHODIST MUFFINS

Jennifer was one of the sweetest little girls when we met. When I visited her family in Los Angeles, she was only eleven, but already a good cook. Jennifer gave me several of her recipes. This is one we use all the time. Refrigerate the made-up batter, and take only as much as you need to serve with your meal. Add raisins, nuts, dried or fresh fruit to make a pan of hot muffins quickly, when you are in a hurry.

Pour boiling water over the Nabisco 100% Bran and let stand. In a bowl, cream the shortening and sugar. Add the eggs, butter-milk, and then add the Nabisco 100% Bran. Mix the flour, soda, and salt together in a large bowl and then add Kellogg's All Bran. Next add the creamed shortening and 100% Bran mixture all at once. Fold in only until the dry ingredients are moistened. Leave for 30 minutes. Fill greased muffin tins ⅔ full and bake in a preheated 400° F. oven for 15–20 minutes.

Makes 30 muffins

1 cup boiling water
1 cup Nabisco 100% Bran
½ cup shortening
1½ cups granulated sugar
2 eggs, beaten
2 cups buttermilk
2½ cups unsifted all-purpose flour
2½ teaspoons baking soda
½ teaspoon salt
2 cups Kellogg's All Bran

OATMEAL BREAD

We serve only fresh home-baked breads in the restaurant: white, brown, oatmeal, and dill are the favorites. Once a group came just as the bread was being taken from the oven. Their enthusiasm knew no bounds and each table consumed 4 baskets of bread. I prefer to use stone-ground flour in baking bread.

Put the flour and salt in a large mixing bowl. Combine the boiling water and milk in a large saucepan. Stir in the oatmeal, molasses, and shortening until well blended. Let cool until lukewarm to the touch. Add the dissolved and proofed yeast (the yeast is proofed when it froths slightly and forms tiny bubbles on the surface, proving it is active). Pour into the flour-salt mixture and knead for 10 minutes until the dough is smooth and elastic. Add the 2 eggs, 1 at a time, kneading well after each addition.

Cover the dough with a moist tea towel and let rise about 1½ hours until double in bulk. Punch the dough, then knead again for about 5 minutes until all air bubbles have been kneaded out. Grease two 8½" x 4½" bread pans. Divide the dough. Shape into loaves and put one in each pan. Brush the tops of loaves with beaten egg white and sprinkle with the rolled oats. Bake in a pre-heated 350° F. oven for 45 minutes to 1 hour. The bread is done when it pulls away from the side of the pan. Remove the loaves from the pans and let them cool on a wire cake rack, resting on one side. If a heavy-textured bread like this is cooled in an upright position, the moisture will settle to the bottom of the loaf, and it will not be tender or easy to cut.

Makes 2 loaves

5½ cups all-purpose flour, or, preferable, bread flour
1 tablespoon salt
1¾ cups boiling water
2 cups powdered dry milk
2 cups quick-cooking oatmeal
½ cup molasses or honey
⅓ cup vegetable shortening
2 tablespoons active dry yeast dissolved in ¼ cup 110°–115° F. water
2 eggs
1 egg white, lightly beaten
2 tablespoons rolled oats

SWEDISH TEA RING

In a small bowl mix the sugar and cinnamon. After the second rising of the dough, roll it into an oblong shape approximately 9″ x 18″ on a lightly floured board. Spread soft butter evenly over the dough and sprinkle with the sugar and cinnamon mixture. Sprinkle with raisins. Roll the dough tightly, beginning at the wide side. Pinch the edges to keep the sugar and raisins inside. Place on a lightly greased baking sheet with the sealed edges down, forming the roll into a circle. Seal ends together. Cut ⅔ of the way from the outside toward the center of the ring about 1″ apart, to form slices. Turn each cut ½ turn so the raisins are visible. Allow to rise for 35 minutes in a warm place. Bake in a preheated 375° F. oven for 25–30 minutes. Frost with Confectioners' Sugar Icing.

Makes 1 large ring

½ cup granulated sugar
1 teaspoon ground cinnamon
Basic Sweet Dough (see Index)
3 tablespoons soft butter
½ cup raisins

PFLATZLINGS

Pflatzlings are thin tender pancakes, like a French crepe, of German origin. This recipe came from the Ulrich Gettig family. My friend Ruth Gettig Pearson told me that when she was little, each child in her family could choose the dinner they liked most for their birthday. Ruth always asked for pflatzlings. She could eat as many as 7 or 8. In fact, she would eat until she almost rolled away from the table, and had to save her birthday cake for later.

Ruth's mother had a special way of serving pflatzlings. She would roll them, then put them in a bowl and pour beef stock on top. The pflatzlings were then served with cold sliced beef, or with ham and milk gravy. I asked our cook, Erma Engle, if she'd ever heard of pflatzlings. When I described them, she said her husband, Ez, had been looking for this recipe for years. His mother called them "thin pancakes" or fancy pancakes. In Ez's family, they were for Sunday-night supper, or on a special occasion with honey or sugar and lemon juice, or with a sweet filling, as a dessert. This is also the way the English serve these thin pancakes on Pancake Tuesday, that is, sprinkled with sugar and lemon juice and rolled up. It seems strange how people eat the same food in such very different ways. After my son Charlie returned from the Culinary Institute, he let the batter stand after he had mixed it. When I asked why, he said, "Why, Mother, everyone knows crepe batter stands to let the gluten expand and the batter gets thicker and more tender," and I said, "No, everybody does not know that." I am passing this tip on to help you make better pancakes, too.

Beat the flour, eggs, milk, and salt together until smooth and lump-free in a large mixing bowl, using a whisk or electric hand mixer. Cover the bowl with plastic wrap. Allow the batter to stand at least 1 hour.

For each pflatzling, pour ¼ cup of the batter into a very hot greased frying pan. If available, use a crepe pan, but a small skillet with rounded sides will do. Tilt the pan so that the batter covers the bottom completely. Put on high heat and cook until golden brown on one side, flip over, and brown on the other side. This should take no more than a minute. Tip pflatzling out of the pan onto a plate and roll up tightly. Place the rolled pflatzlings side by side in a heated serving bowl. When the bowl is filled, pour the hot beef stock on top. Serve with cold sliced beef in summer, or with hot sliced beef in winter.

VARIATION

If desired, thicken the stock with 2 tablespoons cornstarch.

Makes 6 servings

BATTER

2 cups unsifted flour

3 whole eggs

3½ cups milk

1½ teaspoons salt

4 cups rich beef stock, heated to boiling

Sliced cold beef

SPICY POPOVERS

Popovers are marvelous with roast beef, or with any roast, pork chops, or steak. Basically, this is a Yorkshire pudding batter, but the dried salad herb mix adds a lovely spicy flavor. For a change, try Krazy Salt instead of the dried herbs. In that case, omit the ¼ teaspoon salt in the recipe.

Combine the eggs, milk, flour, dressing mix, and salt in a bowl. Mix well with a whip. Add the oil and mix thoroughly. Grease 5 custard cups, or 8 muffin tins. Fill each cup or tin half full with batter. Bake in a preheated 475° F. oven for 15 minutes. Reduce the oven temperature to 350° and bake 25 minutes longer.

Makes 5 large or 8 small popovers

2 eggs
1 cup milk
1 cup all-purpose flour
1 tablespoon dry Italian Salad Dressing Mix or 1 teaspoon Krazy Salt
¼ teaspoon salt
1 tablespoon cooking oil

MORAVIAN COFFEE CAKE

Divide the dough in half, and place in 2 buttered 9″ pie pans or round cake pans. Sprinkle each with ⅓ cup of the brown sugar and 4 tablespoons of the butter. Punch the dough with your fingertips about halfway down into the pan, to make a multitude of small holes all filled with sugar and butter. Sprinkle with cinnamon. Set in a warm place to rise for about 25–30 minutes. Bake in a preheated 375° F. oven for 30 minutes. Serve warm.

Makes 2 (9″) pies

Basic Sweet Dough (see Index)
⅔ cup light brown sugar
8 tablespoons butter
½ teaspoon ground cinnamon

STICKY BUNS

After the second rising of the dough, roll it on a lightly floured board into an oblong shape, approximately 9″ x 18″. Spread the butter evenly over the dough. Mix the sugar and cinnamon together, and sprinkle evenly over the dough. Next, sprinkle with the raisins. Roll up the dough tightly, beginning at the wide side. Pinch the edges together to keep the sugar and raisins inside. With a sharp buttered knife, cut the roll into 1″ slices. Put melted butter, brown sugar and nuts into 2 (9″) round or square pans, or in 1 large baking pan. Place the slices in the butter-sugar mixture. Set in a warm place and allow to rise for 35 minutes. Bake in a preheated 375° F. oven for 30 minutes, or until well-baked. Immediately turn pan upside down on a serving dish to let the sugar-butter mixture run around the rolls. Leave pan on top of rolls for at least 3 minutes before removing. Serve warm or at room temperature.

Makes 18 buns

Basic Sweet Dough (see Index)
- **3** tablespoons soft butter
- **½** cup granulated sugar
- **1** teaspoon ground cinnamon
- **½** cup raisins
- **½** cup melted butter
- **¾** cup light brown sugar
- **½** cup coarsely chopped nuts, preferably pecans

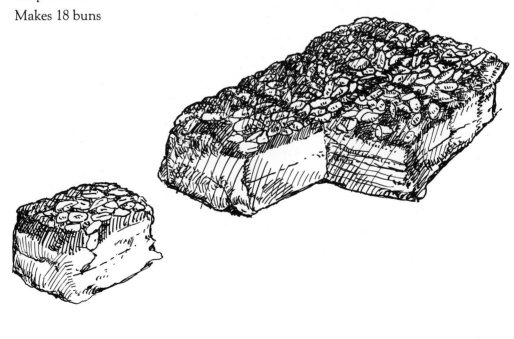

BREAD TURTLE

Divide dough in two after it has risen for the second time. Form ½ into an oval loaf, flattening it a little, to form the body of a turtle. Place on a buttered baking sheet. With a sharp, buttered knife blade, cut a diamond square design on top of the dough. Use small pieces of dough to form legs and a tail. Make a larger piece of dough for the head. Let rise for 25 minutes. Bake in a pre-heated 375° F. oven for 35 minutes. After removing from the oven, lightly butter the top of the bread to make it shine.

Makes 2 turtles or 1 turtle and 2 loaves

Basic White Bread or Basic Whole Wheat Bread (see Index)

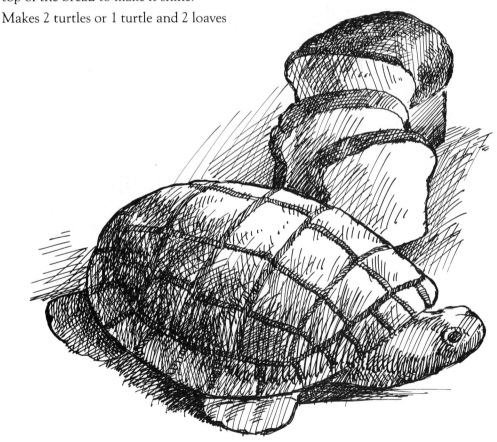

WAFFLES

In Lancaster County, waffles are very popular. They are used in any number of different ways. Many a fire engine has been paid off through chicken-and-waffle suppers sponsored by the fire company's women's auxiliary in this area. We never tire of waffles. The antique irons used to make waffles in the past are very sought after and expensive.

My family always served waffles with chicken and gravy or with syrup. A dinner guest from Alaska told me she serves waffles with sour cream and brown sugar over fresh fruit. Crab meat in cream sauce is another variation. Use your imagination for additional ideas.

In a small bowl, beat egg yolks until light. Add the milk. In another bowl, sift together the flour, salt, and baking powder. Gradually add these dry ingredients to the egg yolks and milk. Add the melted butter. Mix until smooth. Beat the egg whites until stiff and fold in. Blend thoroughly.

Preheat the waffle iron. It is ready to use when a drop of water bounces on it. Pour a ladleful of batter onto the iron, starting in center. Be sure that there is only a thin coating of the batter. It will rise and spread to the edges as it bakes.

Makes 6 servings

- 2 eggs, separated
- 2 cups milk
- 2 cups unsifted flour
- 1 teaspoon salt
- 3½ teaspoons baking powder
- 4 tablespoons melted butter

BEER BATTER

Mix all the batter ingredients in a blender or mixer. Cover and chill for at least 30 minutes.

- 1¼ cups all-purpose flour
- ½ teaspoon salt
- 1 tablespoon baking powder
- ¼ cup milk
- 8 ounces beer
- 1 egg
- ◆ Dash pepper

Johannes Lang

Was born in America, state of Pennsylvania, county of Northumberland, township of Auguster on the 27th day of November, 1805. He is the godchild of Johannes Mellich and Elizabeth Borckert. His parents are John George Lang and Catharina Lonrath Lang daughter of Jacob Lonrath.

Father
John George Lang

Mother
Catharina Lonrath Lang

DECORATIVE CERTIFICATE, BIRTH FRAKTUR

The Birth Fraktur records the birth of a child. Such a joyous occasion recorded in paint and ink is treasured for generations to come.

11

PICKLES & RELISHES

PICKLES & RELISHES

Basic Sour Pickling Syrup
Basic Sweet Pickling Syrup
Bread-and-Butter Pickles
Chow Chow
Corn Relish
Cranberry-Orange Relish
Dill Beans
Dill Pickles
Erma's Pickled Cauliflower
Jessie's Green Tomato Relish
Green Tomato Relish
Mrs. Swink's Pepper Relish
Jackie's Relish
Letitia's Lime Pickles
Mother's Refrigerator Pickles
Mother's Spiced Kumquats
Spiced Cantaloupe
Nancy McNiff's Marinated Mushrooms
Green Tomato Pickles
Pickled Green Beans, Carrots, and Cauliflower
Pickled Herb Beets
Pickled Beet Eggs
Reba Hammond's Sweet-Sour Carrots
Seven-Day Crisp Sweet Pickles
Pickled Watermelon Rind with Ginger
Stuffed Pickled Peppers
Three-Bean Relish
Two-Day Sweet Pickles
Pickled Celery
Mother's Ripe Tomato Relish

BASIC SOUR PICKLING SYRUP

Combine all ingredients and bring to a boil. Simmer for 5 minutes, adding whatever spices the recipe calls for.

2 cups sugar
2 cups cider vinegar
2 cups water
1 tablespoon celery seed
1 tablespoon mustard seed

BASIC SWEET PICKLING SYRUP

Combine all ingredients and bring to a boil. Simmer for 5 minutes, adding whatever spices the recipe calls for.

4 cups sugar
2 cups cider vinegar
2 cups water
1 tablespoon celery seed
1 tablespoon mustard seed

BREAD-AND-BUTTER PICKLES

These have been a favorite in the dining room. They are simple and quick. Cracked ice freshens the cucumbers, onions, and peppers and keeps them crisp.

Toss the cucumbers, onions, and peppers with the salt in a large bowl and cover with cracked ice. Let stand 4 hours. Bring the syrup, with the spices and dillweed, to a boil in a heavy pan. Rinse the vegetables in cold water. Add them to the boiling syrup. Boil 3 minutes. Pack in hot sterilized jars and seal.

Makes 6 pints

7 large unwaxed cucumbers, sliced
5 white onions, sliced
1 green bell pepper, chopped
1 red bell pepper, chopped
¼ cup salt
Cracked ice
6 cups Basic Sweet Pickling Syrup
1 tablespoon mustard seed
1½ teaspoons celery seed
¾ teaspoon turmeric
¼ teaspoon dillweed

CHOW CHOW

Cook each fresh vegetable separately in a saucepan, covering with water and boiling only enough to make the vegetables tender, not mushy. Do not cook the canned or frozen vegetables. Place in layers in a large pan in whatever order you prefer. Gently mix with your hands, or a very large pierced spoon, being careful not to break the vegetables, or it may become mushy. Pour off all liquid before spooning vegetables into sterilized jars, filling within 1″ of the neck. Pour in Syrup to fill jars to neck.

2 cups canned Great Northern Beans, drained
2 cups canned Red Kidney Beans, drained
2 cups fresh or frozen lima beans
2 cups fresh or frozen green beans cut into 1″ pieces
2 cups fresh or frozen yellow wax beans cut into 1″ pieces
2 cups fresh or frozen cauliflower buds
2 cups coarsely chopped celery
2 cups coarsely chopped red bell peppers
2 cups coarsely chopped green bell peppers
2 cups sliced carrots
2 cups fresh or frozen corn kernels
2 cups tiny white onions, or chopped yellow onions
2 cups coarsely chopped cabbage
2 cups sliced or chopped sweet pickles

SYRUP

5 cups sugar
2½ cups cider vinegar
1½ cups water
2 tablespoons mustard seed
1 tablespoon celery seed
1 teaspoon turmeric

Combine all ingredients in a large kettle and bring to a boil, stirring until the sugar is dissolved. Ladle the syrup over the vegetables. Seal jars with lids and covers and process in the canner for 12 minutes, timing from the moment the water comes to a full boil.

Makes 6 quarts or 12 pints

CORN RELISH

Put the corn, cabbage, onion, and peppers in an 8-quart kettle. Put the vinegar, sugar, celery seed, and mustard seed in a 2-quart saucepan and stir until dissolved. Pour over the vegetables. Place the large kettle over medium heat. Bring to a boil and cook for 8 minutes. Ladle into hot sterilized jars, filling to the neck of the jar. Seal. Do not move jars until completely cooled—approximately 12 hours.

Makes 4 quarts or 8 pints

8 cups fresh or frozen corn kernels
2 cups chopped cabbage
1 cup chopped onion
1 cup chopped bell peppers, both red and green if available
4 cups cider vinegar
4 cups sugar
1 teaspoon celery seed
1 tablespoon mustard seed

CRANBERRY-ORANGE RELISH

Wash cranberries. Quarter the oranges and remove seeds. Core and quarter the apples. Put the cranberries, oranges, and apples, peels and all, in a food processor or food grinder. Add the sugar and blend thoroughly. Let stand for several hours before serving. This relish will keep for weeks in the refrigerator. It also freezes well.

Serves 10–12

6 cups fresh cranberries
3 large oranges
3 large apples
2 cups sugar

DILL BEANS

These beans are delicious, crisp and crunchy, and good to serve as an hors d'oeuvre or at a buffet instead of pickles. Pickle them in quart jars, as they store well after they are opened. Extra time and effort are required to pack whole beans in small jars, but it is well worth the effort.

Soak the beans for 1 hour in a pot with ½ cup salt and water to cover. Rinse and cover with fresh cold water. Bring to a boil and cook, uncovered, for 2 minutes only. Drain in a colander. When cool enough to handle, pack the trimmed whole beans lengthwise, carefully, in hot sterilized jars. Tuck a sprig of tarragon (or put ½ teaspoon dried tarragon) in each jar. Combine the vinegar, water, dill seed, and dillweed in a saucepan, bring to a boil, and boil 2 minutes. Pour over the beans in the jars and seal.

Makes 4 quarts

4 **pounds whole firm young green beans, trimmed**
½ **cup salt**
Water to cover
6 **cups white vinegar**
4 **cups water**
2 **tablespoons dill seed**
2 **teaspoons dillweed**
4 **sprigs fresh tarragon, or 2 teaspoons dried tarragon**

DILL PICKLES

Wash the cucumbers. If cucumbers are waxed, rinse in hot water to remove wax, rubbing dry. Cut in desired shape: slices, chunks, or quarters for strips. Arrange cucumbers in sterilized canning jars. Add the dill, mustard seed, and garlic. Put the vinegar, water, and salt in a 1-quart saucepan. Bring to a boil. Pour over the cucumbers, filling jars to the neck. If additional liquid is needed to fill jars to necks, use boiling water. Seal jars with lids and covers and process in the canner for 5 minutes, timing from the moment the water comes to a full boil.

Makes 1 quart, or 2 pints

4 **medium-size pickling cucumbers, 3"–4" long**
2 **teaspoons dill seed**
1 **sprig fresh dill or 1 more teaspoon dill seed**
1 **teaspoon mustard seed**
½ **teaspoon minced garlic**
¾ **cup cider vinegar**
¾ **cup water**
1½ **tablespoons salt**

ERMA'S PICKLED CAULIFLOWER

Cauliflower will not stay white when it is canned. Erma, therefore, uses a little turmeric in this recipe. We feel it is better to give the cauliflower a nice yellow color than to use additives to keep it white.

Clean and trim the cauliflower. Break the heads into buds. Dissolve the salt in the water, pour it over the cauliflower buds in a large bowl, and soak overnight. Drain and rinse with cold water. Combine the vinegar, sugar, and spices in a large pan and bring to a boil. Add the cauliflower and cook for 8 minutes. Pack into hot sterilized jars and fill with syrup to neck of the jar. Seal.

Makes 12 pints

5 medium heads cauliflower
1 cup salt
1 gallon water

SYRUP

4 cups vinegar
4 cups sugar
1 teaspoon ground turmeric
2 teaspoons celery seed
1 tablespoon mustard seed

JESSIE'S GREEN TOMATO RELISH

Jessie Babcock shared this recipe with me several years ago and I am very grateful for it. If the green tomatoes are picked just before the first frost, they are inexpensive, yet ideal for relish. This recipe is very old, and an excellent standby.

Put the cheesecloth in a colander. Place the tomatoes and onions in layers in the cloth. Lightly salt each layer, repeating until all ingredients are used. Tighten cheesecloth with string and place colander in a crock or stainless steel kettle. Put a heavy weight on top and cover. Let stand overnight. The contents of the bag should be well drained and dry by morning; if not, let it stand a few hours longer.

Heat syrup to boiling point in a kettle. Add the tomatoes and onions, and simmer 15 minutes. Ladle into sterilized jars and seal.

Makes about 10 pints

5 pounds green tomatoes, cored and sliced
2½ pounds onions, sliced
1 tablespoon salt
6 cups basic sour pickling syrup (see Index)
Cheesecloth and white string

GREEN TOMATO RELISH

Just before the first frost, the tomato stalks in vegetable gardens are laden with green tomatoes. At that time, green tomatoes are easily available at farm markets—and at an excellent price. Consequently, fall is the ideal time to make this recipe.

Put the tomatoes in a large bowl and sprinkle with salt. Allow to stand for 4 hours, then drain. Bring the vinegar and sugar to a boil in an 8-quart pot. Add the tomatoes, onions, bell peppers, and spices, and simmer gently for 1½ hours on low heat until thickened. Remove the infuser or bag of spices. Pack the relish into hot sterilized jars and seal.

Makes 12 pints

- 12 pounds firm green tomatoes, cored and cut into ½″ slices
- ½ cup salt
- 1½ quarts white vinegar
- 3 cups sugar
- 4 cups chopped onion
- 5 cups chopped green bell peppers
- 2 tablespoons whole mixed pickling spices, in a tea infuser or cloth bag

MRS. SWINK'S PEPPER RELISH

Our friend Rita shared this tasty recipe with me because of the different method of preparing the relish. It sounds difficult, but it is not.

Clean and trim the vegetables. Put through a food grinder on a coarse setting. Put into a 5-quart kettle and cover with boiling water, mixing well. Let stand 5 minutes; drain thoroughly. Return to the kettle. Add the 2 cups water and the vinegar. Bring to a boil and immediately remove from heat. Let stand 10 minutes, then drain thoroughly. Return vegetables to the kettle again. Now add the remaining ingredients. Bring to a hard boil for 3 minutes. Pour into hot sterilized jars and seal.

Makes 7 pints

- 12 large green peppers
- 12 large red peppers
- 16 medium onions
- 2 cups water
- 6 cups vinegar
- 3 cups sugar
- 3 tablespoons coarse (kosher) salt
- 3 tablespoons mustard seed

JACKIE'S RELISH

My neighbor Jackie, an excellent cook, is very adept at canning and pickling. This relish may be used as a sandwich spread, or it is equally delicious on hot dogs, hamburgers, grilled cheese sandwiches, and cold meat. In the fall, green tomatoes and peppers must be picked before the first frost. This is an excellent way to use them.

Clean all the vegetables carefully, Grind with the coarse disk of a food grinder. Drain well. Save all vegetable juices to combine with water for the syrup.

Blend all the syrup ingredients together in a saucepan until smooth. Bring to a boil. Add the ground vegetables. Simmer on low heat for 10 minutes. Mix in the mayonnaise and simmer for 12 minutes on low heat, stirring constantly. Pour into hot sterilized jars and seal.

Makes 6 pints

6 green bell peppers, seeded
6 red bell peppers, seeded
6 green tomatoes, cored
1 small onion
2 cups commercial mayonnaise

SYRUP

1 cup cider vinegar
1 cup water (part may be juice from the ground vegetables)
½ cup flour
1¼ cups sugar
½ teaspoon celery seed
½ teaspoon salt
1 cup prepared mustard

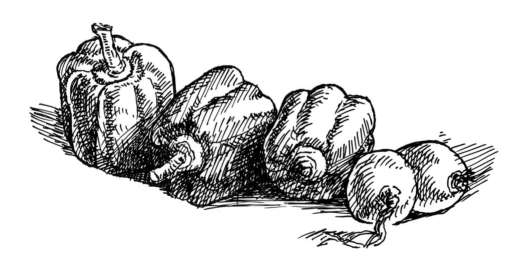

LETITIA'S LIME PICKLES

Soon after Good Earth and Country Cooking was published, I received a letter from Letitia Kraxburger Thomas of Ohio, telling me all about her Mennonite family background. She enclosed some of her grandmothers's recipes. The love of good food does seem to bring people together, and I am always delighted when someone wants to share a recipe with me. I have mislaid Letitia's address, but if she should happen to see this, a warm thank-you for this superb recipe, which has become a restaurant favorite. This recipe and the one for green tomato pickles call for pickling lime, or calcium hydroxide. It is a white powder used in pickling to keep cucumbers and green tomatoes crisp. If you are a gardener, you will recognize this to be sweet, or slaked, lime, used on the garden, and on the lawn to make the grass grow. Instead of buying it in a drugstore, buy it at a garden or farm supply store in 5-, 10-, or 50-pound bags. Obviously, this is a good saving. Be sure to rinse the vegetables well after soaking to remove all traces of lime. Large cucumbers are always available and, if unwaxed, do not need to be peeled. If peeled, a drop or 2 of green food coloring will make the pickles look more attractive.

Put the sliced cucumbers in an enamel pot, stone jar, or stainless steel pot with the water mixed with pickling lime. Do not use aluminum. Soak for 24 hours, stirring occasionally with a wooden spoon. This will keep the cucumbers very crisp. Next day, rinse thoroughly in several changes of water and cover with clear, cold water. Leave for 3 hours.

Combine the syrup ingredients, not including the food coloring, in a large stainless steel pot and bring to a boil. Be sure that the sugar dissolves. Add the food coloring. Drain the cucumbers. Cover with the hot syrup for 35 minutes until the pickles are translucent. Pack into hot sterilized jars and seal.

Makes 8 pints

17 cucumbers, peeled if waxed, otherwise unpeeled, sliced ½" thick
2 gallons water
2 cups pickling lime (calcium hydroxide)

SYRUP

2 quarts white vinegar
9 cups sugar
1 teaspoon celery seed
1 teaspoon salt
1 teaspoon whole cloves
1 teaspoon whole mixed pickling spices
◆ Drop or 2 green food coloring (optional)

MOTHER'S REFRIGERATOR PICKLES

Excellent pickles which will keep indefinitely in the refrigerator without being sealed. The alum makes the cucumbers crisp.

Prepare enough salt brine to cover the cucumbers, using 1 cup salt to 1 gallon water. Put in a large bowl. Leave the cucumbers in this brine for 3 days. Drain. Soak the cucumbers in cold water for the next 3 days, changing the water every day. Drain and cut each cucumber into 3 or 4 pieces. Combine the 1 pint vinegar, 1 pint water, and alum in a pot. (Do not use aluminum.) Add the cucumbers and simmer in this solution for 2 hours. Drain and pack in clean glass jars or in a large crock.

In a pan, combine the sugar, cider vinegar, spices, and food coloring. Boil for 8 minutes. Pour this syrup over the pickles. Cool and store in the refrigerator.

Makes 10 pints

Salt
Water to cover
8 pounds medium unwaxed
  cucumbers
1 pint vinegar
1 pint water
1 tablespoon alum
4 pounds sugar
6 cups cider vinegar
1 ounce stick cinnamon
  (about 10 [3-inch] sticks)
½ ounce whole allspice
  (4 tablespoons)
2 drops green food coloring

MOTHER'S SPICED KUMQUATS

Mother and I always used to make spiced kumquats for special occasions and to give as gifts for Christmas. Kumquats are usually a good value in the markets during the holiday season. You will also find them arranged around the oranges in fruit gift baskets. Many people cannot decide how to serve them. This recipe is really a gourmet treat. Be sure not to give a jar of spiced kumquats to the children or the whole jar will disappear in a flash. After all the work involved preparing this recipe, you will want to serve your spiced kumquats sparingly.

Our recipe is somewhat different because we cut the kumquats in half and remove the seeds.

Cut the kumquats in half and remove all seeds. Mix the salt and water to make a brine. Pour this brine over the kumquats and leave overnight. Drain, rinse and drain again. Cover the kumquats with fresh water and just bring to a boil. Drain.

Put 2½ pounds of the sugar, the vinegar, water and the spice oil or spices, in a pan, and bring to a boil. Pour this syrup over the drained kumquats and again leave overnight. Drain off the syrup, add the remaining 1½ pounds sugar to it, and boil for 5 minutes. Pour over the kumquats. For the next 2 days, once a day, drain off and reboil the syrup, and then pour it over the kumquats again. Each time leave overnight. On the third day, cook the fruit and syrup together for 2 minutes. Pack the fruit loosely in hot sterilized jars. Cover with the syrup and seal.

NOTE: Spiced kumquats are very sweet and syrupy. A serving of 1 or 2 per person is sufficient. For a slightly different flavor, add a little grated orange or lemon zest to the syrup.

Makes 6 pints

3 quarts kumquats
½ cup salt
2 quarts water

SYRUP

4 pounds sugar
2 cups white vinegar
2 cups water
⅛ teaspoon equal parts oil of cinnamon and oil of clove, mixed, or 2 teaspoons whole cloves and 2 teaspoons broken cinnamon stick in a metal tea-ball infuser

SPICED CANTALOUPE

Wash the cantaloupe, cut it in slices, and remove the seeds and rind. Cut melon into 2″ pieces and pack into sterilized jars. Combine the sugar, water and vinegar in a saucepan and bring to a boil. Stir until all the sugar is dissolved. Pour the hot syrup over the melon in the jars. If necessary, add boiling water to fill jars completely. Add the oil to the syrup. Place self-sealing lid and ring on the jar. Process in a home canner for 15 minutes, timing from the moment the water comes to a full boil.

Oils of cinnamon and cloves may be purchased at a drugstore. Ask the druggist to mix them and to put them in a bottle with a dropper. I use the oils because they do not discolor the melon.

2 pints or 1 quart

2 pounds firm ripe cantaloupe
1 cup sugar
½ cup water
⅔ cup cider vinegar
4 drops oils of cinnamon and cloves (equal parts)

NANCY MCNIFF'S MARINATED MUSHROOMS

When Nancy and Jim entertain, they like to serve new recipes they have discovered. However, they always include this mushroom recipe—it is marvelous.

If the mushrooms are large, cut into thick slices; if tiny, leave whole. Combine all the marinade ingredients and pour over the mushrooms. Put in a covered container. Marinate for 3–4 days, shaking the container daily to blend the flavors. After using the mushrooms, use the liquid as a salad dressing.

1¼ pounds mushrooms
MARINADE
½ cup wine vinegar
⅔ cup salad oil
1 tablespoon chopped fresh or 1 teaspoon dried oregano
1 clove garlic, minced fine
½ teaspoon sugar
½ teaspoon salt or 1 teaspoon Krazy Salt
½ teaspoon freshly ground black pepper
1 tablespoon lemon juice

GREEN TOMATO PICKLES

This is a pickle everyone loves, and a good way to use unripe, or green, tomatoes. Best are green tomatoes of the firm, small Italian plum variety. Be sure to rinse the tomatoes thoroughly, after soaking, to remove any lime which may lodge in the seeds. Green tomatoes have a dull color. A drop or 2 of green food coloring helps to make them prettier.

Combine the water and lime in a large enameled or stainless steel pan, stirring to dissolve the lime. Add the sliced tomatoes and soak for 4 hours. Rinse well in several changes of water, then cover with fresh water, shake the pan, and drain. Repeat this procedure 3 times.

Combine the sugar, vinegar, and spices in a large pot or canner. Bring to a boil and add the food coloring. Drain the tomatoes. Pour the syrup over them and leave overnight. Next day, bring the tomatoes and syrup to a boil. Do not stir, or the tomatoes will break up. Simmer for 1 hour. Pack in hot sterilized jars and seal.

Makes 6 pints

- 2 gallons water
- 3 cups pickling lime (calcium hydroxide)
- 6 pounds small firm green tomatoes, sliced ⅛" thick

SYRUP

- 5 pounds sugar
- 1½ quarts white vinegar
- 1 teaspoon ground cloves
- 1 teaspoon ground allspice
- 1 teaspoon celery seed
- ◆ Few drops green food coloring

PICKLED GREEN BEANS, CARROTS, AND CAULIFLOWER

This pickle may be made at any time, which is a good recommendation for the recipe. Green beans, carrots, and cauliflower are always available, although cauliflower is more expensive in the spring. The turmeric turns the cauliflower slightly yellow and adds a nice spicy flavor.

Clean all the vegetables. Chop into bite-size pieces. Put each vegetable in a separate pan with water to cover and salt: 2¼ teaspoons salt for the cauliflower, 1 teaspoon salt for the beans, and 1½ teaspoons salt for the carrots. Bring to a boil and cook about 8 minutes, until just crunchy. Drain. In a pan combine the turmeric, mustard seed, celery seed, and syrup and bring to a boil. Add the drained vegetables and boil 3 minutes. Pack in hot sterilized jars and seal.

Makes 8 pints

2 pounds cauliflower
1½ pounds green beans
2 pounds carrots
Salt
1 teaspoon turmeric
1½ teaspoons mustard seed
1¼ teaspoons celery seed
10 cups sweet or semisweet pickling syrup

PICKLED HERB BEETS

Wash but do not peel the beets. Place in a large (5–6 quart) kettle. Add the water and bring to a boil. Cook on medium heat until the beets are tender. Remove and let cool enough to handle. Peel and slice to desired thickness. Fill sterilized jars with the sliced beets, filling to 1″ of the neck. Put the sugar, vinegar, beet broth, water, salt, pepper, and chopped herbs in a 2-quart saucepan. Stir until the sugar is dissolved, then bring to a boil. Boil the syrup for 2 minutes. Ladle syrup over the beets, filling the jars to the neck, and seal. Do not move to storage area until completely cooled—at least 12 hours.

VARIATION

For Pickled Beet Eggs, marinate hard boiled eggs in beet liquor for at least 12 hours in refrigerator.

Makes 6 pints or 3 quarts

5 pounds fresh beets
6 cups water
1 cup sugar
1 cup cider vinegar
2 cups beet broth
1 cup water
3 teaspoons salt
1 teaspoon black pepper
2 tablespoons chopped herbs (thyme, dill, oregano, etc.)

REBA HAMMOND'S SWEET-SOUR CARROTS

Put sliced carrots in a 2-quart saucepan and cover with water. Bring to a boil and cook approximately 10 minutes over medium heat until tender. Drain. Layer the carrots and onion in a large salad bowl. In a small bowl, blend the soup, salad oil, sugar, and vinegar until thoroughly mixed. Pour over the carrots and onions. Cover with plastic wrap and refrigerate for several hours. Serve chilled. This will keep in the refrigerator for 3–4 weeks.

Makes 8 cups

2 pounds carrots, washed, peeled, and cut into ½" slices
1 medium onion, sliced
1 (11½-ounce) can tomato soup
½ cup salad oil
½ cup sugar
½ cup vinegar

SEVEN-DAY CRISP SWEET PICKLES

Seven days may sound like a long time, but this pickle recipe is not too difficult to make. All that is needed is small unwaxed pickling cucumbers, 3"–4" long and about 1½" thick, which we always call "pickles." In our terminology, cucumbers are the "biggies," while pickles are the small variety. Pickles are odd. When they are small they are covered with sharp little prickles. If you are lucky enough to find small prickly pickles, put them under running water and rub the prickles off.

Wash the cucumbers and put them in a large crock. Cover with boiling water and allow to stand 24 hours. Drain. Repeat every day for 4 days, using fresh boiling water each time. On the fifth day, cut the cucumbers in ¼" rings. In a saucepan, combine the vinegar, water, 4 cups of the sugar, the salt, spices, and food coloring and bring to a boil. Pour this over the sliced cucumbers and leave for another 24 hours. On the 6th day, drain off the syrup. Add 2 cups sugar to this syrup and bring to a boil. Pour over the cucumbers and let stand 24 hours. On the seventh day, drain off the syrup again and add the remaining 2 cups sugar. Bring to a boil. Add the cucumber slices and bring back to the boiling point. Pack in hot sterilized jars and seal.

Makes 10 pints

5 pounds medium pickling cucumbers, 3"–4" long
3 cups cold cider vinegar
1 cup water
8 cups sugar
2 tablespoons salt
2 tablespoons whole mixed pickling spices
2 drops green food coloring

PICKLED WATERMELON RIND WITH GINGER

When buying watermelon, be sure to save the rind. If it is at least ½" thick, it will make delicious watermelon pickle. When taking off the rind, leave about ¼" of the pink flesh—enough to show that it is indeed watermelon—but no more, as watermelon does not pickle well.

The rind is bulky until it is boiled down. Large containers are needed to soak the rind overnight. A large enameled pot will do, but aluminum is not advisable as it may discolor the rind. For the same reason, I use oil of cinnamon and cloves rather than whole spices. The oil is expensive but worth the investment, and a little goes a long way. If you use whole spices, put them in a metal tea-ball infuser so they can be removed easily. Use fresh ginger root, which has a much more pungent flavor. However, dried ginger root soaked in water will reconstitute perfectly. Although fresh ginger is perishable, it may be stored for a year or 2 in the refrigerator. Simply scrape it with a knife, put it in a screw-top jar, and cover with vodka, dry sherry or mild white wine to preserve it.

Cut the peeled watermelon rind into 2" pieces. Mix the salt and water and pour it over the rind, which has been placed in a large plastic or enameled container. Do not use aluminum. Leave to soak overnight. Next day, drain and rinse in cold water. Drain again. Cook in fresh water to cover until the rind is translucent and tender when pierced with a fork. Drain well.

In a large stainless steel or enameled saucepan, combine the sugar, cider vinegar, 1 cup water, cloves and cinnamon oils (or the spices in the tea infuser). Bring to a boil, stirring until the sugar dissolves. Pour this syrup over the drained rind. If you used a plastic container, transfer the rind to an enamel pot. Next day, drain off the syrup, cook it for several minutes, and again pour over the rind. Repeat this process for 3 days, each time leaving the rind in the syrup overnight. This will make the rind clear. On the last day cook the rind in the syrup for 3 minutes, pour into hot sterilized jars, and seal.

Makes 6 quarts, or 12 pints

5 **pounds watermelon rind, peeled (with ¼" of pink flesh left on for color)**
½ **teaspoon salt**
2 **quarts water**

SYRUP

2½ **pounds sugar**
2 **cups cider vinegar**
1 **cup water**
⅛ **teaspoon equal parts oil of cinnamon and oil of cloves, mixed, or use 2 teaspoons whole cloves and 2 teaspoons broken cinnamon stick in a nonaluminum metal tea-ball infuser**
6 **slices peeled fresh ginger root, or ½ teaspoon dried ginger root, reconstituted**

STUFFED PICKLED PEPPERS

Stuffed baby peppers are quite a delicacy in the Pennsylvania Dutch country. Although it takes a long time to prepare them, these peppers are both colorful and tasty. Serve on gleaming crystal.

Clean the peppers carefully. Fill with cole slaw and set upright in a deep skillet. Bring syrup to a boil in a separate pan. Pour over the peppers. Simmer, covered until peppers are tender when pricked with a fork. Ladle very gently into pint jars open end up. Fill jars with syrup and seal.

Grate cabbage and pepper in food processor. Stir in sugar, vinegar, oil, and salt till well blended.

Makes 3–4 pints

3 cups Cabbage Slaw
24 very small bell peppers, green, yellow, and red

CABBAGE SLAW
1 firm head cabbage
1 medium green bell pepper
½ cup sugar
⅓ cup cider vinegar
¼ cup salad oil
½ teaspoon salt

SYRUP
1 cup sugar
1 cup cider vinegar
3 cups water

THREE-BEAN RELISH

This relish is one we use practically all year round, together with bread-and-butter pickles, dill pickles, and pepper relish. Everyone loves it.

Put all the ingredients except the kidney beans in a large enameled or stainless steel pot and bring to a boil. Reduce the heat and simmer for 15 minutes. Add the kidney beans for the last 5 minutes. Pour into hot sterilized jars and seal.

Makes 8 pints

4 cups green beans cut into 1" pieces
4 cups yellow beans cut into 1" pieces
2 cups chopped onion
1 tablespoon mustard seed
1 tablespoon celery seed
½ cup salad oil
2 quarts Basic Sweet Pickling Syrup
4 cups canned red kidney beans, well rinsed and drained

TWO-DAY SWEET PICKLES

If time is short, this recipe is a good substitute for the Seven-Day Crisp Sweet Pickles. Cucumbers may be substituted for the small pickles if the unwaxed kind is available. When using cucumbers, be sure to quarter them. However, they do not look as attractive as the smaller variety. There is something special about the small pickles, which are firmer and not as seedy.

Dissolve the salt in the 2 gallons water. Put the cucumbers in a large crock and cover with this brine solution. Let stand for 24 hours. Drain. Puncture each cucumber with a 3-tined fork. In a large pot, combine 6 cups of the sugar and the 12 cups vinegar, with 2 cups of water and the pickling spices. Bring to a boil, and simmer for 30 minutes. Add the pickles and boil for 15 minutes. Leave the pickles in the syrup for 2 days in a 3-gallon crock, or in 3 (1-gallon) jars. Drain, saving the syrup. Add the remaining 6 cups of sugar to the syrup and boil for 5 minutes. Pack the pickles in hot sterilized jars. Pour the boiling syrup over the pickles and seal.

Makes 12 pints

2 cups salt
2 gallons cold water
10 pounds medium pickling cucumbers, 3"–4" long
12 cups sugar
12 cups cider vinegar
2 cups water
4 tablespoons pickling spices

PICKLED CELERY

The most requested of all the relishes we make is pickled celery. It is economical to make since it is made with the green outer stems of the celery, which are so often trimmed off in the markets. The greener it is, the prettier! If you are on good terms with the manager of your local produce market, ask him to save his celery trimmings. The celery may also be pickled in long spears and served as an hors d'oeuvre.

Put the celery in a 6-quart pot with the salt and water to cover. Bring to a boil. Reduce the heat and simmer about 6 minutes until the celery gives a little when pressed with the back of a fork. Be sure not to pierce the celery. Drain thoroughly. Heat the pickling syrup to boiling. Add the celery and simmer 2 minutes. Pack into hot sterilized jars and seal.

Makes 8 pints

10 **cups celery, cut into ½" pieces**
1 **tablespoon salt**
6 **cups Basic Sweet Pickling Syrup (see Index)**

MOTHER'S RIPE TOMATO RELISH

This relish is delicious on hamburgers. Be sure to select firm peppers without wrinkles or spots. Many people are unaware that red peppers are green peppers which have turned red, not a different variety. Sometimes in the fall you can also find yellow peppers, which look very pretty in this relish.

Combine all the ingredients in a large pot. Bring to a boil and simmer for 20 minutes, stirring occasionally. Pack into hot sterilized jars and seal.

Makes 6 pints

6 **cups cored and chopped ripe tomatoes**
1 **cup finely chopped celery**
¼ **cup finely chopped onion**
¼ **cup finely chopped red bell pepper**
¼ **cup finely chopped green bell pepper**
¼ **cup (scant) salt**
1 **cup sugar**
1 **tablespoon ground nutmeg**
1 **teaspoon ground cinnamon**
½ **teaspoon ground cloves**
1 **teaspoon dry mustard**
1 **pint cider vinegar**

FLOWER BASKET, Counted Cross Stitch

Beautiful flowers are a wonderful joy to
share with friends. In this Flower
Basket design we have gathered
some of our very best blooms.

12

DESSERTS

CAKES

Banana Cake
Applesauce Cake
Blueberry Cake
Blueberry Tea Cakes
Carrot Cake
Coconut Layer Cake
Dottie Kreider's Date and Nut Cake
Gold Cake Extraordinary
Prune Cake
Dottie Kreider's Strawberry-Glazed Cheese Cake
Lemon Chiffon Cake
Mother's Yellow Caramel Cake
Nectarine or Pineapple Upside-Down Cake
Oatmeal Cake
Peach Upside-Down Cake
Sauerkraut Cake
Pumpkin Cake
Swedish Crumb Cake
Rich Walnut Cake
White Cake
Yellow Cake with Chocolate Cream Filling
Gingerbread
Tea Cake with Spring Flowers
Chocolate Cake

COOKIES

Jennifer's Peanut Butter Incredibles
Crunchy Cookies
Dorothy's Oatmeal Cookies

ICE CREAM

Peach Ice Cream
Vanilla Ice Cream
Lemon-Orange Ice

PIES

Betty's Lemon Chiffon Pie
Blueberry Crumb Pie
Banana Cream Pie
Apple Pie
Fresh Strawberry Pie
Boston Cream Pie
Caramel Pie
Charles-Louis's Blueberry Cheese Pie
Cherry Pie
Cherry Cream Pie
Chocolate Cream Pie
Coconut Molasses Custard Pie
Funny Pie
Erma's Grape Pie
Hot Mince Pie
Kitty Schroeder's Rhubard Custard Pie
Mary's Coconut Custard Pie
Peach Glaze Pie
Ruth Clark's Amish Vanilla Pie
Shoofly Pie
Rhubarb Sponge Pie
Coconut Custard Pie

PUDDINGS

Vanilla Pudding
Blueberry Pudding
Chocolate Pudding
Cottage Pudding
Cracker Pudding
Dottie Hess's Banana Pudding
Rice Pudding
Tapioca Pudding with Pineapples

MISCELLANEOUS

Apple Brown Betty
Apple Dumplings
Apple or Dandelion Fritters
Broiled Pear Halves with Chocolate and Brandy
Baked Apples with Apple Snow
Basic Dessert Crepe Recipe
Apple Pan Dowdy
Basic Pie Crumb Topping
Basic Pie Dough
Thelma's Foolproof Pie Crust
Blueberries in Sour Cream
Blueberry Torte
Cream Puffs
Curried Fruit
Flambéed Strawberry Soufflé Crepes
Canned Apricots
Fresh Cranberry Crunch
Dottie's Glazed Oranges
Glaze for Fresh Fruit
Fresh Peach Cobbler
Fried Apple Turnovers
Meringue-Nut Kisses
Mim Good's Homemade Yogurt
Mim's Sesame Candy
Turtle Dessert
Peach Dumplings with Chocolate Surprise
Mim's Yogurt Sherbet
Whoopie Pies
Vanilla Soufflé

FROSTINGS

Boiled Frosting
Broiled Icing
Butter Frosting
Chocolate Cream Frosting
Confectioners' Sugar Icing
Cream Cheese Frosting
Thin Chocolate Frosting

BANANA CAKE

This is a very moist cake. It may be frosted with a cream cheese frosting* or powdered with sugar.

In a large bowl cream the sugar, egg yolks, and butter till frothy. In another bowl add the vinegar to the milk. Sift together the flour and cream of tartar in a third bowl. Beat the egg whites until stiff. Moisten baking soda with water and add to egg yolk mixture. Add milk and flour alternately until well blended. Fold in the beaten egg whites and mashed bananas until well blended. Pour into a greased 9½″ x 13″ cake pan. Bake in a preheated 350° F. oven for approximately 50 minutes or until cake pulls away from sides of pan.

MICROWAVE: Pour into a greased microwave Bundt pan and microwave on high 10 minutes.

Serves 12

* *See under recipe for Carrot Cake.*

2	cups granulated sugar
5	eggs, separated
1	cup butter
1	teaspoon vinegar
1	cup milk
4	cups unsifted flour
1	teaspoons cream of tartar
1	teaspoon baking soda
2	tablespoons water
1	cup mashed ripe bananas

APPLESAUCE CAKE

This moist cake needs no icing, just powdered sugar on top. For a special look, put a paper doily over the cake and sprinkle the powdered sugar through it, to make a design.

In a bowl, cream the sugar and shortening until light and fluffy. Mix in the eggs, 1 at a time. In another bowl, sift the flour with the spices and salt. Beat into the creamed mixture. Next, beat in the dissolved baking soda. Fold in the raisins (or nuts and raisins), applesauce, and vanilla. Pour into 2 greased and floured 9″ x 13″ cake pans. Bake in a preheated 350° F. oven for 50 minutes.

MICROWAVE: Pour into a greased Bundt pan and bake for 12 minutes.

Makes 10–12 servings

- 1 cup granulated sugar
- ½ cup vegetable shortening
- 2 eggs
- 2 cups all-purpose flour
- 1 teaspoon powdered cloves
- ½ teaspoon ground nutmeg
- 1 teaspoon salt
- 1 teaspoon baking soda dissolved in 2 tablespoons hot water
- 1 cup raisins or ½ cup each raisins and coarsely chopped walnuts
- 1½ cups canned or homemade applesauce
- 1 teaspoon vanilla extract

BLUEBERRY CAKE

Sift the flour, baking powder, salt, and sugar in a large mixing bowl. Gradually add the butter, milk, vanilla, lemon juice, and half the grated lemon rind. Beat until smooth. Add the eggs and beat until mixed. Pour the batter into a greased 11" x 13" cake pan. In a small bowl, toss the blueberries, the sugar, and the remaining lemon rind together until blended. Sprinkle over the batter. Bake in a preheated 350° F. oven for 50 minutes until golden brown. Serve warm with whipped cream or ice cream.

MICROWAVE: Sprinkle some of the blueberries and sugar in the bottom of a greased microwave Bundt pan, pour in batter, and place remaining blueberries in the batter. Microwave on high for 12 minutes.

Makes 1 cake, 11" x 13"

- 2 cups sifted flour
- 2½ teaspoons baking powder
- ¾ teaspoon salt
- 1 cup granulated sugar
- ⅓ cup soft butter
- ¾ cup milk
- 1 teaspoon vanilla extract
- Juice of ½ lemon
- Grated rind of 1 lemon
- 2 eggs
- 1½ cups blueberries
- 5 tablespoons sugar
- Whipped cream (optional)
- Ice Cream (optional)

BLUEBERRY TEA CAKES

Mary Davis of York, Pennsylvania, gave me this recipe because of the joke about the ton of blueberries. An excellent recipe.

Sift together the flour, baking powder, and salt. In another bowl, cream the butter and sugar together until fluffy, then add the egg. Gradually add in the milk and beat until smooth. Slowly add the flour mixture, continuing to beat until smooth. Fold in the blueberries. Pour batter into cupcake tins. If you are not using paper cupcake liners, first grease the tins. Sprinkle a small amount of the Crumb Topping on each cupcake. Bake in a preheated 375° F. oven for 40–45 minutes until cupcakes pull away from the sides of the pan.

Makes 24 cupcakes

2 cups sifted flour
2 teaspoons baking powder
½ teaspoon salt
¼ cup butter
¾ cup granulated sugar
1 egg
½ cup milk
2 cups blueberries

CRUMB TOPPING
½ cup granulated sugar
¼ cup flour
½ teaspoon cinnamon
¼ cup butter

CARROT CAKE

It is hard to realize there are carrots in this cake, since it tastes so much like a spice cake. It is excellent topped with a cream cheese frosting. As an alternative, use a broiled icing.

Sift the flour, baking soda, sugar, salt, and cinnamon into a bowl. Beat in the eggs and oil, then fold in the carrots and, if included, the nuts or raisins. Pour into a greased and floured 9″ x 13″ oblong cake pan. Bake in a preheated 350° F. oven for 50 minutes. Remove the cake from the pan and cool on a wire cake rack. While the cake is cooling, beat all frosting ingredients together until satin-smooth. Frost the cake after it has cooled.

NOTE: This frosting is delicious also on spice cake or gingerbread.

MICROWAVE: Pour into a greased microwave Bundt pan and microwave for 10 minutes.

Makes 8 servings

2 cups all-purpose flour
1 teaspoon baking soda
2 cups granulated sugar
1 teaspoon salt
¼ teaspoon ground cinnamon
4 eggs
1½ cups salad oil
3 cups grated carrots
½ cup chopped walnuts or whole raisins (optional)

CREAM CHEESE FROSTING

3 ounces cream cheese
6 tablespoons butter
1 cup confectioners' sugar
1 teaspoon vanilla extract

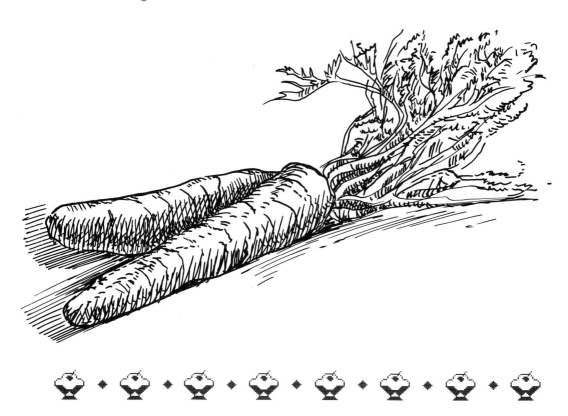

COCONUT LAYER CAKE

In a mixing bowl, cream the butter and shortening. Gradually add in the sugar, beating until very light. Add the egg yolks, 1 by 1, beating well after each addition. In another bowl, sift the flour, baking powder, and salt together. Add this and the milk alternately to the egg mixture. Beat until smooth, then add the vanilla. In a medium bowl, beat the egg whites until stiff. Fold into the batter. Pour the batter into 2 greased and floured 9″ layer cake pans. Bake in a preheated 350° F. oven for approximately 30 minutes until a wooden toothpick inserted in the cake comes out clean. Remove cakes from pans and cool on racks. Put layers together with coconut. Frost the top and sides of the cake with boiled frosting. Press coconut on the frosted cake.

2 (9″) layer pans

⅓ cup butter
⅓ cup vegetable shortening
1 cup granulated sugar
3 egg yolks
2 cups sifted cake flour
2¼ teaspoons baking powder
½ teaspoon salt
⅔ cup milk
1 teaspoon vanilla extract
3 egg whites, stiffly beaten
Boiled Frosting (see Index)
1½ cups shredded coconut

DOTTIE KREIDER'S DATE AND NUT CAKE

Mix dates, boiling water, and baking soda in a medium bowl and set aside.

Cream the eggs, shortening, and sugar in a large mixing bowl until fluffy. Gradually add the flour, salt, and vanilla. Fold in the chopped nuts. Mix in the dates until well blended. Pour into a greased 9″ x 13″ pan. Bake in a preheated 350° F. oven for 45 minutes.

2	cups pitted and chopped dates
2	cups boiling water
2	teaspoons baking soda
2	eggs
4	tablespoons vegetable shortening
2	cups sugar
3	cups flour
½	teaspoon salt
1	teaspoon vanilla extract
1½	cups chopped nuts

BUTTER FROSTING

3	tablespoons butter
1	tablespoon cream
1½	cups confectioners' sugar
½	teaspoon vanilla extract

Cream the butter in a small bowl until soft. Add the cream, sugar, and vanilla. Beat until smooth and creamy. Spread on the cake.

1 cake, 9″ x 13″

GOLD CAKE, EXTRAORDINARY

Cream the sugar and butter in a large mixing bowl until fluffy. Add the egg yolks 1 at a time, mixing until well blended. In a separate bowl, sift the flour, baking powder, and salt. Add to the sugar-butter mixture alternately with the water. Whip the egg whites into soft peaks and fold them and the vanilla into the batter. Pour the batter into greased layer pans or into a 9″ x 13″ pan. Bake in a preheated 350° F. oven for 40 minutes for layer pans, 50 minutes for 1 large pan. The cake should spring back when lightly touched, and pull away from the sides of pan.

This cake may be used in many ways: for Boston Cream Pie, Upside-Down Cake, Etc.

Makes 2 layers or cake 9″ x 13″

1½ cups granulated sugar
½ cup butter
3 egg yolks
2½ cups cake flour
2 teaspoons baking powder
1 teaspoon salt
¾ cup water
3 egg whites
1 teaspoon vanilla extract

PRUNE CAKE

Prune Cake and Applesauce Cake make very good desserts. They are moist, heavy cakes, unlike light and fluffy cakes such as Lemon Chiffon.

Blend the sugar and oil. Beat in the eggs, 1 at a time. Mix well, then add the vanilla. In a bowl, sift the flour, baking soda, spices, and salt together. Beat into the sugar-oil-egg mixture a little at a time, alternately with the buttermilk. Blend well, then fold in the prunes. Pour the batter into a well greased and floured loaf cake pan, or into 2 (8″) cake pans. Bake in a preheated 350° F. oven for approximately 1 hour.

Makes 10 servings

1½ cups granulated sugar
1 cup salad oil
3 eggs
1 teaspoon vanilla extract
2 cups all-purpose flour
1 teaspoon baking soda
1 teaspoon ground cinnamon
1 teaspoon ground allspice
¼ teaspoon salt
1 cup buttermilk
1 cup chopped prunes

DOTTIE KREIDER'S STRAWBERRY-GLAZED CHEESECAKE

Thoroughly mix all ingredients in a mixing bowl by hand or with a pastry blender. Press on the bottom and sides of 9″ springform pan.

Combine beaten eggs, cream cheese, sugar, salt, and almond extract in a large bowl. Beat until smooth. Blend in the sour cream. Pour into crust in the springform pan and bake in a preheated 375° F. oven for 35 minutes, or until set. Chill 4–5 hours.

Mix the sugar, cornstarch, and water in a saucepan until smooth. Bring to a boil. Simmer for 3 minutes. Color with food coloring. Remove from the heat. When cool add the strawberries and spread on the cheesecake. Chill for 1 hour. Serve.

Other fruit may be substituted for the strawberries, such as blueberries or pineapples (using the pineapple juice instead of the water).

CRUST
1¾ cups graham cracker crumbs
¼ cup finely chopped English walnuts
½ teaspoon ground cinnamon
½ cup melted butter

FILLING
3 eggs, well beaten
16 ounces cream cheese, at room temperature
1 cup granulated sugar
¼ teaspoon salt
1 teaspoon almond extract
3 cups sour cream

GLAZE
¾ cup cold water
½ cup granulated sugar
2 tablespoons cornstarch
◆ Few drops red food coloring
1 pint fresh strawberries, cleaned and stemmed

LEMON CHIFFON CAKE

There is a funny story to this cake. In Good Earth and Country Cooking, *I talked about winning a baking contest at 13 with my lemon chiffon cake—and then forgot to include the recipe in the book. Since the book was published, many people have asked for the recipe. It is hard to believe that there is no lemon juice in this cake, because it is so lemony. However, I use only the zest, the yellow part of the rind.*

Sift the flour, sugar, baking powder, and salt into a large mixing bowl. Make a well in the center of the dry ingredients with a wooden spoon. Add, in the following order, the oil, egg yolks, water, vanilla, and lemon zest. Stir with spoon until the batter is smooth. In another bowl, beat the egg whites with the cream of tartar until stiff peaks form. Pour the batter over the egg whites in a gentle stream, then fold in very gently with a rubber spatula. Pour the batter into a footed 10″ tube pan 4″ deep. Take a table knife and, starting in the center, around the tube, cut several circles in the batter around the pan until you reach the outer edge. This takes out the air bubbles, and prevents holes in the finished cake.

Bake the cake in a preheated 375° F. oven for 55 minutes, then lower the heat to 350° and bake for 12 minutes longer. Turn the cake pan upside down to cool, but do not remove the cake from the pan for at least 1 hour. When cool, dust the top of the cake with confectioners' sugar.

NOTE: An easy way to cool a cake baked in a tube pan is to turn the pan upside down and insert the neck of a catsup bottle into the center tube.

MICROWAVE: Bake on high 10 minutes in microwave Bundt pan.

Makes 12 servings

2¼ cups sifted cake flour
1½ cups granulated sugar
3 teaspoons baking powder
1 teaspoon salt
½ cup salad oil
6 eggs, separated
⅔ cup cold water
2 teaspoons vanilla extract
Grated zest (yellow part only) of 1 lemon
½ teaspoon cream of tartar
Confectioners' sugar to dust cake

MOTHER'S YELLOW CARAMEL CAKE

Cream the sugar and butter in mixing bowl until fluffy. Add the egg yolks and mix well. In another bowl, sift flour, baking powder, and salt. Add flour mixture and water alternately to the sugar and butter mixture. Add the vanilla. Slowly pour the caramel syrup into the cake batter while mixing with slotted spoon. Fold in the stiffly beaten egg whites and mix gently. Batter should be light and fluffy, with crystals of caramel. Pour the batter into 2 greased and floured layer cake pans, or into 1 (9" x 13") cake pan and bake in a preheated 350° F. oven for 40 minutes for 1 large pan, or for 35 minutes for layer pans, until the cake pulls away from the side of the pan.

In a small saucepan, boil the sugar and water approximately 7 minutes until it turns dark brown. Remove from heat, but keep warm, so it will not crystallize before being poured into the cake batter.

MICROWAVE: Pour batter into a greased microwave Bundt pan and microwave on high for approximately 10 minutes.

Makes 1 (9" x 13") cake

1½ cups granulated sugar
½ cup butter
3 egg yolks
2½ cups unsifted flour
2 teaspoons baking powder
1 teaspoon salt
¾ cup water
1 teaspoon vanilla extract
¼ cup Caramel Syrup
3 egg whites, stiffly beaten

CARAMEL SYRUP
½ cup granulated sugar
⅓ cup water

NECTARINE OR PINEAPPLE UPSIDE-DOWN CAKE

Melt the butter in a heavy 10″ skillet or baking pan. Sprinkle with brown sugar. Place nectarine halves with nuts in centers, cut side up, on top of the sugar. Set aside.

Mix the Cake Batter: In a large bowl, cream the eggs and sugar until fluffy. Gradually add the milk (pineapple juice may be substituted for milk) and lemon flavoring. In a medium bowl, sift the flour, baking powder, and salt together. Add to the egg mixture and blend until smooth. Pour over the fruit. Bake in a preheated 350° F. oven for 45–50 minutes until wooden toothpick inserted in the cake comes out clean. Remove from oven and turn upside down on serving dish immediately, to let syrup run around the sides of the cake. Allow pan to remain on top of cake for a few minutes. Serve warm, with whipped or pouring cream.

MICROWAVE: Microwave on high for 12 minutes, turning just ¼ turn every 3 minutes. Test and let stand 10 minutes before inverting on a serving platter. Insert wooden toothpick into center of cake. When it comes out clean, it's done.

⅓ cup butter
½ cup light brown sugar
7 or 8 nectarine halves or 6 canned pineapple slices
Nuts for the center of each nectarine half

CAKE BATTER

2 eggs, beaten
⅔ cup granulated sugar
⅓ cup milk
1 teaspoon lemon flavoring
1 cup cake flour
⅓ teaspoon baking powder
⅓ teaspoon salt
Whipped or pouring cream (optional)

OATMEAL CAKE

Pour boiling water over the oatmeal and let it stand at least 5 minutes. In a large mixing bowl, cream the shortening, brown sugar, and granulated sugar. Add 1 egg at a time, beating well after each addition. Stir in the oatmeal. Beat well. Sift flour, soda, cinnamon, nutmeg, and salt together, and add to creamed oatmeal mixture. Add vanilla and beat until well blended. Pour batter into a greased and floured 9″ x 13″ cake pan. Bake in a preheated 350° F. oven for 50–55 minutes, or until a toothpick comes out clean. Frost with Broiled Icing.

1¼ cups boiling water
1 cup unprepared Quaker oatmeal
4 tablespoons shortening or margarine
1 cup light brown sugar
1 cup granulated sugar
2 eggs
1½ cups all-purpose flour
1 teaspoon baking soda
¾ teaspoon ground cinnamon
¼ teaspoon ground nutmeg
½ teaspoon salt
1 teaspoon vanilla extract

BROILED ICING

4 tablespoons melted butter
5 tablespoons evaporated milk
⅔ cup light brown sugar, packed
½ cup coconut (medium shred)

In a small mixing bowl, combine all ingredients. Spread on the warm cake. Do not remove the cake from the pan. Place the cake on the medium rack of the oven. Broil approximately 6 minutes until it bubbles and is golden brown.

Makes 1 cake, 9″ x 13″

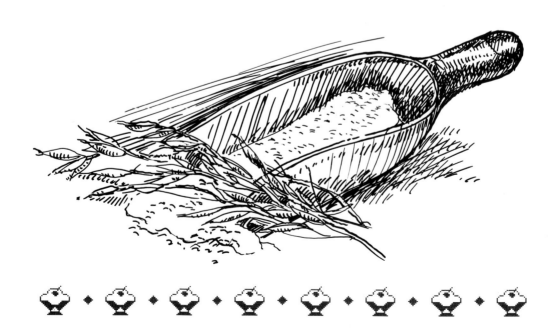

PEACH UPSIDE-DOWN CAKE

Melt the butter and spread evenly around the sides and bottom of an 11″ x 13½″ cake pan. Sprinkle the brown sugar all over the butter. Peel the peaches and cut in half. To each peach cavity add ¼ slice lemon or cherry and place upside down in the sugar.

Beat the egg whites until fluffy. Gradually add ½ cup of the sugar and beat until the eggs hold firm peaks. In another bowl, cream the butter and add the remaining ½ cup sugar, beating until light. Combine and sift the flour, salt, and baking powder. Beat these dry ingredients and the milk alternately into the butter-sugar mixture, beating well after each addition. Fold in the egg whites and the vanilla. Pour the batter over the peaches, and bake in a preheated 350° F. oven for 60 minutes. Remove and cool for 10 minutes. Take a knife blade around sides of the cake to loosen and reverse it onto a serving tray.

MICROWAVE: Microwave on high for 15 minutes, turning ¼ turn every 3 or 4 minutes. Test cake. Let stand 10 minutes before inverting on a serving platter.

Makes 1 cake, 11″ x 13½″

4 tablespoons melted butter
½ cup light brown sugar
8 peaches
4 slices lemon or 4 maraschino cherries

CAKE
4 egg whites
1 cup granulated sugar
⅓ cup butter or vegetable shortening
1¾ cups cake flour
¼ teaspoon salt
1 tablespoon baking powder
½ cup milk
½ teaspoon vanilla extract

SAUERKRAUT CAKE

This is one of those surprise cakes that really throw people. It is really a chocolate cake, but the sauerkraut just dissolves and makes it something special.

Cream the margarine and sugar until light and lemon-colored. Beat in the eggs, 1 at a time, then add the vanilla. Sift the cocoa, flour, baking powder, baking soda, and salt together and beat into the creamed mixture alternately with the water. Stir in the sauerkraut. Pour into 2 greased and floured 8″ cake pans. Bake in a preheated 350° F. oven for 30 minutes.

NOTE: This can be made into cupcakes. Bake 15 minutes.

MICROWAVE: Pour into a greased microwave Bundt pan and microwave for approximately 9 minutes. Test. Let stand for 10 minutes before inverting on a serving platter.

Makes 8 servings

⅔	cup margarine
1½	cups granulated sugar
3	eggs
1	teaspoon vanilla extract
½	cup cocoa
2¼	cups sifted cake flour
1	teaspoon baking powder
1	teaspoon baking soda
¼	teaspoon salt
1	cup water
⅔	cup sauerkraut, rinsed, drained, and chopped

PUMPKIN CAKE

Cream the sugar and shortening in a large mixing bowl. Add the eggs, blending until smooth. Slowly add the pumpkin and vanilla. In a separate bowl, sift the flour, soda, cloves, cinnamon, nutmeg and allspice. Gradually add the flour mixture to the pumpkin, stirring until well blended. Pour the batter into a greased 10″ tube pan. Bake in a preheated 350° F. oven for 50 minutes on the low rack of the oven until the cake pulls away from the side of the pan. Cool in pan. Frost, or sprinkle with powdered sugar.

MICROWAVE: Pour the batter into a greased microwave Bundt pan and microwave for 12 minutes. Let stand for 5 minutes before inverting on a serving platter.

Serves 12

3 cups granulated sugar
1 cup shortening
3 eggs
2 cups pumpkin pulp
1 teaspoon vanilla extract
3 cups all-purpose flour
1½ teaspoon baking soda
1 teaspoon powdered cloves
1 teaspoon ground cinnamon
1 teaspoon ground nutmeg
1 teaspoon ground allspice
Frosting (see Index) or powdered sugar (optional)

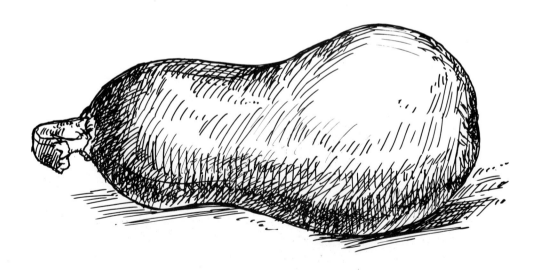

SWEDISH CRUMB CAKE

In a heavy 1-quart saucepan, soak the apricots in the water for 1 hour. Add the sugar and bring to a boil. Simmer for approximately 15 minutes until the apricots are very soft. In a large bowl, combine the flour, oatmeal, brown sugar, shortening, soda, and salt and cut with pastry blender or by hand until well mixed. Spread ½ the crumbs in a greased 9″ x 13″ cake pan. Pour in the apricot mixture. Top with the remaining crumbs. Bake in a preheated 350° F. oven for 30 minutes. Serve warm or cold with whipped cream or ice cream.

MICROWAVE: Spread ½ the crumbs in a greased microwave Bundt pan; pour in the apricot mixture. Top with remaining crumbs and bake for 7 minutes. Test. Let stand 10 minutes before inverting on a serving platter.

9″ x 13″ cake pan

- 1 cup dried apricots
- 1 cup hot water
- 1 cup granulated sugar
- 2 cups all-purpose flour
- 1½ cups uncooked oatmeal
- 1 cup light brown sugar
- ½ cup butter
- ¼ cup margarine
- 1 teaspoon soda
- ¼ teaspoon salt

Whipped cream or ice cream (optional)

RICH WALNUT CAKE

Cream butter and sugar in mixing bowl until fluffy. Gradually beat in the eggs. Sift together the sifted flour, baking powder, and salt. Stir in the flour mixture alternately with milk and vanilla until well blended. Fold in the nuts and pour into greased and floured tube pan. Bake in a preheated 350° F. oven for approximately 60 minutes until it springs back when touched lightly.

1 cup butter
2 cups granulated sugar
3 eggs (⅔ cup)
3 cups plus 2 tablespoons sifted cake flour
2½ teaspoons baking powder
1¼ cups milk
1 teaspoon vanilla extract
1½ cups coarsely cut English walnuts
Greased and floured 10″ tube pan

WHITE CAKE

In a large mixing bowl, cream the sugar, butter, and shortening until fluffy. In another bowl, sift together the flour, baking powder, and salt. Stir the flour alternately with the milk, water, vanilla, and lemon extract into the sugar mixture. Fold in the stiffly beaten egg whites. Pour the batter into 2 greased and floured 9″ layer pans. Bake in a preheated 350° F. oven for 35 minutes until it pulls away from sides of pans. Cool and frost with favorite frosting, or with boiled frosting (see Index).

2 (9″) layers

2 cups granulated sugar
½ cup butter
½ cup vegetable shortening
3¼ cups cake flour, sifted
4¼ teaspoons baking powder
1 teaspoon salt
1 cup milk
⅓ cup water
1 teaspoon vanilla extract
1 teaspoon lemon extract
6 egg whites (¾ cup), stiffly beaten

YELLOW CAKE WITH CHOCOLATE CREAM FILLING

In a large mixing bowl, cream the sugar and butter or shortening until light and fluffy. Add the beaten egg yolks and beat well. In another bowl, sift together the flour, baking powder, and salt. Add to the sugar mixture alternately with milk, beating until the batter is smooth. Add the lemon extract and mix well. Pour batter into 2 greased and floured 9″ layer pans. Bake in a preheated 350° F. oven for 30 minutes until the cake pulls away from the sides of the pan. Cool. Put Chocolate Cream Filling between layers and frost.

Combine the sugar, cornstarch, salt, and cocoa in the top of double boiler. Slowly add the hot water, stirring until smooth. Gradually add the milk and egg. Place over boiling water and cook approximately 8 minutes until the mixture thickens. Remove from heat and add the vanilla. Cool and put between layers of cake.

When cooling cream filling, place waxed paper or plastic wrap over top to prevent drying.

2 (9″) layer pans

1¼   cups granulated sugar
¾   cup butter or shortening
8   egg yolks, beaten until light
2½   cups sifted cake flour
4   teaspoons baking powder
½   teaspoon salt
¾   cup milk
½   teaspoon lemon extract
Chocolate Cream Filling
Boiled Frosting (see Index)

CHOCOLATE CREAM FILLING

⅓   cup granulated sugar
2   tablespoons cornstarch
◆   Pinch salt
2½   tablespoons cocoa
¼   cup hot water
1   cup milk
1   egg, beaten
1½   tablespoons butter
½   teaspoon vanilla extract

GINGERBREAD

In a large mixing bowl, cream the butter, shortening, and brown sugar. Gradually add the eggs and thick milk. In a smaller bowl combine the salt, soda, cinnamon, ginger, nutmeg, and flour. Gradually add the flour mixture and the molasses, alternately, to the egg mixture. Blend well. Pour this batter into a greased and floured 9″ x 13″ baking pan. Bake in a preheated 350° F. oven for 1 hour. Serve with Lemon Rum Sauce or whipped cream.

Serves 12

⅜ cup butter
⅜ cup vegetable shortening
2 cups light brown sugar
3 eggs
1 cup thick milk or butter-milk (add 1 tablespoon lemon juice to milk to make it thick and let stand 5 minutes)
1 teaspoon salt
1 teaspoon baking soda
1 teaspoon ground cinnamon
1 teaspoon ground ginger
1 teaspoon ground nutmeg
3¾ cups flour
¾ cup molasses
Lemon Rum Sauce (see Index)
Whipped cream (optional)

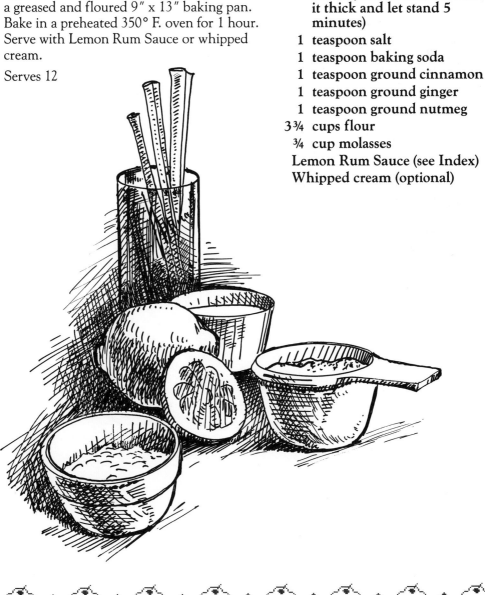

TEA CAKE WITH SPRING FLOWERS

In a large mixing bowl, cream the eggs and sugar until fluffy. In a separate bowl, sift the flour, baking powder, and salt. In a pan, heat the milk and add the butter. When butter has melted, add this and the flour alternately to the creamed egg-sugar mixture. Mix until blended. Do not overbeat. Add the vanilla. Pour into well greased baking pans lined with waxed paper. The batter should be only ½″ deep to make tiny pieces. Bake in a preheated 350° F. oven for approximately 20–25 minutes until it springs back when lightly touched. Remove waxed paper when cake has cooled. Place cake on a large tray and frost with White Icing. After frosting, take a sharp knife and cut in squares or finger-size rectangles before decorating. Decorate with icing flowers, using fresh spring colors. You can use fresh violets or other small flowers instead.

2 (9″ x 13″) cake pans or 1 large jelly roll pan

4 **eggs**
1½ **cups granulated sugar**
1½ **cups flour**
1 **teaspoon baking powder**
¼ **teaspoon salt**
⅔ **cup hot milk**
1½ **tablespoons butter**
1 **teaspoon vanilla extract**
White Icing (see Index)

CHOCOLATE CAKE

In a large mixing bowl, cream the sugar, butter, shortening, and eggs until light and fluffy. Add the sour milk or buttermilk and beat until well blended. In a separate bowl, sift together the salt, flour, soda, and cocoa. Add gradually to the egg mixture. Slowly add the water or coffee and the vanilla and beat well. Pour into a greased and floured 9″ x 13″ cake pan. Bake in a preheated 350° F. oven for 40 minutes until wooden toothpick inserted in the center comes out clean. Frost with your favorite frosting.

2 cups granulated sugar
⅓ cup butter
⅓ cup vegetable shortening
2 eggs
1 cup sour milk or buttermilk
1 teaspoon salt
2 cups cake flour
1 teaspoon baking soda
5 tablespoons cocoa
¾ cup hot water or hot coffee*
2 teaspoons vanilla extract

1 cake, 9″ x 13″

Coffee brings out the flavor in the chocolate, and I prefer it. You may use instant coffee if you wish.

JENNIFER'S PEANUT BUTTER INCREDIBLES

Melt margarine or butter and add peanut butter. Stir until smooth. Add sugar and cracker crumbs. Stir with a wooden spoon until well blended. Press crumbs into buttered jelly roll pan or on 9″ x 13″ baking pan. In the top of double boiler, melt the chocolate chips. Pour over the crumb mixture. Refrigerate until the chocolate is set. Remove and cut into bars. Do not store in the refrigerator, or white spots will develop on the chocolate. These bars freeze well, but should be eaten as soon as they thaw, to prevent this spotting.

Makes 36 bars

⅔ cup butter or margarine
1 cup peanut butter
2 cups confectioners' sugar
1½ cups fine graham cracker crumbs
12 ounces milk chocolate chips

CRUNCHY COOKIES

In a small bowl, combine flour, soda, and salt. Set aside. In a large bowl cream the butter and sugar. Gradually add the egg and vanilla. Stir in the flour mixture. Mix well and fold in Rice Krispies, chocolate bits, and nuts. Drop by tablespoons on lightly greased cookie sheets. Bake in a preheated oven at 350° F. for 12–15 minutes.

Makes 36–42 cookies

1¼ cup flour
½ teaspoon baking soda
¼ teaspoon salt
½ cup soft butter
1 cup granulated sugar
1 egg, slightly beaten
1 teaspoon vanilla extract
2 cups Rice Krispies
6 ounces (1 cup) chocolate bits
¼ cup each chopped pecans and almonds, mixed

DOROTHY'S OATMEAL COOKIES

In a large mixing bowl, combine the oatmeal, flour, raisins, nuts, cinnamon, and sugar. Gradually add the melted butter, stirring with a wooden spoon. Add the soda, milk, and eggs and stir until well blended. Form into small balls. Bake on cookie sheets in a preheated 350° F. oven for 10–15 minutes.

Makes about 48 cookies

3 cups uncooked oatmeal
2 cups flour
½ cup raisins
½ cup broken nuts
1 teaspoon ground cinnamon
2 cups granulated sugar
1 cup melted butter
1 teaspoon baking soda
5 tablespoons milk
2 eggs, slightly beaten

PEACH ICE CREAM

In a large mixing bowl, cream the eggs, sugar, and salt until fluffy. Stir in the evaporated milk, cream, milk, peaches, and flavorings. Pour this into the freezer can of a 4-quart ice cream freezer and cover with the lid. Pack with crushed ice and rock salt and turn until ice cream is hard. Using rock salt instead of table salt cuts the turning time. Add crushed ice as it melts, keeping ice right up to the top of the outside of the freezer. Take care that the salt does not get into the ice cream mixture inside the freezer can.

4-quart freezer

4 eggs
2⅔ cups granulated sugar
⅓ teaspoon salt
2 (13-ounce) cans evaporated milk
1½ cups heavy cream
1 cup milk
1½ cups crushed, fresh or canned peaches
1 tablespoon vanilla extract
1 teaspoon lemon flavoring

VANILLA ICE CREAM

In a large mixing bowl, cream the eggs, sugar, and salt until fluffy. Stir in the evaporated milk, cream, milk, and vanilla. Pour this into the freezer can of a 4-quart freezer and cover with the lid. Pack with crushed ice and rock salt and turn until ice cream is hard. Using rock salt instead of table salt cuts the turning time. Add crushed ice as it melts, keeping ice right up to the top of the outside of the freezer. Be careful that the salt does not seep into the ice cream mixture inside the freezer can.

4-quart freezer

4 eggs
2⅔ cups granulated sugar
⅓ teaspoon salt
2 (13-ounce) cans evaporated milk
1½ cups heavy cream
2½ cups milk
1½ tablespoons vanilla extract

LEMON-ORANGE ICE

Blend all the ingredients and pour into a cake pan, or into ice cube trays. Freeze until firm. Remove and serve in sherbet glasses.

Serves 6

1 cup concentrated frozen orange juice
¼ cup lemon juice
1 tablespoon grated orange zest
1 tablespoon grated lemon zest
1 pint 7-up
1 pint grapefruit soda or Tom Collins mix
♦ Several dashes grated nutmeg

BETTY'S LEMON CHIFFON PIE

This is a delightful light, refreshing dessert.

In the top of a double boiler, mix the egg yolks, ½ cup sugar, salt, and lemon juice. Place over boiling water and stir until thick, about 10 minutes. Put the gelatin in a small bowl with the water and stir until dissolved. Add the lemon zest. With a whisk, beat the gelatin mixture into the double boiler ingredients. Remove from heat and cool for 10 minutes. Beat the 3 egg whites with the cream of tartar until fluffy. Gradually beat in the 6 tablespoons sugar, beating until the mixture stands in stiff peaks. Fold into the lemon-egg mixture until well blended. Pour into the pie shell and refrigerate. Just before serving, garnish with thin slices of lemon or grated lemon zest.

VARIATION

Lime Chiffon Pie
Substitute limes for lemons. Add 1 or 2 drops green food coloring. Garnish top with sugared whole slices of lime.

Makes 6 servings

1 baked 9″ pie shell
3 eggs, separated
½ cup plus 6 tablespoons granulated sugar
½ teaspoon salt
¼ cup lemon juice
2 packages unflavored gelatin
1 cup water
2 tablespoons grated lemon zest (yellow part only)
¼ teaspoon cream of tartar
Thin slices of lemon or grated lemon rind for garnish

BLUEBERRY CRUMB PIE

Place pie shell in a preheated 350° F. oven for 10 minutes until the dough begins to puff. Remove and set aside. This will keep the dough from becoming soggy when baked.

In a large bowl, combine the sugar, flour, nutmeg, and butter. Stir in the blueberries and add the lemon juice. Pour into the pie shell and top with crumbs. Bake in a 375° F. oven for 10 minutes. Reduce heat to 350° and bake for 35 minutes until fruit bubbles around the edges of Crumb Topping.

Combine the flour, sugar, butter, and salt in a mixing bowl. Cut with a pastry cutter or with your hands until crumbs are fine. Put on top of fruit.

Makes 1 (9") pie

  1 **unbaked 9" pie shell**
  ⅞ **cup sugar**
  4 **tablespoons flour**
  ¼ **teaspoon grated nutmeg**
1½ **tablespoons softened butter**
  3 **cups blueberries**
  1 **teaspoon lemon juice**
     Crumbs for topping (see recipe below)

CRUMB TOPPING

¾ **cup flour**
¼ **cup granulated sugar**
¼ **cup butter**
◆ **Pinch salt**

BANANA CREAM PIE

In the top of a double boiler, combine the sugar, cornstarch, and salt. Gradually stir in 1½ cups of the milk. Place over boiling water, cooking approximately 12 minutes until thickened. Beat the egg yolks with the remaining ½ cup milk and add to the hot mixture, cooking 2 minutes longer. Remove from heat and stir in the butter and vanilla. Cool.

Arrange sliced bananas in the bottom of the pie shell and cover with the cream mixture. In a bowl, beat the egg whites and cream of tartar until they form soft peaks. Gradually add the sugar and salt and continue to whip until they form stiff peaks. Cover the cream with this meringue, making sure it covers the pie completely, or it will shrink during baking. Bake in a preheated 350° F. oven for 6 minutes until the peaks are a light golden brown. Serve cold or at room temperature.

Makes 1 (9") pie

- ⅔ **cup granulated sugar**
- 3 **tablespoons cornstarch**
- ¼ **teaspoon salt**
- 2 **cups milk**
- 3 **egg yolks**
- 1 **tablespoon butter**
- 1 **tablespoon vanilla extract**
- 1½ **cups sliced bananas**
- 1 **baked 9" pie shell**
- 3 **egg whites**
- ¼ **teaspoon cream of tartar**
- 5 **tablespoons granulated sugar**
- ◆ **Dash salt**

APPLE PIE

Roll out ½ of the pastry and fit in a 9″ pie pan. Roll out the remaining dough. Use a knife or fork to make designs in the center to let steam escape. Set aside to use as top of pie.

Combine the sugar, flour, cinnamon, nutmeg, and salt in a bowl. Gradually add the light cream. Combine the sugar mixture with the sliced apples and put in the pie shell. Dot with butter. Moisten the edges of the crust. Top with the second crust and crimp the edges, making sure they are well sealed. Bake preheated in a 375° F. oven for 50 minutes. Serve warm or cold.

Makes 1 (9″) pie

Pastry for 2 (9″) pie crusts
- 3½ **cups peeled, cored, and sliced apples**
- ¾ **cup granulated sugar**
- 3 **tablespoons flour**
- ½ **teaspoon ground cinnamon**
- ◆ **Dash ground nutmeg**
- ¼ **teaspoon salt**
- ½ **cup light cream or milk**
- 2 **tablespoons butter**

FRESH STRAWBERRY PIE

Mix the cleaned strawberries with the glaze. Spoon into the baked pie shell. Chill for 30 minutes. When ready to serve, top with whipped cream or slice and place on a serving dish, then add whipped cream to each serving.

Makes 1 (9″) pie

- 3 **cups fresh strawberries, whole or sliced in half**
- 1 **baked 9″ pie shell**

Glaze for Fresh Fruit (see Index)

Whipped cream for topping

BOSTON CREAM PIE

Cream the sugar and shortening in large mixing bowl until fluffy. Gradually add the eggs and beat until well blended. In another bowl, sift the flour, baking powder, and salt together and add to the egg mixture alternately with milk. Add vanilla and blend. Pour into a greased 9″ pie pan and bake in a preheated 350° F. oven for approximately 30 minutes. When cooled, split and fill with Cream Filling. Top with favorite topping.

Serves 6–8 (1 [9″] pie pan)

CAKE

- ¾ cup sugar
- ⅓ cup soft shortening (half butter and half shortening)
- 2 eggs
- 1¼ cup sifted cake flour
- 1½ teaspoons baking powder
- ½ teaspoon salt
- ½ cup milk
- 1 teaspoon vanilla extract

CREAM FILLING

In the top of a double boiler, combine the sugar, cornstarch and salt. Gradually add milk, stirring until smooth. Add the eggs. Cook over boiling water for approximately 8 minutes, stirring constantly until thickened. Remove from heat and add vanilla. Place between the layers of the cake.

Top with thin chocolate frosting.

- ¼ cup granulated sugar
- 1½ tablespoons cornstarch
- ⅓ teaspoon salt
- ¾ cup milk
- 2 eggs, slightly beaten
- 1 teaspoon vanilla extract

CARAMEL PIE

In a 1½-quart heavy saucepan, melt the butter and add the sugar. Cook over medium heat till the sugar is medium brown. Add dissolved cornstarch, salt, and 1½ cups water. Cook over medium heat, stirring constantly until thickened. Beat egg yolks with a whisk. Take 1 cup of the thickened sauce and add to the beaten egg yolks. When blended, add egg mixture to the remaining sauce and cook 1 minute until thickened. Add vanilla. Cool. To keep caramel from becoming hard on top, cover with waxed paper until cool. Pour into baked pie shell. Pile meringue on top and bake in a preheated 375° F. oven approximately 7 minutes until golden tips appear on the meringue.

Combine egg whites and cream of tartar and beat until fluffy. Gradually add sugar and continue to beat until very stiff. Pile lightly on caramel filling.

Makes 1 (9″) pie

1	baked 9″ pie shell
1½	cups light brown sugar
½	cup butter
3	tablespoons cornstarch dissolved in ¼ cup water
½	teaspoon salt
1½	cups water
3	eggs, separated
1	teaspoon vanilla extract

MERINGUE

3	egg whites
¼	teaspoon cream of tartar
3	tablespoons granulated sugar

CHARLES-LOUIS'S BLUEBERRY CHEESE PIE

Of all our recipes, this has probably been requested the most frequently! Credit for the recipe goes to our son Charlie and his friend, Louis Graybill. Louis's ancestors were originally from Lancaster County. However, for several generations, the family has lived in Denver.

While Charlie attended the Culinary Institute, he would bring Louis home on weekend vacations. Since both were studying food preparation, they always came to the kitchen to help. Charlie and Louis suggested adding a little nutmeg to the cheese mixture and the filling in this recipe. This helps to bring out the blueberry flavor beautifully.

Beat ⅓ cup of the sugar and cream cheese until rich and smooth. Gradually mix in the milk. Add 2 dashes grated nutmeg. Mix until well blended. Whip the cream and fold into the mixture. Pour into the baked pie shell and refrigerate for at least 30 minutes, while making the topping.

Mix the arrowroot, water, remaining ⅓ cup sugar, lemon juice, and a dash of grated nutmeg in a 1-quart saucepan until smooth. Bring to a boil and cook until thickened. Add the blueberries and boil for 2 minutes. Cool. Pour over the cheese filling in the pie shell. Refrigerate for 1 hour. Serve plain or with whipped cream.

Makes 6 servings

⅔ cup granulated sugar
1 cup softened cream cheese
¼ cup milk
Grated nutmeg
1 cup heavy cream
1 baked 9″ pie shell
1½ tablespoons arrowroot
⅓ cup water
1 teaspoon lemon juice
1 cup blueberries

CHERRY PIE

In a 1½-quart saucepan, combine the sugar and arrowroot, gradually adding the water or cherry liquid to make a smooth paste. Bring to a boil over medium heat, stirring constantly, until slightly thickened. Remove from heat and add the lemon juice, cinnamon, and cherries. Pour into the unbaked pie shell and dot with butter, fluting the edges if you are using pastry cutouts. If using strips of dough, or a top, moisten the edges of the pie and place top on. Slit the top crust to allow the steam to escape. If using the strips, place about 1″ apart, forming a lattice, then flute the edges. Bake in a preheated 400° F. oven for 10 minutes, then reduce the heat to 350° for approximately 45 minutes until the juice begins to bubble through slits in crust, or over the edges of the fluting. Serve slightly warm, or at room temperature.

For Washington's birthday, use cutouts of hatchets to decorate the top of the pie.

1 (9″) pie

1 **cup granulated sugar**
3 **tablespoons arrowroot or cornstarch**
½ **cup cold water or cherry liquid from canned cherries**
1 **teaspoon lemon juice**
½ **teaspoon ground cinnamon**
2½ **cups pitted fresh or canned cherries**
1½ **tablespoons butter**
Pastry to line 1 (9″) pan, plus either a pie top or lattice strips of pie dough to cover top

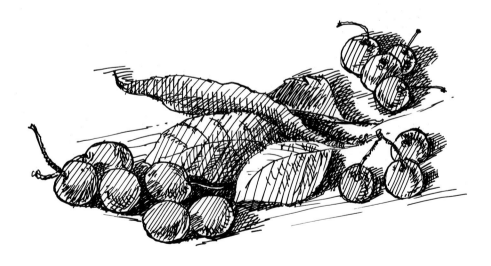

CHERRY CREAM PIE

In the top of a double boiler, combine the sugar, cornstarch, and salt. Gradually add the milk, stirring until smooth. Add the eggs and cook over boiling water for approximately 8 minutes, stirring constantly, until thickened. Remove from heat and add butter and vanilla. Cool. Pour into the baked pie shell. Cover with Cherry Pie Topping.

1 baked 9″ pie shell
⅓ cup granulated sugar
2 tablespoons cornstarch
⅓ teaspoon salt
1 cup milk
2 eggs, slightly beaten
1 tablespoon butter
½ teaspoon vanilla extract

CHERRY PIE TOPPING

½ cup granulated sugar
1½ tablespoons arrowroot or cornstarch
¼ cup water (when using canned cherries, use the cherry liquid and add 1 drop red food coloring)
½ teaspoon lemon juice
1½ cups pitted cherries

In a 1-quart saucepan, combine the sugar and arrowroot, gradually adding the water to make a smooth paste. Bring to a boil over medium heat, stirring constantly until slightly thickened. Add the lemon juice and cherries and cook for 5 minutes. Remove from heat and cool. When cool, pour over the cream mixture and chill for at least 30 minutes before serving.

This topping may be used for Boston Cream Pie or instead of blueberries for the torte recipe on page 274.

Makes 1 (9″) pie

CHOCOLATE CREAM PIE

Blend the sugar, flour, and salt in the top of a double boiler. Gradually add the milk and egg yolks. Place pan over hot water and cook over medium heat for 15 minutes. Add chocolate and cook about 10 minutes until thickened. Add vanilla. Fill the baked pie shell with the mixture and top with the meringue. Bake in a preheated 375° F. oven for 7 minutes until the meringue is golden brown. Serve cold.

Combine egg whites and cream of tartar and beat until fluffy. Gradually add sugar and beat until stiff. Pile lightly on chocolate mixture.

Makes 1 (9″) pie

1 cup granulated sugar
5 tablespoons flour
¼ teaspoon salt
2 cups milk
3 egg yolks, lightly beaten (save whites for meringue)
1½ squares unsweetened chocolate
½ teaspoon vanilla extract
1 baked 9″ pie shell

MERINGUE
3 egg whites, stiffly beaten
¼ teaspoon cream of tartar
3 tablespoons granulated sugar

COCONUT MOLASSES CUSTARD PIE

Mrs. Angus Douple, one of Abe's distant relatives, shared this recipe with me several years ago, and I use it frequently.

In a large bowl combine the sugar and flour. Add the beaten eggs. In a separate bowl mix the soda and the milk until the soda is dissolved. Add the milk mixture to the flour and eggs and blend well. Then add the molasses, sour cream, and coconut. Blend well and pour into 2 unbaked 9″ pie shells. Bake in a preheated 450° F. oven for 10 minutes. Reduce the heat to 350° and bake 30 minutes longer.

This recipe is recommended when you want 1 pie for serving and 1 for freezing. It reheats well in a microwave oven.

Makes 2 (9″) pies

½ cup light brown sugar
½ cup granulated sugar
2 tablespoons flour
2 eggs, slightly beaten
¼ teaspoon baking soda
½ cup sweet milk
1 cup molasses (old-fashioned barrel molasses or table molasses—not strong, black baking molasses)
1 cup sour cream
1 cup coconut
2 unbaked 9″ pie shells

FUNNY PIE

Sallie Harner, of Cincinnati, sent me this recipe for Funny Pie. It is a take-off on Shoofly Pie, with a chocolate rather than a molasses base. Sallie's family used to live in Bucks County. Funny Pie is as popular with the Pennsylvania Dutch in that area as Shoofly Pie is with us.

To make the bottom, stir the sugar, salt, and cocoa together in a saucepan. Slowly add the hot water and blend until smooth. Bring to a boil and simmer for 5 minutes. Remove from the heat and add the vanilla. Cool while preparing batter for topping.

Cream the butter and sugar in a mixing bowl. Beat in the eggs, 1 at a time. Sift the flour, salt, and baking powder into another bowl. Gradually beat into the butter-sugar-egg mixture, alternately with the milk, until smooth. Add the vanilla.

Pour the cooled liquid bottom mixture into the unbaked pie shells. Drop the batter evenly over it. Bake in a preheated 375° F. oven for 50–60 minutes until the filling is firm when the pan is moved.

Makes 2 (9″) pies

LIQUID BOTTOM MIXTURE

- 1 cup granulated sugar
- ½ teaspoon salt
- ½ cup cocoa
- ¾ cup hot water
- 1 teaspoon vanilla

BATTER FOR TOPPING

- ½ cup butter, at room temperature
- 2 cups granulated sugar
- 2 eggs
- 2 cups flour
- ½ teaspoon salt
- 2 teaspoons baking powder
- 1 cup milk
- ¾ teaspoon vanilla extract
- 2 unbaked 9″ pie shells

ERMA'S GRAPE PIE

A pie made with grapes may be unfamiliar to you, but it is a genuine taste treat! And Erma Engle's grape pie is the best I have tasted. It may appear to be tedious to pop the skins off the grapes and then to put them through a colander, but one bite will prove it was worth the effort! After all, time should not be important when preparing something special for someone you love! Soon after we moved to Mount Joy, when Erma invited us to her home, she served grape pie. Abe was very bashful in those days, but he blurted out, "Any woman who can bake a pie like this deserves a kiss." The very next week, Erma brought Abe a grape pie—and collected. It was probably the first kiss Erma ever received from a neighbor, and the blush on her face was something else!

2 cups Concord grapes
¾ cup granulated sugar
¼ cup water
1 tablespoon lemon juice
3 tablespoons cornstarch dissolved in ¼ cup water
1 tablespoon butter
Pastry for a 2-crust, 9" pie

Remove the pulp from the grape skins by popping the grapes with your fingers. This can only be done with "slipskin" grapes such as Concords. Pop the pulp directly into a 1-quart saucepan. Reserve the grape skins. Add the sugar and water to the pulp. Bring to a boil and boil for 1 minute. Strain the sweetened pulp through a fine colander to remove the seeds. Put the skins, the strained pulp, and the lemon juice into a saucepan and bring to a boil. Add the cornstarch dissolved in water and continue to cook, stirring constantly, until thickened. Add the butter.

Roll out enough of the pastry to line the bottom of a 9" pie pan. Pour the grape filling into the shell. Wet the edges of the dough and top with the remaining rolled-out pastry, placing it loosely over the top of the filling. Carefully crimp the edges of the pie. Prick the top crust with a fork or mark in a design with the point of a sharp knife. Bake in a preheated 350° F. oven for 50 minutes. This pie freezes well.

VARIATIONS

Use a crumb topping instead of a pastry topping. Use pink Catawba grapes instead of Concords.

Makes 6 servings

HOT MINCE PIE

Making a good mincemeat is so much work that it is a good idea to make enough at one time to last an entire season. It freezes or cans well, even in pie crust, but I prefer to make my pies fresh each time.

Cook the hamburger in a heavy skillet over medium heat, breaking it up with a wooden spoon, until all traces of pink have disappeared. The meat should be cooked through but not browned.

Grind the soaked dried apples coarsely in a meat grinder or food processor. Grind the lemons, peel and all. This may be done in a blender.

Combine the hamburger, ground fruit, and remaining ingredients in a heavy pot. Bring to a boil. Reduce the heat and simmer for 30 minutes, stirring to combine well. Ladle into sterilized quart jars and cool. Seal and freeze.

Divide pastry dough in half. Roll out 1 crust. Place in a 9″ pie pan. Fill crust with mincemeat and wine. Roll out the remaining dough and slit it, making a design, to let the steam escape. Moisten the edges of the pastry, then top with slit crust. Crimp the edges to seal. Bake in a preheated 350° F. oven for approximately 45 minutes until juice bubbles out of pierced holes in top. Serve hot.

Makes about 8 quarts

MINCEMEAT

- 5 pounds lean hamburger
- 2 quarts dried apples, soaked
- 5 pounds fresh apples, cored and peeled
- 4 lemons
- 1 pound raisins
- 1 pound currants, or raisins if currants are unavailable
- 1½ pounds light brown sugar
- 1 quart light table molasses
- 1 cup cider vinegar
- 3 cups strong-flavored wine
- 1 teaspoon ground cinnamon
- 1 teaspoon grated nutmeg
- 1 teaspoon ground cloves
- ½ teaspoon ground mace

TO MAKE A MINCE PIE

Pastry for 2 (9″) crusts
- 2½ cups mincemeat
- ½ cup wine or whiskey

KITTY SCHROEDER'S RHUBARB CUSTARD PIE

Kitty Schroeder and her husband, Murray, are two exceptionally nice people. Murray is a fun-loving man and I enjoy teasing him. When we first met, I took one look at him and said, "I bet your name is Charlie." He replied, "If that's what you want to call me, go ahead." That started it. It seemed that I could never remember his real name when we met, and Kitty went along with the joke. The Schroeders faithfully attended all my cooking demonstrations in this area. When Kitty heard I was writing another cookbook, she gave me this recipe. It's one of her favorites, and a lovely dessert for spring. Rhubarb is simple to clean: cut off the white at the bottom and the leafy tops, and if the rhubarb is rather old, pull off the strings. Use the inedible bottom parts and leaves for mulch in the garden. If you like rhubarb, you are sure to enjoy this recipe as much as we do.

Put the rhubarb in the unbaked pie shell. Heat the milk with the butter. In a bowl, cream ¾ cup of the sugar, the egg yolks, the salt, and the flour until fluffy. Pour the hot milk into the egg mixture, stir, and pour over the rhubarb. Bake in a preheated 450° F. oven for 10 minutes, then reduce the heat to 325° and bake 30 minutes longer. Remove, and cool pie.

While the pie is cooling, beat the egg whites with the cream of tartar until fluffy. Gradually beat in the 3 tablespoons sugar. Continue to beat until the egg whites stand in stiff peaks. Spread this meringue over the pie and sprinkle the top with a little sugar. Bake in a preheated 375° oven about 5 minutes until light golden brown, watching the meringue closely. When serving, slice with a knife dipped in hot water to keep the meringue from sticking to the blade.

NOTE: The sugar baked on top of the meringue makes it easier to cut.

Makes 6 servings

- 1¼ **cups finely cut raw rhubarb**
- 1 **unbaked 9″ pie shell**
- 1½ **cups milk**
- 2 **tablespoons butter**
- ¾ **cup plus 3 tablespoons sugar**
- 3 **eggs, separated**
- ¼ **teaspoon salt**
- 2 **tablespoons all-purpose flour**
- ¼ **teaspoon cream of tartar**

MARY'S COCONUT CUSTARD PIE

Combine sugar, egg yolks, coconut, flour, and melted butter in a large mixing bowl. Gradually add the milk and mix thoroughly. Gently fold in the stiffly beaten egg whites and pour into the 2 unbaked pie shells. Bake in a preheated 425° F oven for 15 minutes. Reduce heat to 350° and bake for 20 minutes longer.

Makes 2 (9") pies

2   cups granulated sugar
4   egg yolks
2   cups coconut (medium flake)
½   cup flour
1   tablespoon butter, melted
4   cups milk
4   egg whites, stiffly beaten
2   unbaked 9" pie shells

PEACH GLAZE PIE

Slice the peeled peaches and mix with the glaze. Spoon the peaches into the baked pie shell and allow to set a little. When ready to serve, top with whipped cream or cut and place on serving dishes. Then add a generous spoonful of whipped cream to each serving.

When using canned peaches, substitute peach juice for water for the glaze, and reduce the amout of sugar to a scant ¼ cup.

Makes 1 (9") pie.

1   baked pie shell
2½–3   cups sliced fresh peaches (depending on how high you want the pie)
Glaze for Fresh Fruit (see Index)
Whipped cream for topping

RUTH CLARK'S AMISH VANILLA PIE

In a 1-quart saucepan, combine the molasses, sugar, egg, and flour and mix well. Gradually add the hot water. Cook over medium heat until thickened, stirring constantly. Remove from heat and add the vanilla. Cool and pour into the unbaked pie shells. Top with Crumb Topping.

In a large bowl, mix all the ingredients with a pastry cutter or by hand. Combine until the crumbs are fine. Divide in half, using half on each pie. Bake in a preheated 375° F. oven for 10 minutes, then reduce heat to 350° and bake 30 minutes longer until the center of the pie is firm.

Makes 2 (9") pies

2　**unbaked 9" pie shells**

BOTTOM

1　**cup golden table molasses or barrel molasses (not baking molasses)**

½　**cup sugar**

1　**egg slightly beaten**

2　**tablespoons flour**

2　**cups hot water**

1　**teaspoon vanilla extract**

CRUMB TOPPING

1　**cup sugar**

½　**cup butter**

2　**cups flour**

½　**teaspoon baking soda**

½　**teaspoon cream of tartar**

SHOOFLY PIE

Combine the flour, brown sugar, and shortening in a bowl and cut with a pastry blender or rub together until it forms fine crumbs. While preparing the liquid, put the unbaked pie shell in a preheated oven at 350° F. for about 5 minutes. This prevents the bottom from getting soggy.

To make the liquid, dissolve the soda in the boiling water in a bowl. Add the molasses and salt and stir to blend well. Pour the liquid mixture into the prebaked pie shell, and sprinkle the crumb topping evenly on top. Bake in a preheated 375° F. oven for 10 minutes. Reduce the heat to 350° and bake 30 minutes longer until the center does not shake when it is moved.

Serve warm with whipped cream or ice cream, if desired.

These pies freeze very well.

Makes 1 (9″) pie

1 unbaked 9″ pie crust

CRUMB TOPPING
1 cup flour
½ cup light brown sugar
¼ cup vegetable shortening

LIQUID BOTTOM
1 teaspoon baking soda
1 cup boiling water
1 cup golden table molasses
¼ teaspoon salt
Whipped cream or ice cream (optional)

RHUBARB SPONGE PIE

Place the unbaked pie shell in a preheated 350° F. oven for 10 minutes until the dough begins to puff. Remove from oven and set aside. This prevents the crust from becoming soggy.

In a mixing bowl, cream the sugar and butter until fluffy. Add the flour and egg yolks and mix thoroughly, then gradually add the milk. Stir in the cut rhubarb. Whip the egg whites until stiff and fold into the rhubarb mixture. Pour into the pie shell. Bake in a preheated 450° F. oven for 10 minutes. Reduce heat to 350° and bake 30 minutes longer. Test with a wooden toothpick. When it comes out clean, the pie is ready.

Makes 1 (9″) pie

1 unbaked 9″ pie shell
1 cup granulated sugar
1 tablespoon butter
2 tablespoons flour
2 eggs, separated
1 cup milk
1 cup coarsely cut rhubarb

COCONUT CUSTARD PIE

Place unbaked shell in a preheated 350° F. oven for approximately 10 minutes until the dough begins to puff. Remove from oven and allow to cool while preparing the filling.

In a mixing bowl, cream the sugar and eggs until fluffy. Mix in the salt, milk, and coconut. Pour into the pie shell and bake in a 425° F. oven for 10 minutes. Reduce the heat to 375° and bake for 35 minutes longer until a knife blade comes out clean when inserted in the center of the pie.

Makes 1 (9″) pie

1 unbaked 9″ pie shell
¾ cup sugar
3 eggs
½ teaspoon salt
¾ cup milk
1 cup coconut (medium shred)

VANILLA PUDDING

Scald the milk in the top of a double boiler. In a bowl, combine the sugar, cornstarch, salt, and beaten eggs. Add to the hot milk. Cook over boiling water for approximately 5 minutes, stirring constantly, until thickened. Remove from heat. Add the butter and vanilla. Serve warm, or cold with fruit.

Serves 6

1 quart milk
1 cup granulated sugar
3 tablespoons cornstarch
½ teaspoon salt
4 eggs lightly beaten
1 tablespoon butter
1 teaspoon vanilla extract

BLUEBERRY PUDDING

This is Ann Risser's recipe. She served it when we visited her in Lancaster.

In a heavy saucepan, mix the sugar and flour. Gradually add the water, stirring until smooth. Add the lemon juice and blueberries. Bring to a boil and boil approximately 5 minutes until thickened. Pour blueberry mixture into a buttered 2-quart casserole or baking dish. Pour batter on top.

In a bowl, cream the sugar and butter. In a separate bowl, sift the flour, salt, and soda. Add the milk and the flour mixture alternately to the sugar and butter until well blended. Drop this batter by the tablespoon on top of the blueberry mixture. Do not mix. It may sink, but will rise again to the top and brown while baking. Bake in a preheated 350° F. oven for 60 minutes. Serve with whipped cream.

Serves 6–8

1 cup granulated sugar
3 tablespoons flour
1 cup water
2 teaspoons lemon juice
2 cups blueberries
Butter
Whipped cream

BATTER

½ cup granulated sugar
3 tablespoons butter
1 cup flour
¼ teaspoon salt
1 teaspoon baking soda
½ cup milk

CHOCOLATE PUDDING

This chocolate pudding was Dick and Martha Barrs' favorite.

Blend the cornstarch, sugar, and salt. Gradually add milk, stirring constantly. Melt the chocolate in the hot water and add it to the above mixture. Cook in top of 2-quart double boiler for approximately 10 minutes, stirring occasionally. Remove from the heat and beat with a wire whisk for approximately 2 minutes until light. Add the stiffly beaten egg whites and vanilla and fold until well blended. Pour into serving dish and cool. Serve chilled. Whipped cream may be used as a topping if desired.

NOTE: To keep pudding from becoming hard on top while cooling, cover with waxed paper immediately after pouring into serving dish.

Serves 6

3 tablespoons cornstarch
½ cup granulated sugar
¼ teaspoon salt
2 cups milk
1½ squares (1½ ounces) chocolate
3 tablespoons hot water
2 egg whites, stiffly beaten
1 teaspoon vanilla extract
Whipped cream (optional)

COTTAGE PUDDING

In a mixing bowl, combine the sugar, salt, flour, and baking powder. Add the egg and mix well. Gradually add the milk and vanilla. Beat until fluffy. Fold in the melted butter. Pour batter into greased cupcake tins or a small pie pan. Bake in a preheated 350° F. oven for 15 minutes. Serve with Chocolate Sauce or Vanilla Sauce (see Index). Best served warm.

This is very much like a moist cake.

Makes 4–6 servings

½ cup granulated sugar
¼ teaspoon salt
1 cup flour
2 teaspoons baking powder
1 egg
½ cup milk
½ teaspoon vanilla extract
3 tablespoons melted butter

CRACKER PUDDING

In a heavy 3-quart pot or Dutch oven, heat the milk almost to the boiling point. In a bowl, beat the egg yolks and sugar together until frothy and light. Gradually add to the hot milk. Reduce heat to medium. Crumble the crackers into the milk (1 package of crackers makes 2 cups). Stir constantly until the mixture comes to a boil. Add the coconut and stir until the pudding bubbles thickly like the Hot Springs of Arkansas. Remove from the heat and add the vanilla. Fold in the stiffly beaten egg whites. Serve warm or cold.

If you want to make this fancy, top with meringue and bake until golden brown.

Serves 6–8

1 quart milk
2 egg yolks
⅔ cup sugar
2 cups broken saltine crackers (not rolled into crumbs)
1 cup grated coconut (fine or medium shred)
1 teaspoon vanilla extract
2 egg whites, stiffly beaten

DOTTIE HESS'S BANANA PUDDING

Cook Vanilla Pudding as directed. Cool. Whip the cream and add sugar and vanilla. Slice 3 of the bananas and add to cool pudding. Fold in ⅔ of the whipped cream and ⅔ of the vanilla-wafer crumbs. Combine ingredients thoroughly. Pour into a chilled serving dish. When ready to serve, garnish with the remaining sliced banana and the rest of the whipped cream and crumbs.

Serves 6–8

Vanilla Pudding (see Index)
1 cup heavy cream, whipped
1 tablespoon granulated sugar
1 teaspoon vanilla extract
1 (12-ounce) box vanilla wafers, rolled into crumbs
4 large bananas

RICE PUDDING

Heat the milk until almost boiling in a medium pan. When a skin begins to form on top of the milk, stir in the rice, salt, and butter. Reduce heat to low and simmer 8 minutes, stirring occasionally to keep from sticking. Fold in sugar and beaten egg and simmer 1 minute more. Remove from heat and add vanilla. Stir until well blended. Cover with plastic wrap until ready to serve. Serve warm or cold.

VARIATION

You can add raisins, currants, or 1 tablespoon lemon juice before covering with wrap.

Makes 6 servings

3   cups milk
1½ cups Minute rice
½   teaspoon salt
2   tablespoons butter
3   tablespoons granulated sugar
1   egg, beaten
½   teaspoon vanilla extract
Raisins (optional)
Currants (optional)
1   tablespoon lemon juice (optional)

TAPIOCA PUDDING WITH PINEAPPLES

In a heavy 2-quart saucepan, combine the tapioca, sugar, egg yolks, salt, and milk. Bring to a boil over medium heat, stirring constantly. Boil for approximately 7 minutes. Remove from heat. In a bowl, beat the egg whites until fluffy and add the sugar, continuing to beat until soft peaks form. Fold into the tapioca. Stir in the vanilla. Cool for a few minutes. Serve warm or chilled, topped with drained pineapple chunks.

Serves 6

4   tablespoons Minute tapioca
4   tablespoons sugar
2   egg yolks, lightly beaten
¼   teaspoon salt
2½ cups milk
3   egg whites
3   tablespoons granulated sugar
1   teaspoon vanilla extract
1½ cups pineapple chunks, drained

APPLE BROWN BETTY

Place half the thinly sliced apples in a 9″ x 13″ buttered baking dish. In a bowl toss the bread cubes with the brown sugar, butter, and spices. Layer half of the bread mixture on top of apples. Follow with another layer of apples and the remaining bread-and-sugar mixture, saving enough apple slices to decorate the top of the baking dish. Sprinkle the hot water over the mixture. Bake in a preheated 375° F. oven for approximately 30 minutes until the top is golden brown. Serve hot with whipped cream, Apple Snow, or Lemon Sauce, if desired.

In the top of a double boiler, combine sugar, cornstarch, salt, and nutmeg until well blended. Slowly add the water and cook until mixture thickens, approximately 7 minutes. Add the butter and stir until melted. Remove from heat and add lemon juice and rind. Serve at room temperature.

Serves 8

- 4 cups peeled, cored, and thinly sliced apples
- 2 cups bread cubes
- ¾ cup light brown sugar
- 4 tablespoons butter
- ½ teaspoon ground cinnamon
- ¼ teaspoon ground nutmeg
- ¼ cup hot water
- Whipped cream (optional)
- Lemon Sauce (optional)
- Apple Snow (optional)

LEMON SAUCE

- 3 tablespoons sugar
- 1 tablespoon cornstarch or arrowroot
- ¼ teaspoon salt
- ¼ teaspoon ground nutmeg
- 1 cup boiling water
- 1 tablespoon butter
- 1 tablespoon lemon juice
- Grated rind of 1 lemon

APPLE DUMPLINGS

In a small bowl, combine the ½ cup sugar with 1 teaspoon of the cinnamon. Set aside. In another bowl, sift the flour, baking powder, and salt together. Cut in ⅔ cup of the butter with pastry blender or by hand until the crumbs are fine. While tossing the crumbs with one hand, gently pour the milk into the mixture with the other. Do not overwork—just toss until the dough sticks together. Separate the dough into 3 parts. Generously flour a pastry board before you start to roll out the dough. Roll the dough about ⅛″ thick. Cut the pastry into 7″ squares, or large enough to cover an apple. Peel and core the apples and place 1 on each square of dough. Fill the cavities with the cinnamon-sugar mixture. Wrap the dough around each apple by bringing opposite points of pastry up over the apple. Moisten each corner and press to seal. Place the dumplings at least 1 inch apart in a greased baking pan.

Combine the brown sugar, water, nutmeg, and remaining ⅛ teaspoon cinnamon in a 2-quart saucepan and bring to a boil. Simmer for 5 minutes. Remove from heat. Stir in the remaining ⅓ cup butter. When the butter has melted, pour this syrup over the dumplings. Bake in a preheated 350° F. oven for 60 minutes, basting occasionally with the syrup. Serve hot or warm with chilled cream, whipped cream, or ice cream, if desired.

Serves 6

6 medium baking apples, peeled and cored
½ cup granulated sugar
1⅛ teaspoons ground cinnamon
2¼ cups flour
2½ teaspoons baking powder
½ teaspoon salt
1 cup butter
½ cup milk
2 cups brown sugar
2 cups water
⅛ teaspoon ground nutmeg
Chilled pouring cream, whipped cream, or ice cream (optional)

APPLE OR DANDELION FRITTERS

Apple fritters may be used as a vegetable or served as a dessert. They are truly versatile! I like this recipe made with the apples cut in slices about ⅓" thick, dipped in the batter, and fried to a rich golden brown. We sprinkle confectioners' sugar on our fritters, but maple syrup is good, too. Another way to make this recipe is to cut the apples in tiny pieces and then mix them into the batter. In this version, the apple-batter mixture is dropped into the hot fat by the teaspoonful.

Abe's mother always used this same batter to fry dandelion flowers in the spring. Be sure to find dandelions which have not been sprayed, and snap off the flowers. Dip the flowers in the batter. The taste is similar to fresh oysters. Squash blossoms can also be used.

FRITTER BATTER

1½ cups all-purpose flour
2 teaspoons baking powder
1 teaspoon salt
2 tablespoons granulated sugar
2 eggs
⅔ cup milk, at room temperature
4 tart cooking apples, peeled, cored, and cut into ⅛" wedges, or ⅓" slices, or
Dandelion flowers, without stems
Oil for frying
Confectioners' sugar for topping

Mix the dry ingredients. Gradually mix in the eggs and stir in the milk to make a smooth, lump-free batter. Refrigerate, covered, for 20 minutes before using.

Pour oil into heavy skillet until it is 2 inches deep. Heat to 375° F.

Dip the apple pieces into the fritter batter and drop into the oil. Fry on both sides until golden brown. Remove and drain on paper towels before serving. Sprinkle with confectioners' sugar.

NOTE: Use the fritter batter also for other fruits, such as peach or apricot halves, chunks or fingers of pineapple, or thick slices of banana.

Makes 6 servings

BROILED PEAR HALVES WITH CHOCOLATE AND BRANDY

Put the pear halves in a 9″ baking pan and sprinkle with the brown sugar. Place in a chocolate kiss in each cavity and pour 1 tablespoon brandy over each pear. Place in the middle rack of the oven. Broil for approximately 12 minutes until the edges of the pears are golden.

When using fresh pears, increase the broiling time to 18 minutes.

Serves 6

6 canned Bartlett pear halves
3 tablespoons light brown sugar
6 chocolate kisses
6 tablespoons brandy

BAKED APPLES WITH APPLE SNOW

Peel and halve the apples, removing the core. Fill cavity of each half with brown sugar and 3 cinnamon candies. Arrange the apples in a pan large enough to hold them all. Pour the water around the apples. Add more water to cover the bottom of the pan, if necessary. Sprinkle the tapioca around the apples, allowing some to fall on the brown sugar. Sprinkle the remainder of the candies in the water. Bake in a preheated 350° F. oven for 45 minutes. Serve warm or cold, plain, or with whipped cream or Apple Snow.

Beat egg whites until fluffy. Gradually beat in the sugar. Grate the apple coarsely and add it gradually to the egg whites. Beat until it holds stiff peaks. This makes a fine substitute for whipped cream. It costs less and has fewer calories!

Serves 6

6 Golden Delicious or any other firm apples
6 tablespoons light brown sugar
About 40 cinnamon heart candies
1 tablespoon tapioca
½ cup water
Whipped cream (optional)

APPLE SNOW
2 egg whites
½ cup confectioners' sugar
½ apple, peeled and cored

BASIC DESSERT CREPE RECIPE

Combine all ingredients except salad oil in a large mixing bowl. Cover and refrigerate overnight or for several hours. When ready to make the crepes, season the crepe pan by adding the salad oil and heating the pan until it smokes. Remove pan from heat and sprinkle with salt. Wipe out and pan is ready to use. Pour ¼ cup of the batter into the heated pan. Cook over medium heat and turn when light or very pale brown, depending on the use planned for the crepes.

Serve with lemon juice and powdered sugar, or dribble with honey, rolling crepes up as you make them. Or use any of your favorite jellies or jams as a filling.

Makes 12–14 crepes

1 cup flour, sifted
3 whole eggs
2 tablespoons granulated sugar
½ teaspoon salt
½ cup beer
¾ cup milk
¼ cup water
2 tablespoons melted butter
½ teaspoon lemon extract
1 tablespoon salad oil
Serving fillers (all optional)
Lemon juice and powdered sugar
Honey
Jam or jelly, in your favorite flavor

APPLE PAN DOWDY

Place apples in a buttered 9″ x 13″ baking pan. In a small bowl, blend the molasses, water, butter, spices, and salt. Pour over the apples. Cover with pastry. Cut designs in the pastry to let steam escape and to prevent from bubbling over. Flute the edges and bake in a preheated 350° F. oven for 60 minutes. Serve warm, spooning apples and crust into serving dish. Serve with pouring cream or with a bowl of whipped cream, if desired.

Makes 12 servings

8 large apples, cored, peeled, and thinly sliced (about 8 cups)
1 cup light table molasses
¼ cup water
4 tablespoons softened butter
1 teaspoon ground nutmeg
1 teaspoon ground cinnamon
¼ teaspoon ground cloves
¼ teaspoon ground ginger
½ teaspoon salt
Pastry for top of baking dish, enough for double crust
Pouring cream or whipped cream (optional)

BASIC PIE CRUMB TOPPING

Cut ingredients with a pastry blender or mix by hand until very fine.

Makes 4 (9″) pies

3 cups flour or 2 cups flour and 1 cup fresh bread crumbs
¾ cup butter, at room temperature
½ cup granulated sugar
½ teaspoon salt

BASIC PIE DOUGH

Use pastry cutter to cut the lard and butter into the salt and flour until they are fine crumbs. Carefully drip the ice water over the crumbs with one hand while tossing the crumbs lightly with the other. Use only enough water to hold the dough together. Be sure the water is sprinkled evenly over the flour mixture. As the dough becomes moist, gently press it to the sides of the bowl. The less the dough is handled after it has been moistened, the flakier it will be.

Put the dough on a generously floured board or counter. Gently pat it into a ball. Flatten the ball lightly, and pat the edges so there are no rough dry sides. Roll the dough until it is ⅛″ thick, moving the rolling pin in one direction, then in another. If the circle is not quite round, continue to roll out until it is. When the circle of dough is rounded, cut it 1″ larger than your pie pan. Put the dough around the rolling pin and slide it into the pie pan, cutting off any excess dough. Crimp, or flute, the edges unless there is a top crust. The trimmings may be used to make patty shells, or tart shells.

½ cup lard or vegetable shortening
¼ cup butter
¾ teaspoon salt
2½ cups all-purpose flour
About ⅓ cup ice water

NOTE: Only dampen as many crumbs as are needed for crust. Save the rest in a refrigerated container, adding the water when needed. I keep a gallon container filled with crumbs ready to make into a pie shell at a moment's notice by adding ice water. Usually the amount of crumbs held in both hands is enough for 1 crust.

2 (9″) pie shells

THELMA'S FOOLPROOF PIE CRUST

Mix the flour, shortening, sugar, and salt with a pastry blender or your fingers. In a separate bowl, beat the vinegar, egg, and water together. When the pastry crumbs are fine, gradually pour the liquid on top. Stir or toss the crumbs with a fork until all the ingredients are moist. Form the dough into a ball. Chill in the refrigerator, covered, for at least 15 minutes before rolling out. Divide into 5 balls. Roll each ball on a floured board or between sheets of waxed paper. Place in pie pans and crimp the edges. These freeze well, wrapped in plastic wrap.

To bake, place in a preheated 425° F. oven for 8–10 minutes until golden.

Makes 5 crusts

- 4 cups all-purpose flour
- 1¾ cups vegetable shortening
- 1 tablespoon granulated sugar
- 2 teaspoons salt
- 1 tablespoon vinegar
- 1 egg
- ½ cup water

BLUEBERRIES IN SOUR CREAM

Leta Smith from Wichita, Kansas, gave me this recipe because of the "blueberry incident." She uses it often in her home. I love it.

Wash blueberries and pat dry with paper towels. In a small bowl, mix the brown sugar, nutmeg, and salt with the sour cream until well blended. Pour over the blueberries. Refrigerate, covered with plastic wrap, for several hours. A light dessert, low on calories.

Other fruits may be used— any of the berries, strawberries, raspberries, etc., even fresh apples.

Serves 4–6

- 3 cups fresh (or frozen) blueberries
- 8 ounces sour cream
- 2 tablespoons light brown sugar
- ◆ Several dashes grated nutmeg
- ◆ Pinch salt

BLUEBERRY TORTE

Mae Greider, a friend of mine of long standing, shared this blueberry recipe with me many years ago. That was long before the "blueberry incident." Her recipe is as delicious as it is easy to prepare.

In a small mixing bowl, combine the graham cracker crumbs, use half the sugar, and butter until blended. Put into the bottom of a greased 9″-square baking pan. In a large mixing bowl, whip the cream cheese, gradually adding the remaining sugar until smooth and light. Add the eggs, 1 at a time, and blend thoroughly. Pour over the graham cracker crumbs. Bake in a preheated 350° F. oven for 30 minutes. Cool.

In a heavy 1-quart saucepan, combine the sugar, cornstarch, and nutmeg. Gradually add the water, stirring to make a smooth paste. Add the butter and the blueberries and bring to a boil over medium heat, stirring constantly but gently, to avoid breaking the blueberries. Boil for 2 minutes until thickened. Pour over cooled cheese mixture. Chill and serve plain or with whipped cream.

Serves 6–8 (9″-square pan)

1 cup graham cracker crumbs
¾ cup granulated sugar
¼ cup softened butter
8 ounces cream cheese
2 eggs
2 cups Blueberry Pie Filling
Whipped cream (optional)

BLUEBERRY PIE FILLING
½ cup granulated sugar
2 tablespoons cornstarch or arrowroot
♦ Pinch grated nutmeg
¼ cup water
1 tablespoon butter
1½ cups blueberries

CREAM PUFFS

In a heavy 2-quart saucepan, combine the butter with the boiling water and bring to a boil. When it reaches a full boil, add the flour and salt all at once. Beat vigorously with a wooden spoon until the dough is smooth. Remove from heat and add the eggs, 1 at a time, stirring well after each addition. Drop by the teaspoon on 2 greased cookie sheets, shaping the dough to peak in the center and to round at the bottom. Place the dough about 2″ apart. Bake in a preheated 375° F. oven for 10 minutes. Reduce the heat to 350° and bake for 25 minutes more. Cool and fill with cream filling. An excellent recipe to use is the Thin Chocolate Frosting listed with the Boston Cream Pie recipe (see Index).

In the top of a double boiler, combine the sugar, flour, and salt. Gradually add the beaten eggs and milk. Place over boiling water and cook for approximately 15 minutes, stirring constantly until thickened. Remove from heat and stir in the vanilla and butter. Cool.

Fill a pastry bag with cream and insert it with the large hole tube into each cooled cream puff. Or slit a hole in the side of the puff and fill with a teaspoon. Top with confectioners' sugar, or icing.

Makes 36

1 cup boiling water
½ cup butter
1 cup flour
½ teaspoon salt
4 eggs
Cream Filling
Confectioners' sugar or Thin Chocolate Frosting (optional)

CREAM FILLING

⅞ cup granulated sugar
⅓ cup flour
⅛ teaspoon salt
2 eggs, lightly beaten
2 cups milk
1 teaspoon vanilla extract
1 tablespoon butter

CURRIED FRUIT

Drain fruit and slice bananas. Gently mix all the fruit together. Put in a buttered 2-quart baking dish. Pour melted butter over the fruit. In a small bowl, combine curry, brown sugar, and cornstarch. Sprinkle over the fruit. Bake in a preheated 350° F. oven for 40 minutes. Serve with chicken, pork, or ham.

NOTE: This is delicious served hot or at room temperature.

MICROWAVE: Microwave for 12 minutes in a covered casserole dish, turning ¼ turn and stirring every 3 minutes.

Serves 6

¾ cup cooked pears cut into 1″ pieces
¾ cup cooked peaches cut into 1″ pieces
¾ cup cooked pineapple cut into 1″ pieces
1 cup pitted black cherries
½ cup maraschino cherries
4 bananas, cut into bite-size pieces
¼ cup butter, melted
1 teaspoon curry powder
½ cup light brown sugar
2 tablespoons cornstarch

FLAMBÉED STRAWBERRY SOUFFLÉ CREPES

Make crepes according to directions. Add approximately ⅓ cup of the Vanilla Soufflé in the center of each crepe. Next add ¼ cup of the sliced stawberries. Fold crepe to seal. Moisten the corners to keep the filling inside and place smooth side up, on a buttered and sugared baking pan. Bake in a 425° F. oven for 10 minutes. Reduce heat to 375° and bake for 20 minutes longer. Crepes should be golden and puffy. Sprinkle with orange liqueur and immediately light liqueur with a match. Be sure to use a heat-resistant platter, or flambé in the baking dish.

Makes 8–10 crepes

Basic Dessert Crepes
Vanilla Soufflé
2 cups thinly sliced fresh strawberries
½ cup orange liqueur

CANNED APRICOTS

In a 6-quart saucepan or kettle bring sugar and water to a boil. Add fruit. Boil 7 minutes on medium heat. Spoon fruit gently into sterilized jars and fill to neck with syrup. Seal jars, carefully.

When preserving a few jars of fruit, like apricots, the open-kettle method is best. It saves space and jars, but does not require a lot of time. "Open kettle" simply means cooking the fruit in the boiling sugar water until the fruit becomes clear. When the fruit gives a little when pressed to the side of the pan with a spoon, it is ready to be canned. Spoon hot mixture into sterilized jars. Place lids on jars and seal. To prevent seal from breaking, allow jars to cool before moving them to their storage area.

Fills 3 quart or 6 pint jars

4½ **pounds apricots, washed but not pitted**
2 **cups sugar**
3 **cups water**

FRESH CRANBERRY CRUNCH

Other fruits may be used instead of cranberries, for example, blueberries, cherries, or raspberries.

Mix the sugar, cornstarch, water, vanilla, and salt in a saucepan. Stir in the cranberries and raisins. Bring to a boil over medium heat. Reduce heat, simmer for 5 minutes, then cool slightly.

In a bowl, mix the oats, flour, and brown sugar together. Cut in the butter with a pastry cutter until a crumbly mixture forms. Sprinkle ½ of this mixture over the bottom of a greased 7" x 7" pan or a pie pan. Spread with the cooled cranberry filling. Top with the remainder of the oatmeal mixture. Bake in a preheated 350° F. oven for 45 minutes. Serve warm with vanilla ice cream.

Makes 6 servings

1 **cup granulated sugar**
1 **tablespoon cornstarch**
½ **cup water**
1 **teaspoon vanilla extract**
◆ **Pinch salt**
2 **cups fresh cranberries**
½ **cup raisins**
1 **cup uncooked oatmeal**
½ **cup flour**
1 **cup brown sugar**
⅓ **cup butter**
Vanilla ice cream (optional)

DOTTIE'S GLAZED ORANGES

My cousin Dottie Hess and I were very close friends. We spent almost every weekend together while we were growing up, and today we enjoy swapping recipes. This recipe has become one of her specialties. Dottie serves this in beautiful antique crystal parfait glasses. It's simple, pretty, and a wonderful holiday treat on ice cream or mixed with blueberries, strawberries, or other fruits. One of the advantages to this recipe is that it can be made in quantity to be kept for later use. When using oranges, navel oranges, though more expensive, are best because they are seedless.

Grate the rind of the oranges on a coarse grater in long and short slivers, but don't grate too deep, since the pith will make it bitter. Grate enough rind to make ¼ cup. Then peel the oranges, removing all white pith. Cut between the membranes to make bite-size sections.

Put the sugar, water, and ¼ cup rind in a 2-quart saucepan. Stir over medium heat until the sugar is dissolved, then boil at the same heat for 8 minutes. Pour the boiling syrup over the orange pieces and cover. Cool and refrigerate for 1–2 days before using.

NOTE: To keep for later use, add the orange pieces to the boiling syrup and boil for 1 minute, then pour into sterilized jars and seal.

Makes 6 servings

6   very large navel oranges
1¼ cups granulated sugar
¾   cup water

GLAZE FOR FRESH FRUIT

A perfect glaze for strawberries, peaches, or any fruit pie using uncooked fruit. The secret is to use arrowroot. It remains smooth and clear, unlike cornstarch, which jells quickly, and may turn cloudy and lumpy. When baking blueberries, toss the arrowroot with the sugar and mix it with the berries. However, for this glaze, I mix the arrowroot with water, often adding lemon juice and nutmeg for flavor. The most economical way to buy arrowroot is by the jar. Both McCormick and French have it available in jars. Once you begin to use arrowroot, you will never want to use anything else. Many people have asked for this recipe, and they appreciated our telling them how to buy arrowroot economically.

Blend all the ingredients in a 1-quart saucepan and bring to a boil. Boil until thickened. Cool before adding to fruit.

Makes about 1 cup

1   tablespoon arrowroot
½   cup water
⅓   cup granulated sugar
1   teaspoon lemon juice (optional)
◆   Dash ground nutmeg (optional)

FRESH PEACH COBBLER

Put the cornstarch, brown sugar, and honey in a 1-quart saucepan. Gradually add the water, stirring constantly until smooth. Place over medium heat and cook until thickened, still stirring constantly. Add the peaches and boil for 1 minute. Remove from heat and add butter and lemon juice. When the butter has melted, stir and pour into a greased 9" x 13" baking pan.

In a mixing bowl, combine all ingredients, beating until well mixed and smooth. Drop batter by the tablespoon over the hot peach mixture. Bake in a preheated 375° F. oven for 60 minutes. Serve warm with whipped cream.

MICROWAVE: Microwave in a baking dish for approximately 12 minutes turning ¼ turn every 3 minutes.

Makes 1 (9" x 13") cake

2 tablespoons cornstarch
¼ cup light brown sugar, firmly packed
¼ cup honey
½ cup water
6 cups sliced peaches
2 tablespoons butter
1½ tablespoons lemon juice

BATTER

1 cup cake flour
1 cup granulated sugar
1 teaspoon baking powder
½ teaspoon salt
2 tablespoons softened butter
1 egg slightly beaten
½ cup milk

FRIED APPLE TURNOVERS

Fried Apple Turnovers are very Pennsylvania Dutch. The little individual pies are often served for lunch. The Amish used to give them to their children to keep them quiet during their long Sunday church service that started at 8 and lasted until 12 noon. The dough is similar to our basic pastry crumbs, but baking powder is added, and enough cold water to make the crumbs stick together. To make a good fried turnover, seal the edges by wetting them and pressing them firmly together. It must be done by hand, not with a plastic pie crimper. To cut the crust, use the lid of a 4"-6" saucepan with a sharp edge.

In a bowl, mix the sugar, spices, and arrowroot. Toss with the apples and lemon juice. Set aside.

To make the pastry, mix the baking powder into the pie crumbs in a bowl. Gradually add enough cold water to make the crumbs hold together. Form into 2 balls and roll out on a well-floured board. Using a 4" or 6" circular cutter, cut the dough into 10 circles. Place some of the apple mixture in the center of each pastry circle to make a half-moon shape. Firmly seal edges by pressing and crimping them together. Heat oil in a deep fryer to 375° F. Drop the turnovers into the oil 1 or 2 at a time, and fry about 3 minutes on each side until golden brown. Remove and drain on paper towels. Keep in a warm oven until ready to serve.

Makes 10 turnovers

APPLE FILLING
- 1 cup sugar
- ¼ teaspoon grated or ground nutmeg
- ½ teaspoon powdered cinnamon
- 1 tablespoon arrowroot
- 4 cups peeled, cored, and thinly sliced baking apples
- 1 teaspoon lemon juice

PASTRY DOUGH
- 1 teaspoon baking powder
- 3 cups Pastry Crumbs (see Index)
- ½ cup plus 2 tablespoons cold water
- Oil for deep frying

MERINGUE-NUT KISSES

Beat the egg whites and cream of tartar in a large mixing bowl until they form soft peaks. Sift together the sugar and salt and gradually beat into the egg whites. Beat until they hold stiff peaks. Fold in the nutmeats and vanilla. Drop mixture by teaspoons onto greased cookie sheets and bake 1 sheet at a time. Preheat the oven to 375° F. When ready to bake kisses, reduce the heat to 350° and bake 7–8 minutes. The peaks should be a pale golden. Do not overbake. The kisses should be dry on the outside, moist on the inside. Cool thoroughly before packing in airtight containers. These freeze well.

Makes 3 dozen kisses

⅓ cup egg whites
¼ teaspoon cream of tartar
2 cups sifted confectioners' sugar
¼ teaspoon salt
½ teaspoon vanilla extract
1 cup coarsely broken unsalted nutmeats (pecans, shellbarks, or walnuts)

MIM GOOD'S HOMEMADE YOGURT

Mix 1 cup of the raw milk, the skim milk, and the yogurt in a blender or bowl. Set aside. Heat the remainder of the raw milk to scalding. Remove from heat. Cool to 115° F. Stir in the yogurt mixture. Pour into custard cups or glass containers. Set uncovered, in a pan of warm water, 115°. Cover the pan with foil and place in a preheated 100° oven. Turn off the oven and incubate for 4–6 hours until firm. Chill, covered. Serve with fruit topping or brown sugar.

Makes 9 cups

2 quarts raw milk
⅓ cup powdered skim milk
¾ cup plain commercial yogurt

MIM'S SESAME CANDY

Mim says, "When children munch on this, they're getting something that will help them to grow."

In a large bowl, combine the seeds, nuts, and coconut. In a heavy saucepan, combine the sugar, water, honey, and butter. Bring to a boil and heat to 265° F. Pour the syrup over the seed mixture and stir quickly to combine all the ingredients. Pour on a buttered platter. Flatten by pressure to ½" thick. Cut into desired size and wrap each piece in plastic wrap or waxed paper. This keeps well in an airtight container.

Makes 2 pounds

1 pound sesame seeds
½ cup sunflower seeds
½ cup chopped nuts
1 cup grated coconut
1 cup granulated sugar
1 cup water
1 cup honey
1 tablespoon butter

TURTLE DESSERT

Melt the chocolate and butter in a small saucepan, on low heat, stirring until well blended. In a bowl, cream the eggs and sugar until fluffy. Add the salt and vanilla. Gradually add the melted chocolate and butter. Stir in the flour and mix thoroughly. Heat a waffle iron to medium heat. Drop batter by ½ teaspoonfuls on the waffle iron at least 2" apart. Close the iron and bake 1¼ minutes. Remove immediately and cool. Trim the edges to look like turtles. Frost generously with Chocolate Cream Frosting. Top with pecans.

Makes 36 turtles

2 ounces unsweetened chocolate
⅓ cup butter
2 eggs
¾ cup granulated sugar
½ teaspoon salt
1 teaspoon vanilla extract
1 cup flour
Chocolate Cream Frosting
1 pound pecans

PEACH DUMPLINGS WITH CHOCOLATE SURPRISE

Roll out pastry about ⅛″ thick, and cut in 6″–8″ squares. Peel the peaches and cut a hole in top. Pit each peach carefully and replace the pit with a chocolate kiss and ½ teaspoon butter. Put the cut-off section back on top of the peach and place on a pastry square. Bring opposite corners of pastry up over the peach, moistening each corner. Seal and secure when all 4 corners are folded up.

Make the syrup by combining all the ingredients in a heavy saucepan and boiling for 3 minutes. Place the peaches in a greased 9″ x 13″ baking dish and pour the hot syrup around the dumplings. Bake in a preheated 425° F. oven for 10 minutes, then reduce the heat to 350° and bake 45 minutes longer. Serve warm with pouring cream, whipped cream, or ice cream, if desired.

Serves 6

Enough pastry dough for 2-crust pie
6 large peaches
6 chocolate kisses
3 teaspoons butter

SYRUP
½ cup granulated sugar
1 cup water
1 tablespoons butter
¼ teaspoon ground cinnamon
¼ teaspoon salt
Whipped cream, pouring cream, or ice cream (optional)

MIM'S YOGURT SHERBET

Soak the gelatin in water in a small bowl for 3 minutes. Heat in a small saucepan until the gelatin has dissolved. Put the strawberries and sugar in a blender or food processor. Pour the hot gelatin mixture on top and puree. Blend in the yogurt. Pour into sherbet glasses or a serving dish. Chill until ready to serve.

Serves 4–6

1 tablespoon unflavored gelatin
½ cup water
2 cups cleaned fresh or frozen strawberries
4 tablespoons granulated sugar
2 cups yogurt

WHOOPIE PIES

Cream the shortening and sugar in a large mixing bowl. Beat in the eggs, 1 at a time. In another bowl, sift the flour with the cocoa, salt, and baking soda. Gradually add this to the creamed mixture alternately with the milk. Mix in the hot water or coffee. Drop by teaspoonfuls onto greased cookie sheets, placing about 3″ apart. Bake in a preheated 375° F. oven for 8 minutes. Store on waxed paper until all the cookies have been baked.

1 cup vegetable shortening or margarine
2 cups granulated sugar
2 eggs
3½ cups flour
1 cup cocoa
2 teaspoons salt
2 teaspoons baking soda
1 cup milk soured with 1 tablespoon cider vinegar
1 cup hot water or coffee

FILLING

2 egg whites
1 tablespoon vanilla extract
4 tablespoons milk
2 cups confectioners' sugar
4 tablespoons flour
1 cup vegetable shortening
½ cup butter

Beat the egg whites until fluffy. Gradually beat in the vanilla, milk, sugar, and flour. Add the shortening and butter and beat until very fluffy.

Take 1 cookie and place a generous tablespoon of filling on the flat side. Top with another. These freeze well if wrapped individually. They look like yo-yos.

Makes about 48–60 finished cookies

VANILLA SOUFFLÉ

In a 1-quart heavy saucepan, melt the butter over medium heat. Add the flour and stir until smooth. Slowly add the milk, continuing to stir. Gradually add the sugar and salt. Cook until the sauce is smooth and thick, stirring constantly. Remove from heat and cool slightly. Beat the egg yolks. Add yolks and the vanilla to the sauce, stirring until well blended. Fold the stiffly beaten egg whites into the sauce. Pour the mixture into a 1½-quart straight-sided soufflé dish which has been generously buttered and sprinkled with sugar. Set the dish in pan of hot water and bake in a preheated 450° F. oven, on the low rack, for the first 15 minutes. Reduce the heat to 375° and bake 25 minutes more.

3 tablespoons butter
2½ tablespoons flour
1¼ cups milk
½ cup granulated sugar
½ teaspoon salt
5 egg yolks
1 teaspoon vanilla extract
5 egg whites, stiffly beaten
Butter
Granulated sugar for sprinkling

VARIATIONS

Fine shredded coconut, thinly sliced almonds, or chopped pecans may be added to the buttered, sugared sides of the soufflé pan. Add only enough to give the soufflé traction as it climbs up the sides of the pan.

Chocolate Soufflé Use basic recipe for Vanilla Soufflé. When adding the sugar to the sauce, add 3 tablespoons cocoa with the sugar, or use 2 squares baking chocolate. Stir in after adding the milk. The chocolate will melt completely as the sauce thickens.

A delicious dessert served plain, or with Lemon-Rum Sauce. For another variation, use the above recipe and add ¼ cup chocolate or coffee liqueur at the time when the mixture is folded into the egg whites.

Serves 4–6

BOILED FROSTING

In a small heavy saucepan, combine the sugar, water, and cream of tartar. Stir and bring to a boil until it registers 242° F. on a candy thermometer. Meanwhile beat the egg whites in a bowl until they hold soft peaks. Beat in 3 tablespoons of the hot syrup, gradually by tablespoons. Pour the hot syrup gradually over the egg whites, beating steadily until the frosting stands in soft peaks. Add the vanilla and continue to beat until stiff enough to frost the cake.

If frosting tends to become sugary, add a little lemon juice.

1½ cups granulated sugar
½ cup water
⅛ teaspoon cream of tartar
2 egg whites
½ teaspoon vanilla extract

BROILED ICING

In a small mixing bowl, combine all ingredients. Spread on the warm cake. Do not remove the cake from the pan. Place the cake on the medium rack of the oven. Broil approximately 6 minutes until it bubbles and is golden brown.

4 tablespoons melted butter
5 tablespoons evaporated milk
⅓ cup light brown sugar, firmly packed
½ cup coconut (medium shred)

BUTTER FROSTING

Cream the butter in a small bowl until soft. Add the cream, sugar, and vanilla. Beat until smooth and creamy. Spread on the cake.

3 tablespoons butter
1 tablespoon cream
1½ cups confectioners' sugar
½ teaspoon vanilla

CHOCOLATE CREAM FROSTING

Melt the butter and chocolate in a small saucepan, stirring until well blended. In a large mixing bowl, combine the sugar, cream, cheese, and vanilla. Slowly stir in the melted butter and chocolate. Beat until very creamy.

⅓ cup butter
3 ounces unsweetened chocolate
3 cups sifted confectioners' sugar
¼ cup light cream or milk
4 ounces cream cheese
1 teaspoon vanilla extract

CONFECTIONERS' SUGAR ICING (for Tea Rings)

Blend all the ingredients except the nuts and cherries together in a small bowl until smooth. Spread on the warm tea ring. Decorate with nut halves and cherries. Serve warm.

1¼ cups confectioners' sugar
2 tablespoons cream
1 tablespoon butter
½ teaspoon vanilla extract
Nuts and cherries

CREAM CHEESE FROSTING

Beat all ingredients together until satin-smooth. Frost cake when cool.

3 ounces cream cheese
6 tablespoons butter
1 cup confectioners' sugar
1 teaspoon vanilla extract

THIN CHOCOLATE FROSTING

In a 1-quart heavy saucepan, melt the chocolate and butter, stirring constantly until smooth. With a wire whisk, blend in the water and sugar, whipping until smooth. This should not be a stiff frosting but should run over the sides of the cake.

Excellent on cream puffs and over filled dessert crepes.

Makes ¾ cup

1 square unsweetened chocolate (1 ounce) or 2 tablespoons cocoa
1½ teaspoons butter
2 tablespoons boiling water
1 cup confectioners' sugar

THE PAST

Betty Groff's education began early and never stopped when she was growing up on the family farm, thanks to the number of able teachers in residence.

The 84-acre farm, on the outskirts of Strasburg, was home to Betty's grandparents, Newton and Amanda Herr, and their sons' families. As was the custom, Newton and Amanda gave their younger son, Betty's Uncle Emory, the farm and main house, called "Down Home." But they also built a hilltop dwelling, called "Up Home," for Betty's dad Clarence and his family. Just a quarter of a mile apart, the families basically lived as one, sharing the income from the farm.

Although Newton had given up heavy farm work, preferring to leave that to his sons and the hired hands, he still commanded the entire family's respect. Betty recalls that at mealtime, he would wait until everyone else was seated before taking his place at the head of the table and leading the prayer.

"Because he had the time to spend with me, he taught me about nature. He'd hoist me up to count the eggs in pigeon nests and together we'd keep a close watch until it was time for us to prepare a meal of squab," Betty said.

The horses, kept on long after they'd been replaced by tractors, were Grandpa Newton's special charges. When he cared for them, Betty was often at his side. And when he used them to work the garden, Betty wasn't far away.

After a day in the garden, Grandpa Herr liked to retire to his favorite quiet place—a stack of hay bales near the horse stables and overlooking the Amish neighbor's fields. He'd chew on a chunk of dried bologna the way some people chew gum or tobacco, contemplate the state of the world and share his thoughts with his granddaughter.

Betty is quick to say that Amanda has always been a role model. "When people say I am a lot like my grandmother was, I consider it quite a compliment," notes one of Pennsylvania Dutch country's most successful businesswomen.

After Newton lost all his fingers in a farming accident, and knowing that to be prosperous, a farmer generally needed two good hands, Amanda made a suggestion. Because the land wasn't all that good (or so she said to protect her husband's feelings), she said she thought it would be a good idea to open a butcher shop. And then Amanda began handling public relations for the shop. "I strongly suspect that many

customers who frequented the butcher shop came as much to sit on the porch and hear what Amanda had to say about events of the day as they came for the meats," Betty said.

But Amanda Herr wasn't all business. She had a decided soft spot for her grand-daughter. At corn-drying time, she'd slip the little girl small amounts of sweet corn when her mother wasn't looking because Betty could never get enough of it. Noted Betty, "I'd eat as many cobs of corn as I could get away with before mother would stop me." Of course, the youngster didn't lose her taste for the corn, even as it dried. The sugary aroma from the drying sweet corn and, later, the caramel-like scent of the nearly finished dried corn, were as tempting as the aroma of freshly popped corn. Grandmother Herr would say, "Just let them melt in your mouth," as she furtively gave Betty some dry, hard corn kernels to suck. Trouble was that although the corn melted in the mouth, it didn't fare as well in the stomach where it stirred the same feelings as sour green apples!

Uncle Emory, a prominent minister as well as a farmer with decided ideas about the way food should taste, is best remembered for two gifts. You've no doubt heard of people with perfect pitch. Well, Uncle Emory had a perfect sense of smell. As soon as he'd step on the farmhouse porch he could tell if Betty's Aunt Ruth (his wife) and her mother had salted the peas they were serving.

He was also the family's master beverage maker. "No matter whether he was making lemonade or root beer, the drinks always tasted better when Uncle Emory made them," Betty commented. He'd bring out the lemonade's flavor with a bit of fresh nutmeg. His grape juice was always generously laced with Seven-Up, ginger ale or lemon to make it extra good. And his fruit punches, made from the juices of canned fruit, never went to waste.

Aunt Ruth, a master at making flaky, good-tasting pastry, taught Betty the basics of pie-baking. A good cook, she also prided herself in superb potpie with soft, doughy square noodles that never stuck together (the trick is dropping each noodle into the boiling broth separately). But one meal of potpie, made for 15 including the family and hired hands, would shake Aunt Ruth's very faith in herself. The noodles were sticking together for no apparent reason.

To keep Aunt Ruth from retiring her apron, Betty sheepishly confessed that she liked her noodles stuck together and had been slipping several at a time into the broth when Aunt Ruth wasn't looking. Because everyone else liked the individual noodles, Betty figured there would be some of the large, all-day noodles left by the time the serving bowl made it to her distant place at the long table. Relieved to know she hadn't lost her touch, Aunt Ruth asked, "Why didn't you tell me you liked them that way? I gladly would have set some aside for you."

Mischievous from the start, Betty found plenty of other ways to amuse herself. Down Home's steep, curving walnut banister provided thrills that made conventional sliding boards seem tame. And when it came to daredevil adventure, climbing the towering silo (something every mother hopes her child won't discover) provided a lofty perch.

When the adults went away for a few hours, Betty and her cousin Dick attacked their chores with unusual enthusiasm because they had big plans. They'd head for the barn and clean off the cradle on a track that normally was used to "muck" the stables and move the manure outside. "We'd quickly hose it down and give a signal to our playmates at the next farm. They'd hurry over and we'd ride back and forth until it was nearly time for our parents to return home," Betty recalled.

Testing parental rules was then, as it is now, all a part of growing up. Betty's father was a stickler about cold drinking water and ruled that the pump had to be pumped 40 times before water could be drawn for the table. "I figured that was a crock and that my father would have no way of knowing if I had pumped the handle 20 times or 40 times. I hurried inside because it looked as if it were going to rain any minute and poured the water into the glasses. After daddy said grace, he picked up his glass and took a sip. He looked at me and asked, 'Who pumped the water?' I said that I did. He pressed on: 'Did you pump 40 pumps?' I said I thought it made no difference."

❦   ❦   ❦   ❦   ❦   ❦   ❦   ❦   ❦

With that, he sent Betty out to refill the pitchers during a downpour—a move her brother Raymond thoroughly enjoyed.

Although she laughs about the incident today, she has many more pleasant memories of her father in those early days. Clarence, widely known for the smoked hams, dried beef and bologna he sold, emphasized quality. Hearty stews could have been made from the meat he turned into bologna. And whenever a customer came to buy a large quantity of meat, the proud butcher always offered to cook a steak for the customer so he could taste the meat being purchased. Naturally, no customer refused such an offer. "He cooked up a steak in a crepe-sized pan, first tossing in some salt and heating it till it popped, and then flash-cooking the steak," Betty said.

When she was old enough to begin working, Betty asked her father why he allowed customers to come at all hours of the day, rather than opening only at certain times. He responded, "When you have your own business, you can do just that. I have chosen this life because I don't have to do the things other people do like advertising or going to market several days a week." Of course, as Betty comments, "The joke has been on me. When daddy sees Abe and me serving our restaurant customers until late at night, he reminds me that our hours are longer than his ever were."

Clarence Herr has always believed that any meal worth eating should be served on linen, and Betty's mother, a stickler for detail, heartily agreed with her husband. She was known throughout Lancaster County for the dinners she served. "I thought everyone ate the way we did until I started to travel. That's when I realized why her invitations were coveted by those who received them," Betty said.

The Up Home kitchen where Betty and her mother worked together was a pleasant place to be schooled for life. "It was warm and sunny with plants on the windowsills and lots of pictures on the walls. There was always a rocker in the kitchen for the guests who came to visit while we worked. The table in the center of the room was used not only to eat at but to work on. When a long project was to be done, it was placed in front of the large windows overlooking the farm in the valley below. One could see the village of Paradise to the northeast, the Strasburg railroad to the east, and a wonderful view of the hills, meadows and old swimming hole. The kitchen was lined with natural chestnut-wood cabinets with just the stove, refrigerator, sink and table serving as the remainder of the furnishings. It was such a pleasant kitchen to be in; it always looked as though someone cared," Betty said.

And her mother did care—particularly about her daughter's schooling. "Mother had a schedule and outline of things for me to be taught and experiences I should have while she was alive," Betty commented.

Bertha Herr was a fanatic about quality and goodness and treated cooking as a culinary art, long before the thought occurred to others. She even gave "love pats" to foods. Explained Betty, "When my mother would see a particularly beautiful food, such as a plump chicken, she'd pat it and say, 'Don't you just love that?'" And she made sure the foods that came into her kitchen qualified for pats.

Peas, asparagus and lima beans were picked young. Tomatoes with fewer seeds were planted and strawberries had lots of straw in and around the plants so the berries were never dirty.

When Mrs. Herr canned fruits and vegetables (virtually everything that was grown on the farm as well as foods bought from neighboring orchards), the canned goods were picture-perfect. Dilled string beans, for example, were never crammed haphazardly into jars. Each bean was meticulously stood on end in the jar for a neater appearance. Finished colorful vegetable and fruit relishes were interspersed with canned meats to present a prettier appearance on the shelves.

Drying foods commanded equal care. If dried corn got too dark, it had a totally different flavor so Betty's mother, grandmother and Aunt Ruth took turns staying up all night to make sure the corn didn't get overdone. Dried apple slices had to be completely devoid of peels and core. Apple butter couldn't get too dark or it, too, would have a different flavor.

When Betty and her mother worked in the kitchen, they'd listen to the radio. They never missed the Bell Telephone Hour. On Saturday mornings, when they were baking or cooking foods for entertaining guests on Sunday, they tuned to the Metropolitan Opera and to "Amos and Andy." "My mother never demanded that I do anything. She would simply say, 'You can do this if you like.' And I liked doing it."

An accomplished yeast dough and cake baker, Mrs. Herr trained her daughter in the arts and left behind a hand-written cookbook that will always be one of Betty's most treasured possessions. And, she offered helpful hints that Betty never forgot.

Mrs. Herr stressed the importance of the appearances of food as well as their tastes. She noted which seasonings could be added to foods and which ones would overpower dishes. She offered the solution to culinary dilemmas like that of the crooked cake layers. The solution—place the layers in the opposite directions or simply trim off the offending slopes.

She carefully demonstrated the way to wield a knife to take the air bubbles out of angel food cakes. And she was a master at pleasing "sneaky" eaters. (The Pennsylvania Dutch use the word "sneaky" to mean "picky" or "fussy.") Whenever she wasn't certain how a new food would go over with the family "Down Home," she and Betty would make the dish first in their own "Up Home" test kitchen. If it passed their taste tests, the dish was sent Down Home for a trial by fire.

Although much of every day was spent on the serious preparation and preservation of foods produced on the farm, Betty's mother also found time for fun foods. An accomplished candy maker who was known for her chocolate creams, she taught Betty to make candy and helped her with other projects like making homemade potato chips and sodas.

"I wanted to make candy Easter eggs for school, but my mother had a migraine headache the afternoon I wanted to do it. I assured her I could do the task on my own. Before lying down on the couch, she cautioned me to make sure I didn't get any water into the chocolate. I thought I was being careful, but somehow, steam or water did get into the chocolate. I didn't know what was the matter and kept adding more chocolate each time the chocolate in the pan crumbled. Finally, when I had a panful of crumbled chocolate, I woke my mother and tearfully told her something had gone wrong.

"Although I had ruined an awful lot of expensive chocolate, she didn't scold me at all. She simply stayed at my side and helped me make another batch. Now that I look back, I'm not surprised by her reaction to the chocolate disaster for mother's philosophy was: Food must be enjoyed not only by the person eating it but also by the one preparing it. It's a thought I'll never forget."

LANCASTER COUNTY SKYLINE, Watercolor

A traditional pattern utilized by quilters has been one entitled
Migration. Showing the source which was the inspiration for
this design, Lancaster County Skyline records the natural
beauty of the Susquehanna River Valley.

13

MENUS FOR ALL
SEASONS & OCCASIONS

SPRING

Glazed Bacon
Roast Chicken with Bread Stuffing
Saffron Noodles
Buttered Beets
Curried Fruit
Banana Cake with White Icing

Crab Soup
Roast Loin of Pork with Apricot-Pineapple Glaze
Superb Sweet Potatoes
Shirley Wagner's Eggplant Casserole
Erma's Pickled Cauliflower
Betty's Lemon Chiffon Cake with Orange Sauce

Fresh Strawberries with Powdered Sugar
Wiener Schnitzel
Mashed Potatoes
Tomato Sauce
Peach Glaze Pie

Sauerbraten
Potato Dumplings
Green Beans with Onions
Cole Slaw
Apple Pan Dowdy

Vera Bragg's Beef Pie
Garden Greens with Eggs and Creamy Sweet-Sour Dressing
Nectarine Upside-Down Cake

Potato Soup
Pork and Sauerkraut with Dumplings
Fresh or Frozen Garden Peas with Browned Butter
Dotty's Glazed Oranges
Vanilla Ice Cream

Quiche
Boiled Fresh Beef Tongue
Puffed Potatoes
Marinated Tomatoes and Onions
Pickled Green Beans, Carrots, and Cauliflower
Cottage Pudding

Matty's Easter Pie
Fresh Baked Ham With Sherry
Superb Sweet Potatoes
Charlie's Lima Beans
Seven-Day Crisp Sweet Pickles
Celery and Cauliflower Salad with Mustard Dressing
Coconut Layer Cake
Peach Ice Cream

Pan-Fried Whiting Fish
Lemon Orange Ice
Parsleyed Potatoes
Sunburst Salad
Angel Food Cake with Orange Sauce

Broiled Grapefruit and Oranges with Brown Sugar
Rolled Brisket of Beef with Horseradish Sauce
Baked Potatoes
Asparagus with Water Chestnuts
Green Tomato Relish
Cherry Pie
Homemade Vanilla Ice Cream

MARCH

St. Patrick's Day

For St. Patrick's Day, we have planned a meal featuring the color green. It is most effective. The various shades of green blend well and are not as "green-green" as you may think. The green noodles are particulary interesting. As you know, I am Pennsylvania Dutch and I ordinarily make yellow noodles with lots of egg yolks. When we cook these noodles, we even use saffron to be sure they are truly golden. To make Green Noodles, you simply add a cup of Spinach. In New Orleans, for a promotion with Del Monte in which I represented the East Coast, I cooked noodles. You may not be familiar with the problems one finds making noodles in a location below sea level. But it does make a difference! Ordinarily when you make noodles, you wrap the dough in plastic wrap, or cover it with a bowl to let it blend till all the flour is absorbed. Below sea level you need more flour; otherwise the noodle dough turns rubbery, like chewing gum. It is really crazy. At the show everybody told my husband, "She will never make noodles using that recipe." It turned out I had to use several extra cups of flour to make the dough. It just stretched as far as my arm would reach. If you make noodles below sea level, be sure to use more flour and see that the mixture is well blended.

The remaining dishes in this meal can be used throughout the year at other times; but when you want an all-green menu, why not make your noodles green with spinach?

Melon Balls—preferably honeydews
Dill Bread and Whipped Chive Butter

Breaded Pork Chops
Parsleyed Potatoes with Cream or
Green Noodles (Spinach Noodles)
Creamed Onions

Bread-and-Butter Pickles
Spiced Cantaloupe

Lime Chiffon Pie

APRIL

Charlie's Spring Feast

This is one of the dinner parties our son Charlie served when he was attending culinary school. The explanation with the Crown Roast of Lamb is quite complete. If you use white Crème de Menthe, you will not have a green hue on the bones of the lamb.

The Apple-Raisin Bread Stuffing is excellent.

Let me add a short story about a Caesar Salad at a dinner pary one night. Charlie and Louis were making the Caesar Salad. While tossing it, some of the lettuce landed in a lady's lap. Without slowing down, Charlie said, "Isn't it great to have Caesar on your lap?" So, if you ever have a similar problem, keep calm and use some imagination to laugh it off. Never worry if something falls on the floor! Just pick it up and throw it away and, if appropriate, laugh about it.

As far as the Strawberry Soufflé is concerned, the crepes are an interesting combination with the soufflé on the inside. And remember, crepes are always better when a little beer is added to the batter and the mixture is allowed to stand overnight. This helps to overcome the slightly floury taste you tend to get otherwise. At a demonstration at John Wanamaker, several different companies were showing their crepe machines. They realized that it was not the crepe maker itself, but they could not decide what it was. I was amused because I had made my batter the day before. You can, too! And it does save time at the last minute. At the demonstration everyone asked, "Why do your crepes taste better than ours, and everyone is eating your crepes?" I suggested, "Maybe it's just the crepe maker." I never gave away the secret that crepes are better if the batter is made the night before. Don't forget it. It does help.

Clams Casino
Onion Soup

Charlie's Crown Roast of Lamb with Crème de Menthe
Apple-Raisin Bread Stuffing
Asparagus with Hollandaise Sauce
Stuffed Broiled Tomatoes

Caesar Salad

Flambéed Strawberry Soufflé Crepes

MAY

Bridal Shower

This month we feature a May bridal shower. The Spiced Tea is one of the few recipes in this book using anything that is instant. However, in this day and age, we all use these items when they are available. We may as well. This Spiced Tea is delicious. Alma Bobb uses it for gifts. It can be served year-round and is especially good if someone has a bad cold; a hot drink will help to perk them up. It is also good served with a shot of whiskey.

The Spiced Kumquats are unusual because they have been seeded. We prefer not to make this recipe with whole kumquats, although most of the gourmet canners do pack spiced kumquats whole. I like to think this dish looks better when the kumquats have been cut in half and seeded. This is the way my mother always prepared them, also.

The Tea Cake with Spring Flowers is another of Kitty Brown's creations. Kitty Brown is an excellent cook and a very dear friend of mine. At one time we took cake-decorating classes together. Kitty came up with the idea of making this beautiful cake in a jelly roll pan, so that it is only about ½″ thick when it is baked. Then she suggested using a cake decorator to decorate it with various spring flowers. It makes an excellent shower dessert and takes little time to prepare. All you need is four decorater tubes with different-colored icings—one with a generous amount of green icing for the stems and leaves, and three other colors for the flowers, possibly white, pink, and yellow.

The menu for this bridal shower is one you can make easily and quickly with little work, yet it is something that guests are not likely to forget.

Spiced Tea

Chipped Ham and Herb Cheese Sandwiches
Watercress and Herb Cheese Sandwiches
Chicken Salad Sandwiches

Mother Groff's Sweet Dill Pickles
Spiced Kumquats
Celery and Carrot Sticks or Curls

Tea Cake with Spring Flowers

Mother's Day

We included a Mother's Day breakfast because every family has some special treats. Mine is Mother's Day. When our children first served me breakfast in bed, it was coffee and toast. As they grew, the breakfasts became more and more elaborate. Finally, when Charlie went to school, the highlight of my being a mother of young children was the day I was served this menu.

Like every mother, I am still amazed how much children can do, and I must confess that it is fun to be served once in a while. The Eggs Benedict were excellent. They are not at all difficult to make. Once you have tried them, you will want to make them often. However, don't count on your eight-year-old cooking this kind of menu. It deserves to be a breakfast prepared by someone who is used to cooking. In fact, it really takes two people to prepare a Benedict Sauce; while one is stirring the sauce, the other pours the butter.

Broiled Grapefruit
Eggs Benedict
Toast and Strawberry Preserves

SUMMER

Corn "Rivvel" Soup
Dried Green and Yellow Beans with Ham Hock
Marinated Tomatoes and Onions
Chocolate Cake
Cracker Pudding

Corn and Clam Chowder
Batter-Dipped Fish or Shrimp
Poulticed Potatoes
Cucumber and Onion Marinade
Carrot Cake with Cream Cheese Frosting

Split Pea and Tomato Soup
Breaded Pork Chops with Fried Apple Rings
Green Noodles (Spinach Noodles)
Batter-Dipped Eggplant
Two-Day Sweet Pickles
Rhubarb Custard Pie

Chicken and Corn Soup
Abe's Roast Round of Veal with Herb Gravy
Mashed Potatoes
Carrots with Nutmeg
Fresh Lima Beans with Thyme
Mother's Ripe Tomato Relish
Bread and Butter Pickles
Coconut Layer Cake

Fresh Vegetables in Sour Cream and Vegetable Dip
Barbecued Ribs
Baked Sweet Potatoes
Baked Corn on the Cob (in the Husks)
Pickled Green Beans, Carrots, and Cauliflower
Blueberry Cake

Chicken Pot Pie
Red Cabbage with Plums and Bacon
Polish Potato and Apple Salad
Mother's Refrigerator Pickles
Blueberry Crumb Pie

Vichyssoise
Fresh Pork Cubes or Chops, Spring Onions, and Sugar Peas
Fresh Cutting Lettuce Leaves with Creamy Sweet-Sour Dressing
Fresh Strawberry Pie

Chilled Melon with Lemon Wedge
Cold Sliced Meats
Oatmeal Bread
Macaroni Salad with Sliced Olives
Dill Pickles
Blueberry Torte

Cream of Mushroom Soup
Salmon Cakes with Lemon Sauce
German Hot Potato Salad
Corn on the Cob
Green Tomato Pickles
Lemon Chiffon Pie

Pan-Fried Liver and Onions
Poulticed Potatoes
Broiled Tomatoes
Three-Bean Relish
Chocolate Pudding

Cream of Watercress Soup
Roast Duck with Orange-Pineapple Glaze
Whole Scraped Potatoes with Browned Butter
French Green Beans and Bean Sprouts
Mother's Spiced Kumquats
White Cake
Sliced Peaches

Broccoli Soup with Chicken Broth
Broil-Fried Chicken with Chives and Lemon
Saffron Noodles
Spinach Salad with Hot Bacon Dressing
Peach Dumplings with Chocolate Surprise

Tomato Juice
Dad's Sausage
Potatoes in Jackets
Italian Green Beans with Water Chestnuts
Marinated Broccoli and Cauliflower
Boston Cream Pie with Chocolate Icing

Creamed Sweet Bologna Gravy
Potato Cakes or Pancakes
Lettuce with Creamy Sweet-Sour Dressing
Coconut Custard Pie

❈ ◆ ❈ ◆ ❈ ◆ ❈ ◆ ❈ ◆ ❈ ◆ ❈ ◆ ❈ ◆ ❈ ◆ ❈

JUNE

A Turtle Party

A June turtle party is lots of fun. Most of you have probably heard about the turtle club, so we won't go into it here. We had the turtle party because our son Charlie and his girl, Cindy, were being married in the fall. I wanted to give a party and Charlie said, "Let's do something different." As a result we had what we called the turtle party for Charlie's rehearsal dinner. We made an announcement, as we toasted the bride-and-groom-to-be, that the turtle stands for lots of things—for instance, a slow beginning is a sure ending; also, wherever you go, you have your house with you. If you never stick your neck out, you will not get anywhere, because the turtle has to do that to move. These are some of the reasons for the turtle party. It seemed appropriate for a rehearsal dinner to start off a successful marriage.

Kitty Brown gave us the recipe for the turtle dessert. The base is a waffle made with chocolate and cut to look like a turtle. The topping is exceptionally good. Don't wait for a wedding to make this turtle dessert. It is easy anytime, but also fantastic for a party.

For our turtle party everything, from trivets to favors, was turtle-shaped. We were amazed how many different turtle-shaped items one can find in a gift shop! Generally, there are more frog-shaped items than there are turtles, but with a little effort you will find plenty of turtles to complement your dinner party arrangement.

The bread turtle made for the start of the dinner is excellent. Fill it with sandwiches, and next day use it as a bird feeder.

Talking of turtles, do try turtle meat sometime. A friend of mine, Charlotte Meredith, told me that she thoroughly enjoyed turtle steak while she was in the Cayman Islands. They raise turtles there commercially. As a matter of fact, there are more turtles on the island than there are human beings. The meat of the turtle supposedly tastes like the meat of seven different kinds of animal—including lamb, veal, beef, and chicken—and it is very delicate. The local turtles in Pennsylvania are not large enough to provide steaks, but the meat itself is very sweet and not at all fishy. Preparing a turtle for cooking is not much fun. I did it only once, using two turtles. Abe killed them for me. By the time I cooked them, I found the odor overwhelming and it was nearly a year before I was ready to eat snapper soup again. A better idea is to buy your turtle meat already prepared. Believe me, cleaning a turtle and preparing the meat is no fun. I'll never complain again when I have to pay a high price for turtle soup. And do remember to try a turtle steak if you are in the Cayman Islands, because it is excellent.

DECEMBER

Holiday Parties

When you have a party and don't know exactly how many people will be there, you will find it best to make everything in quantity. Then you will be prepared no matter how many people arrive.

There is an amusing story concerning the quiche. When he was younger, our son John was watching me cook a recipe one day. He looked at me and asked, "Mom, what are you doing?" I replied, "I am making a snack." John then asked, "What is it?" and I said, "Can't you read the recipe?" After looking at the recipe, John said, "Are you making a quickie?" That is what we call a quiche at our house, and indeed it is also a "quickie," for it is very simple and easy to make.

The Shrimp and Anchovy Puffs have an interesting story to them, too. I have done many cooking demonstrations for John Wanamaker's in Harrisburg. After a while, you want to present different styles of cooking. One year, we presented recipes for a "summer cooler." Ruth Adams' recipe for Anchovy Puffs was excellent. To give the puffs a Dutch accent, they may be made with either shrimp or diced home-cured ham. Ruth Adams, public relations director for Wanamaker's, is an excellent cook and a world traveler, and she has found unusual recipes everywhere. The puff pastry she uses in this recipe is very rich and delicious and may be used with almost any kind of filling. It was featured in the recipe brochure given out at the "summer cooler."

The Steak Tartare is Jim Bobb's recipe. He was formerly chairman of the board of Hershey Estates. Jim has a great love for food and a special interest in serving it beautifully. Over the years, Jim rightly has been given much of the credit for the quality of the food and the success of the Hotel Hershey and the Hershey Country Club.

I have made cream puffs ever since I was a child. Cream puffs are featured in French gourmet cookbooks now. The Pennsylvania Dutch used cream puffs all the time as special desserts. We filled them either with a vanilla pudding or whipped cream for dessert, or with ham or chicken salad when we served them as a sandwich.

Quiche

Ruth Adams' Shrimp and Anchovy Puffs

Jim Bobb's Steak Tartare

Glazed Bacon

Cream Puffs filled with Ham Salad

Chicken Salad Sandwiches

Watermelon Rind with Ginger
Letitia's Lime Pickles
Fresh Cauliflower and Broccoli with Dip
Green and Ripe Olives
Carrot Curls
Pickled Celery

Coconut-Molasses Custard Pie
Brandied Apricots
Fried Apple Turnovers

Christmas Eve Dinner

Our Christmas Eve dinner is always very traditional. I like to cook it myself as long as I have the strength. I hope I can continue to have Christmas dinner with my family on Christmas Eve. To me, the perfect way to spend Christmas Eve is with my family—all the children and grandchildren. At that time, we talk over the blessings of the past year and exchange our gifts. Then on Christmas morning we discuss the Christmas story one more time and we are grateful for another good season.

Usually each person tells me what they would like to have for Christmas Eve dinner. As a result, the dinner does not necessarily turn out to be one where everything blends together, or one where everything is cooked on the top of the stove, or all is done in the oven. But it is a dinner that just seems right for the occasion. Our family loves roast goose with a special bread stuffing and other dishes I am featuring in this menu.

Gingerbread with Lemon Rum Sauce is an excellent recipe, and it gives that special holiday spirit, much like Plum Pudding.

Meringue Nut Kisses are delicate and delectable. They were my mother's specialty. Since Mother passed away, we have continued to make them because we don't want to break that tradition. The trick to making this special delicacy is to keep the inside moist while the outside is dry, and in beautiful peaks, with just a golden top on them. The recipe in this book should guarantee that. Meringue Nut Kisses are not as difficult to make as you may have been led to believe, but they should be eaten within a few days, as they do tend to dry out.

Just a hint for the Chocolate Soufflé. Use leftover Lemon Rum Sauce (from the Gingerbread) to put over the Chocolate Soufflé. It adds a special touch. Be assured that Chocolate Soufflé is not too difficult to make. As a matter of fact, one Christmas Eve I dropped it on the floor. Luckily, it did not turn over, so I picked it up and put it back in the oven. It baked perfectly and we were able to serve it with no problems. So forget that myth about having to breathe quietly around a Chocolate Soufflé.

Shrimp Cocktail with Hot Sauce
Cheese Biscuits

Roast Goose with Gravy
Moist Bread Stuffing
Mashed Potatoes
Tomato and Eggplant Casserole
Brocolli with Cheese Sauce

Greens with Creamy Sweet-Sour Dressing

Gingerbread with Lemon-Rum Sauce
Meringue-Nut Kisses
Salted Nuts

Chocolate Soufflé

New Year's Eve

We have always had New Year's Eve parties. When you make Mulled Cider, be sure that you do not pour the hot cider into a crystal bowl without putting something in the bowl to take away the heat, or the cider will crack the bowl.

It's traditional in this area to have Pork and Sauerkraut to start out a new year. We are not quite sure where this tradition began, but it is believed that the real reason was that the Pennslyvania Dutch, who were very careful to stay in good health and particular in their cooking, felt that if you happened to eat all kinds of rich food though the holidays, the sauerkraut would clean out your system. You would then start the new year with your insides as fresh and new as the year. In our family, therefore, Pork and Sauerkraut has always been our way to start the New Year. Also, for our New Year's Eve party, we serve the old wines that we made many years earlier. We just sip them—then at midnight, our sons shoot ten volleys from their shotguns. We light candles and have a beautiful sit-down dinner, including Pork and Sauerkraut. By cooking the Sauerkraut in beer, this dish becomes easier to digest and free from "after effects" during the night and next day.

Make the little Apple Dumplings ahead of time, then reheat them in the oven that night.

Mulled Cider
Cheese Balls

Roasted Pork Loin
Sauerkraut
Mashed Potatoes
Whole Tiny Buttered Beets

Marinated Mushrooms
Banana-Nut Salad

Apple Dumplings with Cream

Wild Game Dinner

Many people have asked us to prepare a dinner using wild game. You will find Smoked Trout in delicatessens almost everywhere. It is served with a sour cream or herb dressing. The rest of the dishes on this menu are all excellent.

The Venison Stew is one of the best recipes I know, as it takes away the wild flavor of the meat. Some of the less expensive cuts of beef may be substituted for the venison.

When preparing the Roast Pheasant, be sure to get out all the shot if you are using a pheasant that was shot in game season. We buy commercial pheasants, so we do not have that problem.

The Cherry Salad helps to clear your palate before dessert.

Smoked Trout
Corn Bread

Fried Rabbit
Venison Stew
Roast Pheasant with Cranberry Stuffing

Stuffed Baked Potatoes
Fried Eggplant
Buttered Carrots

Cherry Salad

Hot Mince Pie
Grape-Nut Ice Cream

JANUARY

Fireside Dinner

Basically this meal can be cooked in the oven. The heat from the stove will help to warm your kitchen, and the vegetables and other foods may all be found at the market. There is an amusing story concerning the Smoked Ham with the Wine-Raisin Sauce: We had a group of people in the dining room one evening who were nondrinkers; in fact, they abstained totally and were members of the WCTU. I asked them, "Would you like the gravy on the baked ham?" and they said, "Yes, definitely." Of course, I did not mention that there was wine in it. As you can see, the gravy is all wine! Would you believe, they asked for third helpings of the gravy!

Waldorf Salad is one I have been making since I was in high school. Almost everyone is familiar with it since it is a very simple recipe. Just apples, raisins, and celery plus the salad dressing. It is very good for wintertime salads, and you are sure to enjoy it.

Funny Pie goes well with this dinner because it is similar to Shoofly Pie, except that it has a chocolate base. The recipe was given to me by a friend. This dinner should warm up your family by the fireside.

Sour Cream and Potato Soup
Corn Bread Muffins

Baked Smoked Ham with Wine-Raisin Sauce
Sweet Potatoes Supreme
Turnips, Rutabaga, and Kohlrabi

Waldorf Salad

Funny Pie
Vanilla Ice Cream

FEBRUARY

Washington's Birthday

Rolled Brisket of Beef has been a family favorite all my life. We always served it well done. However, I have given you the recipe medium rare. Decide which way you prefer—medium rare or well done, or somewhere in between. The best way to ensure that it is done to your liking is to use a meat thermometer.

It is most appropriate to have little hatchet cutouts on the Cherry Pie for Washington's Birthday. Christmas cookie cutters generally include a "hatchet" cookie cutter.

To make the Cherry Ice Cream, you can use Bing cherries, as I do, or if you prefer, use Maraschino cherries. Both are delicious in ice cream.

Ham and Bean Soup
Jennifer's Methodist Muffins

Rolled Brisket of Beef au Jus
Whole Browned Potatoes
Dried Corn Pudding

Spinach and Endive with Hot Bacon Dressing

Cherry Pie with "Hatchet" Cutouts
Cherry Ice Cream

ACKNOWLEDGMENTS

I would like to express my gratitude to the following people for their contributions to the book:

The narrative portions of this book were written by Diane Stonebeck. The Present, The Family and The Past are examples of her creativity and writing skill in interpreting my memories and experiences.

To the Chefs and all the staff of our Groff's Farm Restaurant and Cameron Estate Inn for their cooperation, enthusiasm and dedication to quality and service.

Frank Costello, for his enthusiasm for the total project and for meeting deadlines.

Chris Kunzler, Jr., one who insures quality in smoked meats "just like home."

Kunzler and Company, Inc.

Bob Shaeffer, for all his kindnesses.

Elsie Swenson for testing the Microwave recipes.

Sharron Quay, for patience and flexibility in working with Flat Tulip Studio to reach our goals for layout and design.

For additional copies, please check your local bookstore or write to:

Pond Press Publishers
650 Pinkerton Road
Mount Joy, Pennsylvania, 17552

or call: 717-653-1115 for additional information.

Index